MW01071601

MEET THE KELLYS

MEET THE KELLYS

THE TRUE STORY OF
MACHINE GUN KELLY
AND HIS MOLL
KATHRYN THORNE

CHRIS ENSS

CITADEL PRESS
Kensington Publishing Corp.
kensingtonbooks.com

CITADEL PRESS BOOKS are published by

Kensington Publishing Corp.
900 Third Avenue
New York, NY 10022

Copyright © 2025 by Chris Enss

All rights reserved. No part of this book may be reproduced in any form or by any means without the prior written consent of the publisher, excepting brief quotes used in reviews.

All Kensington titles, imprints, and distributed lines are available at special quantity discounts for bulk purchases for sales promotions, premiums, fund-raising, educational, or institutional use. Special book excerpts or customized printings can also be created to fit specific needs. For details, write or phone the office of the Kensington sales manager: Kensington Publishing Corp., 900 Third Avenue, New York, NY 10022, attn Sales Department; phone 1-800-221-2647.

CITADEL PRESS and the Citadel logo are Reg. U.S. Pat. & TM Off.

10 9 8 7 6 5 4 3 2 1

First Citadel hardcover printing: June 2025

Printed in the United States of America

ISBN: 978-0-8065-4305-5

ISBN: 978-0-8065-4307-9 (e-book)

Library of Congress Control Number: 2025930763

The authorized representative in the EU for product safety and compliance
is eucomply OU, Parnu mnt 139b-14, Apt 123,
Tallinn, Berlin 11317; hello@eucompliancepartner.com

CONTENTS

———

INTRODUCTION

WHEN THE OUTLAW DUO OF George "Machine Gun" Kelly and his wife, Kathryn Thorne, kidnapped Charles Urschel in July 1933, the couple, and their accomplices, made history. The Kellys were the first to be tried for such a crime since the creation of the Federal Kidnapping Act, the first lawbreakers to be transported by plane to stand trial, and the first to have their trial filmed.

Memphis born, bootlegger, and bank robber, Kelly, and vivacious divorcée, Kathryn, celebrated their third anniversary by abducting a prominent oil tycoon from his home and demanding a $200,000 ransom for his release. Their outrageous actions shocked the Oklahoma City community where Charles Urschel and his wife, Berenice, resided with their children, and frustrated the overburdened Bureau of Investigation and its director, J. Edgar Hoover. Hoover's agency was still on the hunt for the guilty parties involved with the kidnapping and murder of famed aviator Charles Lindbergh's son. The Bureau's inability to close high-profile abduction cases like Lindbergh's quickly, as well as the unsuccessful efforts of federal agents to apprehend any of violent lawbreakers like Al Capone, John Dillinger, and Bonnie and Clyde, damaged the outfit's reputation. The relationship between the Bureau's director and United States Attorney General Homer Stille Cummings was strained as a result of the agency's struggles. Hoover knew the Bureau's days were numbered if he didn't produce results. The Urschel kidnapping case provided him with an opportunity to achieve that goal and, like the Kellys, make history.

The Urschel kidnapping was the first prominent case in which Director Hoover exercised his control of the print media and laid the groundwork for building his legendary status. He not only recruited talented individuals to help develop scientific methods to solve crimes and track offenders but hired publicists to feed information to the press that highlighted the Bureau's accomplishments and the methods employed by relentless agents to apprehend notorious outlaws.

Throughout the investigation into the Urschel abduction, Director Hoover turned every lead, either uncovered by his men or reported by a civilian, into an opportunity to promote the agency as a superior crime-fighting force. He did not want the public to think that the Bureau solved crimes by luck or happenstance. The American people had to believe Hoover's agents' deductions were based solely on their investigative skills. Hoover and his publicist weren't opposed to embellishing the facts. Such was the case with the arrest of the Kellys on September 26, 1933. Much of what the Bureau reported about the capture of the pair was accurate, but some of the events they claimed occurred were fiction. Kelly pointed out the discrepancies to newspaper reporters, but journalists were disinclined to take the gangster's word, and Hoover counted on that.

Kathryn Kelly had a flair for manipulating the press as well, but her talent was discovered too late to improve her circumstances. News of the Kellys' crimes and various law enforcement agencies' pursuits of the pair appeared in newspapers across the country. Hoover and his staff painted Kathryn as a materialistic femme fatale who drove her husband to commit the crimes he did. She tried to change the public's opinion of her by giving interviews with respected journalists and candidly sharing her truth about her relationship with Kelly and how he misled her. George's upper-middle-class background was in sharp contrast to Kathryn's depressed past. She referred to the difference in their upbringing often when she spoke with reporters and was quick to tell them that it was Kelly who intimidated her into breaking the law and not the other way around.

"The first time I ever saw a machine gun was when Kelly had one at my house in Fort Worth," Kathryn told Pulitzer Prize–winning Scripps-Howard staff writer Lee Hills in mid-October 1933. "It is being told that I provided my husband with weapons and that he taught me how to use them. He never taught me to use a machine gun or any other kind. I wouldn't know what to do with one. This talk about him being about to write his name on a wall with machine gun bullets may be so, but I don't know whether he even can shoot." Kathryn herself circulated the rumor about his shooting prowess long before she and Kelly embarked on their first kidnapping. That kind of promotion had served its purpose well when they were deciding to graduate from robbing banks to abducting the wealthy, but once they were caught, Kathryn denied it all to the press. To avoid life in prison, it was important potential jurors saw her as a naïve young woman with ordinary wants and dreams who was taken advantage of by the man she loved.

In the beginning, George Kelly didn't care how he was depicted in the media. The notoriety earned him a fair amount of respect from his fellow gangsters and elicited fear in those he robbed or kidnapped. He didn't pretend he wasn't an outlaw, but after he was captured he embellished on his crimes to make himself seem more ruthless than the public already knew him to be. He did that because he thought he could save his wife. She told the press, the authorities, and a jury that she had no idea her husband was as dangerous as he turned out to be. "George Kelly brought all this trouble on us," she told Lee Hills. "I feel pretty hard against him. If it would save my mother [who was implicated in the abduction], I'd walk up to him now and shoot him. . . ." By making himself out to be more of a heartless thug in the public's eye, Kelly hoped the court would believe he threatened Kathryn and her family if she didn't keep quiet about kidnapping Urschel.

The Kellys' trial was a media circus. Newspaper reporters, photojournalists, and newsreel cameramen covered the event from the swearing in of the jury to the arrival and departure of the main characters and the supporting cast. Numerous people associated with the case were given a moment in the spotlight, including the victim, the prosecuting attorneys, the money launderers, and those who harbored the fugitives. Kathryn Kelly and J. Edgar Hoover were lavished with attention more than any of the others. The publicity proved to be an important windfall for Hoover's agency. Citizens from coast to coast became aware of the valuable services the government police force offered the nation, and that knowledge helped bring about the creation of the Federal Bureau of Investigation.

For George and Kathryn Kelly, the notoriety they received from the press solidified a guilty verdict and served as notice for all who considered defying the law at that time that no one was more powerful than Hoover and the federal government.

CHAPTER 1

IN THE COMPANY OF THE KELLYS

IT WAS A WET, CHILLY EVENING in early May 1934 when thirteen-year-old Geralene Arnold stepped onto the stage at the Glory B Theater in Miami, Oklahoma. The playhouse was filled to capacity. All one thousand seats were occupied and patrons were standing in the aisles. The film *Sucker Money* had concluded moments earlier and a plump, redheaded woman wearing a black chiffon dress and standing beside an ornate pipe organ was serenading the audience with her rendition of the popular tune "Street of Dreams." The song served as an interlude between the showing of the motion picture, directed by Mrs. Wallace Reid, also known as Dorothy Davenport, and the teenager taking her place behind the microphone.

Geralene was new to the footlights. A year prior, the dark-eyed, deeply dimpled young woman was simply a precocious sixth grader who enjoyed school and being with her friends. Had she not been abducted by gangsters George "Machine Gun" Kelly and Kathryn Kelly she would have continued along with her ordinary life, content to let fame pass her by.[1]

Entertainment agent K. Lee Williams conceived of the idea of Geralene embarking on a tour of twenty Oklahoma theaters in conjunction with the showing of the motion picture *Sucker Money*. The controversial film, about the head of a group of grifters who kidnap a woman and hold her ransom, seemed like the perfect vehicle to introduce Geralene's talk, entitled *My Experience in the Hands of*

1

the Kellys. The short recitation was the gripping, true story of how America's two most daring criminals whisked the girl away from her parents and used her for two weeks as a front in their desperate dash from state to state eluding officers of the law.[2]

Geralene's parents, Luther and Flossie, who accompanied her on the statewide tour, were not wealthy people; quite the contrary. The red-and-black outfit the teenager wore, which was frayed and ill-fitting in places, was proof the Arnolds struggled financially. Kathryn Kelly had purchased the garment for her while they were on the run, and it was the nicest dress the girl owned. Geralene was clean and presentable and her shoulder-length hair was curled and held in place with a red barrette. She smiled politely at the audience, who offered their applause after a dignified announcer introduced her.[3]

Geralene scanned the sea of faces eagerly waiting for her to speak. She wasn't nervous or inhibited. "I first met the Kellys at different times," she began. "I first met Mrs. Kathryn Kelly on a highway not far from Waco, Texas. My parents and I were traveling to see one of my great aunts and Mrs. Kelly stopped to give us a ride in her truck. She told us her name was Mrs. Montgomery. She seemed nice and soon confessed her real name then asked my father to help her with something in Fort Worth and Oklahoma. She wanted him to find a lawyer for her parents who had been arrested. My dad agreed and then she and my mother and I drove to San Antonio. That's where I first met George 'Machine Gun' Kelly. He and Mrs. Kelly and another man had kidnapped an oil tycoon named Charles Urschel.[4]

"On September 11, 1933, I left San Antonio with the Kellys. The police were now after them and they needed to get away. Mrs. Kelly told Mr. Kelly the police would only be looking for a couple, not a husband and wife and a child. I was supposed to go with them to Coleman, Texas, because they said I would make a good shield. I was to be back with my mom in San Antonio by four o'clock in the afternoon of the same day. Mrs. Kelly promised my mother, but that's not what happened. When we reached Coleman, a woman there told Mrs. Kelly that the law had been there and that they were looking for Kathryn in a Ford pickup. So, we changed cars and hurried to Chicago.[5]

"While we were traveling, Mrs. Kelly dyed George's hair and she wore a wig. We stayed at the Astor Apartments. Mr. Kelly made frantic phone calls and Mrs. Kelly wrote hurried letters to people. While writing she and Machine Gun Kelly talked about who the letters were going to and about killing those people. The letters, in which I placed the stamps on the envelope, were sent to Charles Urschel, Judge Edgar Vaught, Joseph Keenan, and a lawyer named Herbert Hyde. Both Kathryn and George said they should have taken Charles Urschel to Arizona, killed and buried him there. I was scared and wanted to go home. Mrs. Kelly assured me I would not be hurt and bought me two new dresses. I had no other clothes or anything with me.[6]

"From Chicago we went to Memphis. We made the trip in a brand-new Chevrolet. A friend of the Kellys named Joe Burgle gave them the car along with $200 and a quart of whiskey. When we got to Memphis, Mr. Kelly talked about going back to Coleman, Texas, to get some of the ransom money he buried at Cass Coleman's farm. He decided instead that a man named Langford Ramsey and I should drive to meet another person who would get the money to us. We were then supposed to take it to the Kellys. Mrs. Kelly wanted us to pick up her furs too. She said she wanted them when she returned to Chicago."[7]

Geralene's presentation lasted ten minutes. The audience was mesmerized by the tale and some blinked away tears, imagining how frightened and worried the young girl must have been. Her ordeal didn't end until she was placed on a train in Fort Worth bound for Oklahoma City. When she arrived in Oklahoma, she learned her parents had been arrested. She told the audience of the meeting she had with Bureau of Investigation agents when she reached Oklahoma, and of helping the authorities find the Kellys at their hiding place in Tennessee.[8]

The young woman concluded her presentation with a thank-you to J. Edgar Hoover and the Bureau of Investigation. Ticket buyers applauded and her parents, who had been waiting in the wings, joined her on stage. The couple handed out handbills provided by their daughter's agent that featured a photograph of Geralene under the caption, "Girl Nemesis of the Kellys."[9] Audience members who wanted their handbills signed had a limited time to do so before the next picture started. Articles about Geralene's time in the spotlight appeared in newspapers and magazines across the country. The publications reached hundreds of thousands of readers including the Kellys, both of whom were in federal prison serving life sentences.[10]

Twenty-six-year-old Kathryn Kelly was known as an extravagant, dangerous woman with little regard for the law. Most men she aligned herself with in her early years shared her enthusiasm for reckless living and defying authority. In the summer of 1930, Kathryn was racing through the small towns and back roads of Oklahoma with her boyfriend, bootlegger Steven "Little Steve" Stephens. The passing of the National Prohibition Act restricting the distribution of liquor forced enterprising businessmen and -women to find a way to illegally transport and sell alcohol. Bootlegging was a financially lucrative industry. Not only did Kathryn enjoy the clothing, jewelry, and furs she was able to acquire from the money made hauling liquor but she found outrunning the authorities exhilarating.[11]

"There's no such thing as a little bootlegger, no more than there is a little banker. Bootlegging is immensely profitable," an article in the July 4, 1930, edition of the *Muldrow Sun* newspaper in Sallisaw, Oklahoma, noted about the criminal activity. "The day of the little banker in a small town is past. He is a subsidiary of some big concerns. That's what bootlegging is now. The little fellow can't live in this business on his own, he has to work for someone else. He can't make it, buy his goods, and peddle them on his own. No, he simply makes deliveries, and it's for the chain.[12]

"He is simply an order clerk, or delivery man, or one of dozens of other menial work hands in this great and intricate industry. It's not done by some little fellow with a few hundred dollars capital, it's done by financiers. It takes more capital to invest to ensure the safe delivery of liquor into Oklahoma City, Chicago, Kansas City, and other big cities, and distribute it around than it does to do the same thing with your milk, your bread, or even your meat. They have to control ships, airplanes, and trucks by the hundreds.[13]

"Bootlegging is big business and it takes an unintimidating type who thrills to the chase to make it work."[14]

Kathryn was no stranger to bootlegging. Her stepfather, Robert "Boss" Shannon, and her mother, Ora, participated in the trade. The Shannons lived on a small farm four miles outside of Paradise, Texas, and Boss ran moonshine between his home and Fort Worth. In 1929, Ora, who had a job at a grocery store, joined her husband in the business. The state of the economy in the nation was severely depressed, and the Shannons believed they were doing what had to be done to take care of their family.[15]

The family's criminal behavior extended beyond Kathryn's mother and stepfather's bootlegging enterprise. One of her aunts was a prostitute, and there were uncles who were car thieves and counterfeiters—one of whom was incarcerated at Leavenworth Penitentiary. Director of the Bureau of Investigation J. Edgar Hoover's sentiment about such an upbringing was clear. "Experts say that children are not born criminals, nor pampered parasites," he noted. "They are made that way by the environment in which they live."[16]

Kathryn was born on March 18, 1904, and named Lera Cleo Brooks. Her father's name was James Emory Brooks. "I was born in Tupelo, Mississippi," she told a reporter in October 1933. "Everybody seems to think I was born in Fate, Texas, but that's my mother's birthplace. It would take a month to tell all about what happened since I came into the world in that Mississippi town. I've lived two lives since then."[17]

The Brooks family moved from Mississippi to Brown, Texas, when Kathryn was six years old. James and Ora operated boardinghouses and worked at local grocery stores in both locations. In 1915, they relocated to Coleman, Texas. Kathryn was musically inclined and enjoyed learning to play the piano. Education at public schools bored her, however, and she dropped out after completing the eighth grade. Shortly after leaving school, she met a seventeen-year-old boy named Lonnie Fry. Lonnie's family owned a farm east of Shawnee, Oklahoma, where he worked. He proposed to Kathryn, and the two left Texas in late 1918.[18]

Kathryn and Lonnie were married in Asher, Oklahoma, on November 29, 1918. The following June their daughter, Pauline Elizabeth, was born. According to the neighborhood section of the *Shawnee Morning News*, Kathryn's parents, who had moved to Oklahoma to be closer to her, routinely visited with their daughter, son-in-law, and grandchild.[19] According to the June 18, 1921, edition of the *Shawnee Morning News*, Ora made an emergency visit to help Kathryn care for the baby, who had become "quite sick." The child's full recovery was reported in the June 25, 1921, edition of the paper.[20]

Kathryn and Lonnie divorced two and a half years after they exchanged vows. Kathryn and Pauline moved in with her parents. Sixteen months after the divorce was finalized, Kathryn married Lennie Elbert Brewer, a twenty-seven-year-old man from Wanette, Oklahoma. The couple relocated to Coleman, Texas, with James and Ora, and it was there the Brewers were divorced in 1924.[21]

Kathryn was twenty-three years old when she met and married her third husband, Charles Thorne, in March 1927. At one time, Thorne was a rancher and the owner of more than a hundred fifty acres of land in Bell County, Texas. He also owned the American Café on Commercial Avenue in Coleman. In addition to the eatery, Thorne transported alcohol from one part of the state to another. He always had a considerable amount of cash and showered his young bride with clothing and jewelry. Kathryn accompanied him on his bootlegging runs. She found she liked the lifestyle but realized quickly it wasn't the proper environment for her daughter. Kathryn gave Pauline to her mother to raise and she and Thorne traveled to various speakeasies delivering liquor. On occasion, the pair ventured to Canada where thousands of gallons of grain alcohol were transported. Once it was in the country it was redistributed and turned into synthetic gin, Scotch, rye, and rum.[22]

When the Thornes weren't on the road they were working at the eatery. Both considered the other to be overly flirtatious with the clientele. Kathryn suspected Thorne of being unfaithful but had nothing more than speculation on which to base her feelings. It wasn't until she traveled out of town to visit family that she claimed she had been presented with proof of his infidelity. Kathryn was furious when she made her way back to their home in Coleman. En route, she stopped to fill up the gas tank and engaged in a brief conversation with the service station attendant. While checking the air in her tires, he politely asked where she was headed. She told him she was going to Coleman, Texas, "to kill that *&% damned Charlie Thorne."

Historians note it wasn't the first time Kathryn had threatened to kill her husband. Customers at the café had overheard her promise to end his life should she ever catch him cheating on her. Kathryn accused Thorne of wanting to kill her too. His threats came after having one too many. "He was a terrible drinker," Kathryn stated in an interview later in her life. "He would drink half a gallon of whiskey at a time."[23]

In the early evening on April 29, 1928, after drinking steadily all day at home, Thorne pointed a pistol at Kathryn and announced he was going to kill her. Weary from hearing the threat and arguing, she told him to "go ahead." He decided against it and put the gun away. Frustrated, Kathryn proceeded into the kitchen to wash the dinner dishes. After a few moments she heard the shot of a gun echo through the house. She hurried to find Thorne and when she got to him, he was lying in a pool of blood on the floor of their bedroom. He had shot himself in the right temple and the bullet exited through the top of his skull. An ambulance was quickly called to the scene. The wound hadn't killed him instantly, and he drifted in and out of consciousness until help arrived. "I pleaded with him to get well for my sake," Kathryn later remembered. "He promised he would try."[24]

Charles Thorne died shortly after midnight at the Overall Memorial Hospital. A suicide note scribbled on the back of a letter the twenty-eight-year-old man had received from the First National Bank of Coolidge, Texas, was brief and to the point. "I do not hold no one responsible for my death," Charles had written. "I did it myself for one reason. That reason is because . . . C.G. Thorne."[25]

The note was turned over to the authorities and they verified it had indeed been written by Thorne. Kathryn confessed that the two had been quarreling but could not or would not expand on what they were arguing about. The police found nothing suspicious about the circumstances surrounding his death, and no inquest was held. His body was prepared for burial and funeral arrangements were made. Thorne's service was held at the city cemetery, where he was laid to rest sixteen hours after he passed away. In addition to Kathryn, Thorne's mother, brother, and sister attended the brief graveside ceremony.[26]

There were some residents of Coleman who believed Kathryn had more to do with Charles Thorne's demise than she told the law. Those that knew of her threats to kill him suspected she poisoned him. Rumors circulated that Thorne was illiterate and couldn't write, therefore speculation was that the so-called suicide note had to have been penned by someone else. The speed in which he was buried promoted suspicious minds to surmise Kathryn orchestrated the event to prevent an autopsy from being done. Some believed Thorne's widow was able to perfectly execute his murder because she was romantically involved with the coroner.[27]

Kathryn fled to her mother and stepfather's home near Paradise to escape the gossip. Less than a month after Thorne's passing, Kathryn transferred ownership of a sizable lot she and her husband owned jointly to her mother. A month later, she put a section of cedar timber land in Belton County up for sale. "I'm pricing this land at a great loss," she informed interested buyers. In September 1928, she placed an ad in several newspapers directed at potential business owners. "For Immediate Sale—on account of the death of my husband," the ad read. "The American Café, largest and best up-to-date café in good oil town. Will sacrifice for quick sale, as other business demands my attention."[28]

Kathryn was restless. She craved more than what was offered at the Shannon farm. Using the money left to her from Thorne and the ultimate sale of the timber land and café, the widow traveled to Oklahoma City and Fort Worth, with a few stops in between. She purchased a new wardrobe and a car and stayed at the finest hotels. During Kathryn's time in Oklahoma City, she dated several men, including a jewelry salesman from St. Louis who was in town on business. They met at a salon where she was working as a manicurist. One evening the couple took a drive to a remote lake and parked. Their romantic tryst was interrupted by two men who pulled the salesman from the vehicle, beat, and robbed him. The police suspected Kathryn was collaborating with the thugs and had enticed the naïve man to the location where the crime was committed. She was arrested as an accessory and later released for lack of evidence.[29]

Kathryn was in trouble with the law again in Fort Worth in November 1929. She was arrested for shoplifting on November 30, and when she was taken into custody, she told the police her name was Delores Whitney. According to James Mathers, one of the attorneys who represented her later in her life, Kathryn liked jewels and furs and the way she acquired those things was unimportant to her. The shoplifting charge was eventually dropped and no time was served.[30]

When Kathryn wasn't working or manipulating her way through the legal system, she spent her evenings at jazz clubs and speakeasies around the Texas town. Speakeasies in the block of East 54th Street were well known for recruiting corespondent women in divorce cases. The proprietors charged a $25 fee for arranging the details. Women like Kathryn received a percentage of the fees. The business was so prosperous the women who participated averaged earnings of $100 a week. Kathryn could afford to purchase whatever she needed to maintain a comfortable lifestyle.[31]

Kathryn Thorne wasn't opposed to the admirers she acquired buying her additional fineries. She met a fair number of bootleggers while frequenting various clubs and illegal taverns. Bootlegging was a thriving business and, according to Tarrant County, Texas, District Attorney Robert Stuart, liquor law violators were the best organized of any class of criminal he had ever encountered. They never pleaded guilty and their lawyers routinely arrived at the district attorney's office before the officers making the arrests brought them in to be processed. Their bonds were prepared and signed in most cases without the defendant ever being placed in jail.[32]

Every group of bootleggers in Fort Worth had a leader who stood behind the scenes, directing their operations. Next to the leader was the wholesale dealer who managed the liquor in large lots. He in turn had numerous aides who retailed the liquor in small lots to the consumer. Kathryn was romantically involved with one of those aides, Little Steve Stephens. Referred to as a "hip-pocket bootlegger," Stephens not only sold and transported liquor to customers but arranged for the manufacturing of alcohol. He knew if he was ever caught, he shouldn't make a statement to the police. His reward for his silence was an assurance of the services of an able attorney, employed by the leader to defend him. The penalty for failure to comply could mean his assassination. The women the bootleggers were involved with were also required to say nothing to the police or run the risk of being killed. Kathryn found life as a bootlegger's moll exhilarating. It was immensely profitable, and that meant her cravings for the better things could be fulfilled.[33]

Kathryn was an attractive woman, with dark eyes, auburn hair, a polished smile, and a tall, lean frame that curved in the proper places. She was never lacking for male attention. Little Steve was proud to have her on his arm when they were out and about, and as long as Kathryn was having a good time, she was happy to serve as her paramour's trophy.[34]

"They said that I loved luxury and beautiful possessions. That I was too easy with money," Kathryn noted in a newspaper interview in 1933. "Money never meant anything to me. Of course, I liked to have nice things but I could be just as happy without them. They never bought me happiness." Attorney James Mathers disagreed with Kathryn's assessment of herself. "She was a girl of real beauty, but her whole philosophy of life was based on money and what it could buy. . . . She knew her way around the underworld and made friends with the leading mugs and gangsters of the prohibition era in Fort Worth, Oklahoma City, Kansas City, St. Louis,

Chicago, St. Paul, and New York. She picked her company by the dollar sign, and nothing else mattered.[35]

By 1930, Prohibition was ten years old. Happily for bootleggers like Little Steve and his girlfriend Kathryn Thorne, it had become increasingly difficult to enforce. Congress focused on correcting the issue by transferring the enforcement from the Treasury Department to the Department of Justice. From the moment power was shifted, Prohibition agents began raiding speakeasies across the country. Several hundred thousand pints of beer, whiskey, and other types of liquor were confiscated and destroyed between 1930 and 1931. Some politicians believed it was not enough to defeat the bootleggers. They were convinced leaders and wholesalers should be the chief targets. Stopping the source of supply would put numerous bootleggers out of business. It was the mission of the Department of Justice and the Bureau of Investigation in each state to pursue wholesalers and shut their operations down.[36]

Little Steve wasn't worried the strong-arm approach would keep him out of the money. He drove supplies of illegal alcohol from Chicago to Minneapolis, El Paso to Denver, and Fort Worth to Oklahoma City. He worked for leaders in all those locations. He even worked for Boss Shannon, Kathryn's stepfather. Not only did Shannon manufacture and package his own liquor, he also allowed outlaws needing a place to hide the use of his farm for a fee. Should anything go wrong, Kathryn knew where she and Little Steve could find refuge.[37]

In early 1930, Kathryn and Little Steve left Texas and headed to Oklahoma City. Little Steve was Tulsa's leading bootlegger. Authorities in the Sooner State were less driven to stop the illegal sale of liquor there. Many voters believed Prohibition was an immoral law and welcomed bootleggers, who visited houses at night, hoping to sell their goods to willing consumers. On January 20, 1930, the *Daily Oklahoman* ran an article about how bootleggers in the region were considered folk heroes of sorts. The article included a report from the National Commission on Law Observance and Enforcement that outlined the difficulties in tracking bootleggers like Little Steve and Kathryn Thorne. Critics of the commission noted that enforcement would be a joke until the courts were as "well manned as the speakeasies, booze trucks, and rum boats."[38]

The continued market for liquor in Oklahoma and Texas encouraged bootleggers there to defy Prohibition. Business was good for Little Steve, and the fact that he had avoided arrest gave him incentive to increase his usual runs. By early summer 1930, Kathryn and her companion had returned to Fort Worth, bringing alcohol to thirsty buyers. Little Steve needed help to grow his operation but had yet to meet the person he felt would be a good partner. The solution to the problem presented itself one evening when Little Steve and Kathryn were at one of Fort Worth's most popular supper clubs. Kathryn was adorned in a stylish silk gown that hugged her every curve, an expensive diamond necklace and earrings, and a fur cape draped over her shoulders. Steve was dressed appropriately as well, and the couple alternated between eating the food before them, conversing with each other, and exchanging pleasantries with people they knew at the posh establishment. One of those patrons was a polished, attractive, smartly attired Irishman named George Kelly.[39]

Kelly, like Little Steve, was a bootlegger. He had been imprisoned more than once for smuggling and selling liquor and had a reputation for being an exceptional driver. On February 11, 1928, he'd been sent to serve time at Leavenworth Penitentiary for possession of alcohol. It was there he first made Kathryn's acquaintance. She was at the facility visiting a family member and after a quick introduction, Kelly and Kathryn decided to write to each other. They exchanged only a few letters. Kelly had been out of prison less than a month when he ran into Steve at the supper club. Kelly and Steve had met years prior in Tulsa. The last time they'd seen each other was in late November 1927. Little Steve, his wife Bess, and George were holding a party at the apartment they shared with a woman named Mary Ellen Bodine when Mary fatally shot herself with Kelly's gun. The men parted company after being questioned about the apparent suicide.[40]

Upon meeting again, the two men shook hands and briefly discussed their past, mutual friends, and fields of endeavor. Little Steve

suggested the two get together at another time to discuss the possibility of Kelly coming to work for him. Kelly turned to Kathryn
before agreeing, and Little Steve, remembering his manners, reintroduced the newly released convict to his date. Kelly was charmed.
He nodded politely, expressed his genuine pleasure in seeing her
again, and turned his attention back to the fellow bootlegger's pro-
posal. Before going their separate ways, Kelly risked an admiring
glance at Kathryn. She returned the favor and smiled apprecia-
tively. Little Steve had no idea everything he was about to lose.

CHAPTER 2

BOOTLEGGERS TO BANK ROBBERS

GEORGE KELLY STRUCK A MATCH, touched it to his cigarette, and took a long drag. He expelled the smoke into the perfume-laden air of the fashionable Fort Worth supper club and eyed the attractive patrons dancing to the music provided by a more than capable orchestra. He was leaning against a small, swanky bar when a server placed a drink next to him and then hurried off to wait on others. Kelly lifted the beverage to have a sip and stared across the glass at Kathryn Thorne in Little Steve Stephen's arms. As Little Steve led her around the dance floor, he pressed her close to him. Kathryn didn't resist. She caught Kelly watching her and smiled. Behind her slinky, pursed lips, she offered a look that was a languishing and inviting challenge. Kelly lit up with the sort of grin she knew men wore when they had something mischievous planned. He had made bad choices in his thirty-two years, but falling for Kathryn would have fatal consequences.

George Kelly was born into an upper-middle-class family on July 17, 1900, in Chicago. His mother, Elizabeth, was the daughter of the prominent and affluent Kellys of Memphis, Tennessee. George F. Barnes Sr. was an insurance agent from Texas. He was twenty-five when he married twenty-one-year-old Elizabeth in the summer of 1892. Their first child, Inez, was born in 1896. When George Jr. was two, the Barnes family moved to Memphis. Their home at 2098 Camden Street was an idyllic, two-story structure with a big yard, shade trees, and plenty of extended family to visit.[1]

George adored his mother. She was attractive and kind. His father, on the other hand, was abusive not only to him but to his mother, whose health was failing. He was preoccupied with work and made little time for his wife and children. Fifteen-year-old George channeled his frustration with his home life into making money selling pints of whiskey to neighbors. In 1915, state politicians executed prohibition laws, shut down saloons, and prevented the transportation of liquor between counties. Young George became acquainted with townspeople who wanted him to carry liquor they made to known buyers. The troubled teenager was promised a percentage of the sales and he eagerly accepted the proposition.[2]

While out making deliveries one afternoon, George caught his father with another woman. He visited George Sr. at his office and confronted him with the discovery. George threatened to go to his mother with the news and his father pleaded with him to reconsider. He reminded his son that Elizabeth wasn't well and that the truth could cause her fragile heart to stop. George decided to take advantage of the situation and struck up a bargain with his father. He would keep the secret in exchange for use of the family car whenever he wanted it. George Sr. agreed to his only son's terms.[3]

Kelly's ability to traffic alcohol increased after acquiring a vehicle. He was no longer limited to making deliveries in a confined section of Memphis. He could now make runs to Kentucky and Arkansas, collect the liquor from the source, and deliver it to customers in a five-hundred-mile radius. He was flush with cash on a continual basis. If work didn't interfere with school, he would be in class. His grades didn't reflect the time he spent away from his studies hauling liquor. He liked to read and excelled in math. Except for the embarrassing number of days Kelly was absent during the semesters, there was nothing in his report card that gave his parents reason to be concerned.[4]

Kelly was well-kempt. His clothes were clean and pressed and he was polite. Because he didn't look like a thug or speak in a disrespectful manner, local police were never overly stern with him when they caught him delivering a bottle of whiskey or two. Any discipline that needed to be done was left up to George Sr. whose reprimands were met with sneers and indifference. Kelly would accept his father using his influence in the community to keep him out of jail, but viewed his efforts more to preserve his own reputation than to help his son.[5]

The gulf between George Sr. and Jr. grew wider in early November 1917 when Elizabeth passed away in her sleep. Kelly blamed his father that his mother died of heart failure. She knew somehow that her husband hadn't been faithful to her and felt helpless to do anything about it. The funeral service was held on November 10 at Sacred Heart Church. Kelly and his sister leaned on one another for support. Their father turned to his mistress.[6]

The grieving seventeen-year-old stayed at home until he graduated in the spring of 1918. In the fall that same year, he made good on a promise to his mother to enroll in college. He was accepted at Mississippi State University and planned to pursue a degree in business. He was a good student. He was friendly and made connections easily. He had a robust social life with young women from affluent families. Sadly, academics didn't hold his interest. At the end of his freshman year, he dropped out of school and returned to Memphis. He stopped by his childhood home long enough to retrieve his belongings and exchange his last words with his father. The parting was harsh and what was said was ugly and binding.[7]

Kelly moved into a boardinghouse and reacquainted himself with friends from high school. He alternated his time between driving a cab, bootlegging, and attending summer get-togethers. While attending an engagement party in July 1919, Kelly made the acquaintance of a petite brunette named Geneva Ramsey. The two knew of each other but had never formally met. Kelly introduced himself and asked her to dance. She agreed, and the pair danced together most of the evening. Geneva was charmed by his looks and manners but declined his invitation to court her. She explained that her father, George, who was a reputable contractor responsible for overseeing the building of railways and levees throughout the South, and her mother, Della, a housewife, would never allow it.[8]

Geneva's gracious refusal to allow Kelly to call on her made her that much more attractive to him. He began a relentless campaign to win her heart. He appeared at functions she attended, was at the grocery store when she was there shopping, and at movie theaters where she went with friends. Geneva was flattered by the attention and finally agreed to go on a date with Kelly. The two were then inseparable. [9]

Kelly realized how remarkable Geneva was when he experienced a time of depression over losing his mother. At the time of her death, he was angry at his father and the circumstances he felt led to Elizabeth's demise, and he hadn't allowed himself a long enough time to grieve. The emotions caught up with him in the fall of 1919, and Geneva was by his side to help him deal with the pain. [10]

Kelly and Geneva fell in love with each other, but her parents were against the relationship. When George Ramsey learned that Kelly had a police record for selling liquor, he shared the information with his daughter and forbade her to see him again. Geneva was brokenhearted and insisted Kelly was a good man with potential and admitted how deeply she felt for him. The Ramseys decided to send their daughter to the Columbia Institute for Young Ladies in Columbia, Tennessee. They believed putting distance between the two would effectively end their romance. [11]

A problem with Geneva's health brought the teenager back home to undergo an operation to remove her appendix. In the same town again, Kelly and Geneva rekindled their relationship. The two eloped on October 7, 1919. The October 8, 1919, edition of the *Commercial Appeal* reported on the young couple's impulsive act, misspelling Kelly's name in the process. [12]

"When Miss Geneva Ramsey left home yesterday afternoon, her mother Mrs. George F. Ramsey, thought her daughter was going to the Orpheum Theater," the article read. "But a telegram received last night from Clarksdale, Mississippi, notified Miss Ramsey's parents of her marriage to Mr. George W. Bond [*sic*], and stated that the young couple had left on their honeymoon trip and would be back later." [13]

Mr. and Mrs. Barnes returned to Memphis to face the Ramseys, find a place to live, and gainful employment. Geneva's parents were forgiving and understanding. George Ramsey welcomed his new son-in-law to the family and offered him a job running the warehouse, overseeing all the construction equipment that was kept at his company. Kelly eagerly accepted. He was moved by the gesture and promised his bride that he would work hard and prove to George Ramsey that trust in his abilities was not misplaced.

Kelly learned a great deal from his father-in-law about the family business. He respected and admired the man and wanted to make him proud. George recognized his son-in-law's talents and never missed an opportunity to encourage him. George was the father Kelly had always hoped for, and when Geneva informed her husband that he was going to be a dad, Kelly wanted to be the kind of father to his son that George had been to him. The expectant parents had no idea the happiness they were experiencing would soon turn into heartbreak. On October 22, 1920, a dynamite explosion claimed George Ramsey's life. The accident occurred on a contract levee job on the river between New Madrid, Missouri, and Hickman, Kentucky. George died en route to Memphis for surgical treatment.[14]

The Ramsey family was devastated by the patriarch's death. Kelly was deeply affected by his father-in-law's passing. George had taken him under his wing and made him feel worthwhile. The belief he had in his aptitude had been life-changing. Kelly wept along with his wife, mother, and brothers-in-law and desperately tried to think about the baby on the way. A week after George Ramsey's funeral, Geneva and Kelly welcomed the birth of their first son. They named the boy after his father and grandfather.[15]

Not long after George Ramsey's death, his contracting business was sold to a competitor, and Kelly was left without a job. He was despondent over this quick reversal of fortune, and in a short time all the funds he'd set aside to support his wife and son were depleted. Kelly's mother-in-law noticed the desperate situation and loaned him money to purchase a used car dealership in downtown Memphis. He moved Geneva and George into an apartment near his work and had hopes the business venture would prove successful.

Auto sales were slow in 1921. Kelly was only able to pay his expenses, with little left over for food and rent. He briefly contemplated returning to bootlegging because he knew the trade and knew that a thirsty public would go to great lengths to purchase a drink. Money for a drink was easier to come by than funds for a vehicle. Geneva's view against alcohol kept Kelly from entering the profession again.[16]

Less than a year after opening the lot, Kelly left automotive sales to become a goat farmer. His mother-in-law financially backed that venture as well. That business lost money too. In desperation, Kelly reached out to his father to get him a job selling insurance. Ashamed and humiliated at having to stoop so low as to contact a man he resented drove him to drink. When selling insurance didn't yield the money Kelly needed to support his family in the way he thought necessary, he decided to quit. Selling liquor was an attractive alternative, and after reaching out to a few old contacts, Kelly was back in the driver's seat, distributing alcohol to needy customers.[17]

Geneva believed George's travels out of town were related to selling insurance. She did not know he was bootlegging. She did notice a change in his behavior, however. Kelly was distant and spent little time at home with her and their son. She had a miscarriage in late 1921, and he was too busy to consider the loss or to help Geneva through the tragedy. It wasn't until Kelly was arrested on January 30, 1922, for possession of alcohol that she understood why he'd been withdrawn and disinterested in their family.[18]

"George K. Barnes and P. G. Hammers were arrested yesterday morning by Police Officers Mavo and Jester, and forty quarts of red whiskey were found in an automobile which they had been driving," the January 31, 1922, edition of the *Commercial Appeal* reported. "The car, a Ford coupe, was covered with mud, showing signs of having made a cross-country trip. When first noticed it was parked in front of a local café and the occupants were inside at breakfast. On investigation the officers found the whiskey. The car and the two men were taken to police headquarters.[19]

"There they stated that they had driven from Savannah, Georgia, and a Georgia automobile license was found in the car, and a Tennessee license on the car.[20]

"P. G. Hammers put up a $50 forfeit fine and was released to appear this morning, but up to press time had not been located by the police or the government agents. A prohibition officer, C. H. Boyd, took charge of Barnes and the car, and is holding them for further investigation."[21]

Geneva borrowed the money from her mother to bail Kelly out of jail. She warned him that she would divorce him if he didn't stop selling and transporting alcohol. He agreed to leave it behind, but he had no intention of honoring her request.[22]

Kelly began to drink heavily, and he was a mean drunk. He and Geneva argued, and often their fights would escalate into violence. He was physically abusive to his wife and little boy. Shortly after Geneva decided to leave Kelly and move back to her mother's home, she found out she was going to have another child. Kelly stood trial on the charge of transporting liquor, was fined one hundred dollars, and had to spend sixty days in the county jail. He regretted his actions and when he was released, he tried for weeks to get Geneva to see him so he could apologize. Finally, she relented and agreed to give him another chance.[23]

The Barnes's second son, Robert, was born on January 8, 1925. By March of the same year. Kelly's interest in insurance again began to wane. He dabbled a little with hauling liquor to various locations within the county and was eventually lured back into the lifestyle full time. Geneva knew he had returned to his old ways because he was gone a lot and he always had lots of money. One night he came home drunk, and when Geneva asked him how he could allow the situation to repeat itself, he flew into a rage and slapped her around. She filed for divorce on October 28, 1926. According to the October 29, 1926, edition of the *Commercial Appeal*, paperwork for the dissolution of marriage noted he had deserted her and their children on March 1, 1926. It also noted that Kelly was cruel, drank to excess, and stayed out all night. Try as Kelly did to reach out to Geneva and beg forgiveness, it was too late. After being awarded custody of their two children, she moved, on hoping to never see him again.[24]

Kelly became despondent and searched in vain to find a way to relieve his pain. The thought that his ex-wife would continue on without him, and that he wouldn't be able to see his sons whenever he wanted, made him suicidal. He tried to kill himself by taking an overdose of bichloride of mercury. The poison made him violently ill and he called an ambulance to take him to the hospital. Geneva and Kelly's father were both called to the emergency room. When they learned what had happened, George Sr. was less than sympathetic with his son. When Kelly awoke from the ordeal, his father told him to either straighten himself out or use a gun the next time he wanted to kill himself and do the job right. Geneva wasn't as brutal but did make it clear that nothing he did would change her mind about him. After being released from the hospital, Kelly decided to leave the despair behind and move to Missouri.[25]

The population of Kansas City was more than 325,000 in 1922. The commercial growth in the downtown area was exploding. Prohibition amplified the influence of corrupt politicians who made the city into a wide-open town. Its free-flowing liquor and abundance of vice earned Kansas City the title Paris of the Plains. Kelly fit nicely into the area. He took a job as a clerk at a grocery store but, like always, he found the work didn't pay as well as his illegal pursuits. Kelly regularly stole money from the cash register at the market where he was employed. In time, he had enough to purchase a truck to use to transport liquor for distributors. He told his boss at the store that he had to quit because his family back East had offered him a position at their company and he couldn't turn it down. Kelly knew the bookkeeper at the market would eventually discover the shortage and link it to him. The store owner wouldn't be able to do anything by that time because the guilty party had supposedly left town. It was during this time that George dropped his father's name and began using his mother's maiden name, which was Kelly.[26]

Kelly excelled in the bootlegging trade. He hauled merchandise to Texas, Oklahoma, Mississippi, and New Mexico. He bought three additional trucks during his first five years in Kansas City and hired drivers to expand the delivery service. In most places where he operated, he bribed police officers and politicians to allow him to conduct his business without fear of arrest. He assumed he'd be able to do the same when he drove a shipment of alcohol into New Mexico, but the authorities he tried to pay off refused to be corrupted.

On March 2, 1927, prohibition officers in Alamogordo attempted to apprehend Kelly and his driver speeding through town in a Buick Master Roadster. The bootleggers refused to stop, and a twelve-mile chase ensued. During the pursuit, Kelly and his employee tossed "sacks of booze" from the car. Kelly finally brought the vehicle to a stop on the side of the road. The officers rushed to the car with their guns drawn. Four cases of whiskey were found in the trunk.[27]

In a hearing before the US commissioner, Kelly and his cohort pleaded not guilty and were ordered to appear in federal court in Santa Fe on April 4, 1927. Both were held in jail, their bonds set at one thousand dollars each. By mid-May, circumstances had changed for Kelly. He and his driver were released from jail after having paid a two-hundred-fifty-dollar fine. Associates of Kelly believed he found someone willing to accept an offer of cash in exchange for helping him avoid going to court.[28]

In May 1927, Kelly moved his base of operations from Kansas City to Oklahoma. He worried the federal authorities he dealt with in New Mexico, who knew he worked out of Missouri, would find him and cause trouble. He decided to leave the area to avoid any potential confrontation. Unfortunately, things did not go as Kelly planned. Two months after he established his bootlegging business in Tulsa, he was arrested on a vagrancy charge.[29]

On July 24, 1927, Kelly once again found himself in trouble with the law. This time it was because of his known association with a pharmacist-turned-thief named George Turner. Turner had been arrested for trying to steal the nightly deposit from the drugstore where he was employed. The police knew Turner helped Kelly deliver whiskey on occasion, and they made their way to the home of Little Steve Stephens and his wife, Bess, where Kelly was suspected of being. All three were escorted to the police station to tell the authorities what they knew about Turner. The Stephenses were eventually released, but not before paying a fifty-dollar fine because a sack of empty liquor bottles was found inside their house. Kelly was fined twenty dollars and held over while an investigation was being conducted on a bootlegging charge. Enough evidence was found to send the case to trial, which was scheduled for August.

Kelly was released on a two-hundred-fifty-dollar bond. Five days before the hearing, Kelly was arrested for running away from the police, who were trying to arrest him on the earlier vagrancy charge. He sped away from the officers in his car and they followed him. The chase went on for several blocks before Kelly was captured. By the end of August, all charges were dismissed and no additional fines were imposed.[30]

Kelly's encounters with the law did not inspire him to change his ways. In fact, the dismissal of the offenses demonstrated to him that his charm and, if need be, the bribes he made, could get him out of any difficulties. In January 1928, Kelly was once again socializing with bootlegging competitor Little Steve Stephens and his now ex-wife Bess at the home Stephens purchased while they were married. The police found Kelly at the location when they went searching for him for failure to appear in court on a liquor violation charge in Miami, Oklahoma. He was arrested and held at the Tulsa city jail. The following day, Little Steve was arrested on liquor possession and conspiracy to violate prohibition laws and confined at the same jail. He was furious when the authorities told him where they caught up with Kelly, and the compromising position they found him in with his former wife. Bess too had been arrested on liquor possession and selling charges and had paid 10 percent of the ten-thousand-dollar bond two weeks prior.[31]

According to the January 13, 1928, edition of the *Tulsa Tribune*, Kelly and Bess had been seeing each other for some time. "I sent the money [for the bond] $1,500 to Bess from St. Louis," Kelly told a reporter for the newspaper. Kelly objected to the insinuation that he and the former Mrs. Stephens were more than friends. He insisted he was only at the Stephens home to retrieve the vehicle he had parked on the property.[32]

Kelly, Little Steve, and Bess were tried and convicted for violating the National Prohibition Act. The trio was sentenced to three years in prison. Little Steve was sent to the Atlanta Penitentiary, Bess to the Federal Industrial Institute for Women in Alderson, West Virginia, and Kelly to the Leavenworth Penitentiary.[33]

Leavenworth was the country's largest maximum-security

prison. Founded in 1875 as a military prison, it housed more than fifteen-hundred inmates. The walls were forty feet high, forty feet belowground, and three thousand thirty feet long. Kelly would be keeping company with some of the most notorious criminals of the time. Among the men he became acquainted with were bank and train robbers Thomas Holden and Frank Nash, bank robber Francis Keating, and lawman-turned-outlaw, bootlegger, and bank robber, Verne Miller.

Kelly's stay at Leavenworth would not lead to rehabilitation. He became an eager student gathering as much information as he could from his convict teachers. No one was more honored by the hero worship than Verne Miller. He was happy to answer any questions Kelly had about the jobs he pulled and what he would have done differently to keep from being caught. Kelly wasn't opposed to doing whatever he could to get whatever any of his new friends needed to make life easier on the inside or to get back on the outside. He worked in the records and photography department, where he had access to photographs, fingerprints, and background information on each inmate in the twenty-three-acre facility. Thomas Holden and Francis Keating took advantage of Kelly's services in February 1930 when they had him create paperwork that allowed them to leave the prison on a work detail.[34]

"Using forged outside passes, Thomas Holden and Francis L. Keating, serving sentences of twenty-five years each for robbing a mail car on a Grand Trunk Railroad train at Evergreen Park, in September 1926, escaped from the federal penitentiary here yesterday and still were at large today," an article in the March 1, 1930, edition of the *Manhattan Mercury* read.[35]

"With a new guard at the main entrance of the prison Holden and Keating appeared about 10 o'clock yesterday morning. In some undetermined manner they had procured two pass cards of the regular kind used by trusty prisoners detailed to outside employment. They had obtained photographs of themselves which were pasted on the backs of the cards, as regularly required.[36]

"Satisfied of their proper identification, the guard allowed them to pass through the gate and their escape was not discovered until late afternoon. A half mile west of the prison the heavy duck coats worn by the prisoners were found and nearby were the forged passes.[37]

"Warden Thomas B. White today was conducting a rigid investigation to discover how the men obtained the passes and photographs. The latter are kept only in the photograph room and the office of the records clerk."[38]

The warden's investigation proved inconclusive. Kelly was suspected of having a hand in the convicts' escape but it couldn't be proved. He was removed from the records and photography department. Holden and Keating remembered what Kelly had done for them when he was released four months later.[39]

Kelly returned to Kansas City after being released on July 3, 1930, and picked up where he left off with his bootlegging business. During his absence, he had a crew working for him selling and transporting alcohol. He had amassed a sizable amount of money by the time he regained control of day-to-day affairs. His priorities had shifted during his incarceration. Kelly's interest in bootlegging had diminished. He set his sights on robbing banks. As his ambitions changed, so did his appearance. He invested in a new wardrobe—tailored suits, silk ties and shirts—and he frequented only the finest restaurants and nightclubs. Not only did he focus on how and where he was seen but with whom he was seen. He spent time with beautiful dancers, stage actresses, and lounge singers. When he wasn't making the most of his social life, he practiced shooting pistols and rifles and became proficient using both. Should the need arise, he wanted to be ready to defend himself against anyone who stood in the way of him getting what he wanted.[40]

Kelly traveled to St. Paul, Minnesota, to meet with Holden and Keating on July 10, 1930. Before breaking out of Leavenworth, the escaped convicts told him where to find them when he was free and ready to expand his criminal résumé. St. Paul was a haven for gangsters. Corrupt Police Chief John O'Connor welcomed outlaws to seek refuge in the city. As long as bad guys behaved themselves and agreed to pay bribes to city officials, no one would bother them. Kelly located the duo at a speakeasy called the Green Lantern Saloon, and shortly thereafter took part in the planning of his first bank robbery.[41]

The morning of July 15, 1930, was warm, sunny, and tranquil until it erupted in a hail of bullets as five armed men robbed the Bank of Willmar in Willmar, Minnesota, making off with thousands of dollars in cash and bonds. The holdup did not go as planned. Five men forced the twenty-five people inside the bank during the robbery to lie down on the floor and threatened to kill them if they didn't comply. While two of the five robbers stood guard with guns leveled at the bank customers and employees, the other three went about taking the money from the tellers' drawers and an opened safe. Somehow one of the bank employees managed to trip an alarm that alerted the businessmen in a nearby office to arm themselves and hurry to the scene. One of the robbers hit the bank employee over the head and in the face with the butt of his gun.[42]

After collecting more than one hundred thousand dollars in cash and bonds, the robbers raced out of the bank toward the getaway car waiting in front of the building. By that time, the businessmen from the nearby office had arrived and begun firing shots at the driver of the car. The actions of the daring locals were answered with a barrage of Thompson submachine gun fire. Several people were injured, including two of the thieves. The robbers fled the scene in a four-door sedan that had its windshield and back windows shot out by armed citizens as the vehicle sped away.[43]

Bank employees and patrons of the bank who were there during the holdup were able to give detailed descriptions of the robbers. Several victims of the bank robbery visited the Twin Cities' police department and the office of the State Crime Bureau to look through photographs of known criminals, but none were able to select any that resembled the bandits. Eighteen-year-old teller Howard Hong later said he thought one of the robbers could have been George Kelly, based on the picture he saw at the police station, but he couldn't be sure.[44]

Two hours after the bank robbery took place, authorities found the abandoned getaway car in northeast Minneapolis, more than a hundred miles from the scene of the crime.[45]

According to the Kandiyohi County Historical Society in Willmar, Minnesota, the robbery was never officially solved.

Unofficially, however, it was believed the bandits were Sammy Silverman, Frank Coleman, Robert Steinhardt, Harvey Bailey, Verne Miller, and George Kelly. A month after the brazen daylight crime took place, Sammy Silverman, Frank Coleman, and a third man were found shot to death at White Bear Lake, fourteen miles northeast of St. Paul. Silverman and Coleman were positively identified as two of the robbers who held up the bank in Willmar. Police suspected the thieves quarreled over the division of the money stolen and turned on one another.[46]

On September 8, 1930, Kelly and the crew he worked with on the Willmar bank job, robbed the Ottumwa Savings Bank in Ottumwa, Iowa. Kelly, Verne Miller, Thomas Holden, Francis Keating, and Harvey Bailey entered at ten in the morning, marched to the grated windows, and demanded the staff behind the counters to "stick 'em up." According to the September 9, 1930, edition of *The Gazette*, "This was followed by an order to lie down on the floor which was obeyed by seven employees and four customers.[47]

"The robbers thereupon went back of the counters where they gathered up all the available currency in a deliberate and unhurried manner. As they worked a threat was hurled at one of the girl employees who sought to see what was going on from her prone position on the floor. 'Get your head down there or I'll blow your brains out,' one of the robbers shouted.[48]

" . . . No shots were fired as none of those in the bank made any effort to resist the robbers."[49]

The robbers sped away from the scene in a Buick sedan with more than twenty-five thousand dollars. Descriptions of the five bandits who held up the bank were given to the State Bureau of Investigation and distributed to law enforcement agents from Des Moines to Chicago. The Ottumwa Savings Bank was the twelfth bank robbery in the state in a nine-month period.[50]

Kelly, Keating, Miller, and the other thieves took their shares of the ill-gotten gains and went their separate ways. Kelly decided to lay low in Fort Worth, Texas. In between passing himself off as a banker to the affluent people he met at the exclusive hotel where he was staying, the bootlegger and bank robber frequented the popular nightspots in town. He hadn't planned to fall in love nor find him-self involved with another woman with ties to Little Steve Stephens, but days after being reintroduced to Kathryn Thorne, she was con-suming his every thought.[51]

Kelly and Kathryn traveled to Minneapolis, Minnesota, where they applied for a marriage license. They exchanged vows on Sep-tember 24, 1930. Little Steve wasn't surprised Kathryn and Kelly ran off together. He reportedly told a friend, "I don't mind George tak-ing my girl, but they took my dog. I wish he'd left the dog."[52]

CHAPTER 3

⟨━━◆━━⟩

ADVENTURES IN KIDNAPPING

THE ENORMOUS SUITE AT THE luxurious Dallas hotel where George Kelly and his bride Kathryn were spending their honeymoon was strewn with open boxes and empty shopping bags from several department stores. The floor, dresser, and chairs were cluttered with new dresses, high-heeled shoes, lingerie, silk stockings, fancy hats, and gloves. Kathryn pirouetted in front of an ornate floor-length mirror wearing nothing more than a formfitting lace slip and a mink coat. Kelly watched her model the trousseau he'd purchased for her from the comfort of a wingback chair opposite an unmade bed. He was dressed in a pair of new trousers and a crisp white shirt with an attached soft collar unbuttoned to the nape of his neck. His appreciation for fine clothing matched that of his new wife's.[1]

The Kellys had been married less than a week, and when they weren't locked away in their suite or buying out the stores, they were dining in the city's most expensive restaurants and visiting speakeasies. Kathryn didn't ask her husband where the large roll of bills he frequently unfurled to pay for their lavish living had come from. She knew and she didn't care. She wanted more, and Kelly promised there would be.[2]

On October 2, 1930, Kelly and Kathryn packed their belongings into a top-of-the-line Cadillac and drove sixty-seven miles to the town of Paradise in Wise County, Texas.

Kathryn's family was eagerly awaiting their arrival. The Shannon farm wasn't much to look at. Three dilapidated buildings sat on the property. In addition to the main house there was a shed and a garage of sorts. Each one looked as if a strong wind would bring down the walls. Boss Shannon built the home four miles outside of Paradise on the acreage he purchased with his first wife, Icye. Boss and Icye had two children, and she passed away at the age of twenty-five. Boss's second wife was his deceased wife's sister. They had three children together before she too died.

The Shannon children helped their father work the farm, and for a time they managed to eke out a meager living. The drought that struck the region in the late 1920s transformed the promising homestead. High winds and choking dust swept across the area, and people and livestock were killed and crops failed. Add to that the crushing economic impact of the Great Depression and farms like the Shannons' fell into disrepair. The Shannons' earnings were derived from a variety of sources, the majority of which weren't legal.[3]

In addition to Kathryn's mother and stepfather, Kelly would be meeting seventeen-year-old Armon, fifteen-year-old Oather, and nine-year-old Ruth, Boss's children from his second wife, and Kathryn's daughter, ten-year-old Pauline.[4]

The Shannons stepped out onto the porch when they saw Kelly's car approaching. Kathryn checked her look in a compact she produced from her purse and adjusted the mink draped over her shoulders. The newlyweds seemed out of place in their designer outfits and behind the wheel of their slick automobile. The contrast wasn't lost on the pair. Outside of thinking how much his wife didn't belong in the setting, Kelly was indifferent to the matter, but Kathryn relished it. Proving she was better than what she'd come from meant everything to her.[5]

Kathryn emerged from the vehicle like a starlet arriving at a film premiere. After hugging her mother and daughter, she stretched out her hand to Kelly. Smiling proudly, he took her hand in his and stood at her side as she introduced him to the family. Kathryn hadn't informed her parents that she'd gotten married again, so they were taken aback. Boss was quick to welcome Kelly to the clan, and Ora was equally as inviting. After congratulating the couple, they were ushered inside to share the meal Ora, Pauline, and Ruth had prepared. It was a pleasant evening, with lots of attention paid to Kathryn's fur coat, and the adults sharing a glass or two of Boss's bootleg whiskey. Questions about how the pair met were happily answered, but Kelly hesitated briefly when he was queried about his occupation. Kathryn tried to hide a grin when he announced he was in banking.[6]

The Kellys' visit with the Shannons concluded after two days, and the happy couple returned to Fort Worth. They moved into a modest house on Mulkey Street that Kathryn's third husband had owned and was passed on to her after his death. There was nothing typical about Kathryn and Kelly's home life. They were constantly on the go. They liked parties and attending the theater, and if the action became too tame for them in Texas, they would travel to Miami or Chicago. When Kelly's portion of the money he helped steal from banks in Iowa and Minnesota began to dwindle, he briefly entertained the idea of pursuing a legitimate profession. He had an opportunity to purchase a Ford dealership but decided it wouldn't provide the money he and Kathryn needed to live as they had been. Both relished shortcuts in life—robbing instead of working and stealing whatever they wanted instead of buying.[7]

Unwilling to return to the bootlegging trade because the risk versus reward was too high, and disinterested in nine-to-five jobs, Kelly decided to reach out to the men he'd robbed banks with earlier in the year. He and Kathryn traveled to Kansas City to meet with Verne Miller. Kelly wanted Miller to put in a good word for him with Harvey Bailey, who was also in town. The two hadn't seen each other since robbing the bank in Willmar, Minnesota, and Kelly wanted Bailey to know he was still someone who could be trusted. Miller agreed but urged Kelly to make the initial connection himself, and to do so without Kathryn beside him. Bailey was opposed to wives interjecting themselves into his business. It was common knowledge that Kathryn made a few bootlegging runs with Little Steve, and Kelly and Miller was certain Kelly would have no chance of being invited to participate in future jobs if Kathryn was part of the package.[8]

Mrs. Kelly was on another shopping spree when her husband met with Bailey in his room at the President Hotel on Baltimore Avenue. During their brief meeting where Kelly asked to be considered a part of any future robberies, he admitted to Bailey that he had no money. Bailey gave him one thousand dollars and assured him that he'd be in touch. True to his word, and after a conversation with Verne Miller, Bailey contacted Kelly and recruited him for a bank job in Sherman, Texas. Kelly let Kathryn know about his discussion with Bailey on their way back to Fort Worth. He and Bailey were to meet in Dallas and drive to Sherman together to look over the bank and plan the job. In addition to Bailey, Miller, and Kelly, two other men were recruited to help with the robbery of the Central State Bank on April 7, 1931. There were two getaway cars. Kelly was the driver of one of those vehicles. The thieves split up and later reunited at a well-known hotel in Hot Springs, Arkansas.[9]

The crime made the front page of newspapers from El Paso to San Antonio. "Central State Bank Held Up By Five Unmasked Men," the headline of the *Corsicana Daily Sun* read. "The Central State Bank of Sherman was robbed of $40,000 in cash and liberty bonds at 2:45 p.m. today," the article noted.[10]

"The men were believed to have driven southward toward Dallas. They were pursued by officers and citizens in cars. Ten employees and customers in the bank were compelled by the five unmasked, armed men to march into a back room of the building and turn their faces to the wall.[11]

"A. E. Jamison, cashier, was ordered to open the vault, where the robbers scooped up all currency and money in sight and prepared to make their departure.[12]

"As they were leaving, Barlow Roberts, president, entered. They halted him and searched him, to see if he was armed, then ordered Barlow to join the others in the back room facing the wall. As soon as the robbers were out of sight, the alarm was given and motorcycle policemen sped along streets and highways about the town, searching for the quintet.[13]

"J. S. Knight, traveling salesman, told officers he saw five or six men in a large green sedan driving hurriedly along a street in the outskirts of the city. Another citizen said the sedan nearly overturned in rounding a corner at high speed."[14]

Once the money taken from the bank was divided between the robbers, they went their separate ways, with instructions to keep a low profile for at least a month. The Kellys decided the best place to do that was at the Shannon farm.[15]

Boss Shannon, who himself wasn't immune to shortcuts, suspected Kelly and Kathryn weren't visiting strictly because Kathryn missed her daughter and mother. News of the robbery in Sherman made it to Paradise too, and it seemed to Shannon more than a coincidence that the pair was flush with money and wanted to stay close to the farm. They also spent a lot of time target practicing with a variety of weapons, including a Thompson submachine gun. Kathryn was as good with a gun as Kelly. In a private moment with Kelly, Shannon delicately questioned his stepson-in-law about the timing of their trip. Kelly didn't shy away from the topic but rather confirmed Shannon's suspicions. He offered to pay Shannon to hide out on his property. The money was accepted not only because the Shannon family could use it but because Kelly insisted, making it clear that betrayal had serious consequences.[16]

Kathryn lavished her daughter, stepsister, and mother with gifts, buying them bedroom furniture and a radio. The Kellys purchased a car for Pauline, who wasn't old enough to drive yet. The entire Shannon family used the vehicle. They were grateful for the advantages the Kellys heaped upon them and never questioned the generous attention.[17]

A few months after the Central State Bank robbery, Kelly ventured out to meet with the thieves he'd worked with on the job. The criminals met in Illinois and in Minnesota to plan smaller robberies that would yield enough money to tide them over until they were able to target their next big burglary. Kelly and Kathryn rented apartments in Chicago and St. Paul while he was collaborating with his fellow outlaws. He didn't take his wife with him when he was working. Kathryn understood, but that didn't keep her from getting bored and lonely. Kelly felt bad about leaving her alone and purchased a pair of Pekingese puppies to keep her company. The dogs went everywhere with the couple.[18]

In late 1931, Kelly and Kathryn drove to the outskirts of Denver to meet with a friend Kelly knew from Leavenworth named Albert Bates. Bates had been arrested and jailed more than once for burglary. Kelly liked the man. He was soft-spoken and easy to get along with. He lived in a modest house in the forest and his neighbors believed him to be a traveling salesman hoping to settle permanently in the area. Bates invited the Kellys to his home to discuss robbing a bank in Boulder. Unlike the other bank jobs Kelly had been involved with, Kathryn would take part. She would disguise herself as a man and drive the getaway car. According to Kelly's youngest son, Robert "Bruce" Barnes, although the robbery was well planned, interference from a bank guard on duty kept the trio from getting away with the haul they anticipated. When the guard attempted to draw his weapon, Kelly shot him in the arm. The man was not seriously injured, but the gunplay rattled the thieves. As they hurried away from the scene, Kelly commented on how his nerves couldn't take many more such episodes. He wasn't in a hurry to add murder to his list of sins.[19]

The three returned to Bates's home, split the fifteen thousand dollars they had stolen, and the Kellys took off for Mexico.* During the 1920s, there were numerous banks in every state. FBI records note there was one bank for every one thousand persons across the nation. As the economic depression deepened in the early 1930s, and people had less money to spend, banks began to fail at an alarming rate. In all, nine thousand banks failed during the decade of the thirties. The problems created for bank robbers during this time were twofold: locating a bank that had enough funds in their tills to make it worth burglarizing and being able to execute the crime

---

* The author was unable to substantiate the Boulder bank robbery Bruce Barnes wrote that his father told him about in his biography. FBI records note the first bank robbery George Kelly and Albert Bates participated in together took place in Denton, Texas, on February 6, 1932.

without exchanging gunfire with bank guards and law enforcement agents called to the scene. Bank robbers faced risks of injury or death during the commission of a crime; in fact, the robber was the person most often killed.[20]

When Albert Bates met the Kellys next, they discussed the dangers involved with robbing a bank and decided the time had come to consider a safer way to acquire someone else's money. Reports of prominent, wealthy individuals from Buffalo, New York, to Bakersfield, California, often appeared in newspapers. The May 7, 1931, edition of the Baltimore, Maryland, newspaper *The Evening Sun* announced that St. Louis and Detroit were the kidnapping centers in the United States. "Criminal gangs, with their income curtailed as a result of diminished public thirst for bootleg products, have turned to preying on persons with money," the article noted. "Outfits in St. Louis and Detroit operated in the ransom field with such lucrative results that they are being emulated."[21]

Kathryn, Kelly, and Albert Bates believed kidnapping would not only be safer than robbery but easier in the long run. Kelly and Bates had experience planning or being in on the planning of robbing banks and reasoned the only real work that needed to be done after selecting a wealthy target would be where to hide the victim and arranging the ransom payment. Kathryn was quick to suggest she be allowed to find the right person to be kidnapped. Depending on how well off and influential the individual was would determine how much money they could demand for their release. Kathryn routinely pored over society pages of various newspapers and was confident she could pick a target who would yield a handsome profit.[22]

Howard Woolverton, the secretary treasurer of the Indiana manufacturing company Malleable Steel Range and son of a South Bend bank president, was identified as a promising kidnap victim. Bates decided not to take part in the crime and was replaced with another convict out of Leavenworth and a member of a gang of criminals from Chicago with ties to Al Capone, named Eddie LaRue. Kelly met LaRue at the Kansas institution, and a few of LaRue's associates, such as Eddie Bentz, had worked with Kelly robbing banks. LaRue had ties to Indiana, having robbed a bank there in November 1931.[23]

On January 26, 1932, Kelly and LaRue abducted Woolverton and his wife, Florence, as the couple was driving home from a movie theater. According to the January 27, 1932, edition of the *Reporter Times*, one of the unmasked crooks asked a bewildered Woolverton who he was and what his job title was. Once Woolverton answered the question, LaRue forced Woolverton into the back seat of their car; then Kelly got behind the wheel of the vehicle and drove the victims to an isolated spot two miles east of the city. LaRue followed them in the getaway car. Once the vehicles stopped, Florence was forced out of the Woolvertons' and warned that her husband would be held until she paid a fifty-thousand-dollar ransom. The kidnappers then pulled Woolverton out of his car and loaded him into the back seat of theirs. They handed Florence a note and told her to drive home and wait for instructions on where to take the money. Kelly and LaRue sped off. Florence was stopped by the police en route because she ran a red light. The hysterical woman broke down and told the officer what had transpired.[24]

Patrol cars were immediately dispatched to hunt for the kidnappers' vehicle before they had a chance to get out of the area. "We had eaten dinner and spent the early part of the evening at the country club," Florence later told investigators. "After dinner we drove into town and went to a movie. It was late when the show was over and we stopped at a little lunchroom for a bite to eat and then started to drive home."[25]

"We had driven almost to our house when the kidnappers' machine [car] pulled alongside ours and forced my husband to stop by the curb. Two young men jumped out. They had revolvers in their hands. . . ."[26]

The note Kelly and LaRue gave Florence read as follows:

"On Wednesday at 8 p.m. take your four-passenger Packard auto with license No. 20 and trunk on the rear. Go to Chicago Heights. Before leaving take $50,000 and wrap it into a strong bundle. On your way we will signal you by flashing our headlights nineteen times. We will then be behind you and drive on to Danville and return home from there. Say nothing to the police. If there is any slip up in this plan your husband may be killed."[27]

Woolverton tried to explain to his captors that he did not have fifty thousand dollars for a ransom. Furious, LaRue negotiated with Woolverton's lawyer and family spokesperson Gallitzin A. Farabaugh for a lesser amount. After receiving less than ten thousand dollars, Woolverton was released twenty-four hours after being kidnapped. Farabaugh told the police that days after Woolverton was reunited with his family he received a threatening call from a woman who warned, "You're next, Mr. Farabaugh." Federal authorities believed Kathryn was the woman.[28]

Some historical accounts indicate that by the week of February 4, 1932, Kelly was on to another bank robbery in Denton, Texas, and Kathryn was waiting for him at their home in Fort Worth. Kelly, Albert Bates, and a third man wore masks when they entered the Pilot Point National Bank in Denton County, Texas, on February 6, at ten o'clock in the morning. The bandits blew the safe with explosives and stole eight thousand dollars in cash and eleven thousand dollars in registered liberty bonds. To keep the authorities from being alerted, they cut phone cables and fire alarm wires. The getaway car was seen speeding northward down a dirt road toward Gainesville, Texas. Officially, the bank robbery was never solved. Bureau agents didn't believe Kelly had anything to do with the bank robbery in Denton because he'd never worn a mask during any of his previous bank robberies and never used explosives.[29]

The Kellys' and LaRue's ability to extract cash from Howard Woolverton's family for his release, although for a much lesser amount, whetted Kathryn's appetite for kidnapping. After a careful review of potential victims, she targeted Guy Waggoner, the eldest son of W. T. Waggoner, owner of the Waggoner Ranch and Oil Refinery in Fort Worth. The idea of abducting Guy Waggoner was on Kathryn's mind when planning one of the parties she often hosted. Two of the men on the guest list were police officers she suspected were crooked. She hoped to persuade law enforcement agents K. W. Swinney and Ed Weatherford to help with the crime. Swinney and Weatherford agreed to attend her gathering, hoping they could get her to turn on Kelly and become their informant. They believed she knew about the robberies he'd committed and those he'd planned to take part in.[30]

Katherine was careful not to give away too much information about abducting Waggoner. She said just enough to judge the men's interest in the kidnapping proposition. Swinney and Weatherford declined to take part because they said the job sounded too dangerous. Still convinced the two officers were corrupt, she asked them to do her a favor. She wanted the men to intercede should Kelly or Albert Bates get arrested in another state. If that occurred, she wanted the officers to step in and claim the pair were wanted in Texas for bank robbery. After they had the outlaws in custody, they could let them go free, claiming they escaped. Weatherford and Swinney agreed.[31]

After the party, the policemen returned to their office and made a call to the Bureau of Investigation to inform them that Guy Waggoner was a kidnap target. The Kellys changed their minds about abducting Waggoner when they learned the family had hired security guards to make sure the businessman was safe.[32]

The story that was splashed across the front page of newspapers everywhere on March 12, 1932, took the world by surprise and brought the kidnapping epidemic to the full attention of Congress. The son of aviator Charles Lindbergh and his wife, Anne, was taken from his nursery on the second floor of the Lindbergh home near Hopewell, New Jersey. The boy was only twenty months old. The abduction of the child and his subsequent murder proved to be the shocking catalyst necessary to drive the federal government to rush the creation of a bill to curb kidnappings.[33]

The week before Charles Lindbergh Jr. was carried off and a ransom note delivered to his terrified parents, Congress discussed the kidnapping issue in depth. Tales of kidnapping and torture for ransom crimes in the Midwest were relayed to them during their session. These crimes were reportedly being perpetrated by an alleged ring working in many cities. Offenders were transporting the kidnapping victims from city to city to place the barrier of state lines between the criminal and the law. Members of the House Judiciary Committee were determined to create a law that would ensure kidnappers would receive the death penalty if convicted. The public was behind such a venture. Senators and congressmen were overwhelmed with endorsements from their constituents.[34]

Among the endorsers from the state of Indiana was the man abducted by Kelly and LaRue two months prior to the Lindbergh kidnapping, Howard Woolverton. In a letter to Senator James E. Watson, Woolverton wrote, "Being one of the most recent victims of acts covered by this bill, I cannot urge you too strongly to give favorable consideration. In my estimation from my personal experience these two measures are of extreme importance."[35]

The Kellys had no idea of the impact their first kidnap victim would have on their future. The pair was sickened by the thought of someone abducting a child. There were limits to the crimes the Kellys were willing to commit. Infants and toddlers were off-limits. Adults with healthy bank accounts, or who had parents with healthy bank accounts, were completely acceptable.[36]

With their kidnapping career on hold, Kelly reteamed with Albert Bates and Eddie Bentz to rob the First Trust and Savings Bank in Colfax, Washington, on September 22, 1932. The unmasked men entered the building carrying submachine guns and forced ten bank employees and six customers to lie face down on the floor while they cleared out the teller's drawers and took cash and bonds from the vault. The thieves locked the front door behind them as they entered the lobby, and when their job was done, they fled out the back carrying sacks of stolen money. The loot was loaded into a green Chevrolet sedan in the alley near the rear entrance. Bank officials later estimated the trio took off with more than $71,000 in cash and negotiable securities.[37]

Posses were dispatched immediately and traveled in the direction witnesses reported the bandits were seen going, but the gangsters were nowhere to be found.[38]

By November, the stolen bonds had been recovered by the bank's insurance company and authorities had a lead on the whereabouts of Eddie Bentz and Albert Bates. The description given by the bank employees matched that of Kelly, Bentz, and Bates, and the police were desperately searching for Bentz not only for the Colfax bank robbery but for other bank robberies he had committed in Washington. He was arrested on November 9, 1932, in Fort Worth as a suspect in the Colfax bank robbery and later charged with a bank heist committed in August in Collin County, Texas. Bentz was released after a bond was paid and then disappeared.[39]

Kathryn did not sit idle waiting for Kelly to return from his business venture. She was young, impetuous, and enjoyed visiting private clubs and restaurants where drinks flowed freely and most of the clientele were often at odds with the law. Among acquaintances who knew a little about her background and a lot about her husband's, she was prone to brag about Kelly's various jobs, the men he worked with, and his exceptional skill with a Thompson submachine gun. From time to time, she would distribute spent cartridge cases with Kelly's initials scratched on them to admirers and their friends. As she handed the items to eager people, she would explain that they were souvenirs "courtesy of Machine Gun Kelly." Thanks to his wife, Kelly's criminal celebrity grew at a rate equal to his felony offenses.[40]

The Kellys' last bank robbery in 1932 took place on November 30, at the Citizens State Bank in Tupelo, Mississippi. This time, Eddie LaRue joined Kelly and Bates in the crime. The three were unmasked and Kelly chose a .38 pistol to threaten the bank employees and customers with rather than a submachine gun. According to the December 1, 1932, edition of the *Sun Sentinel*, the robbers fled the scene in a car driven by what witnesses said was a woman disguised as a man. More than fifty thousand dollars in cash and bonds were stolen.[41]

Teller Homer Edgewood, who was forced by the bandits to open the vault and fill a bag with all the cash and bonds in sight, noted that the man he initially identified as Charles "Pretty Boy" Floyd was really George Kelly. He told the police that, "He was the kind of guy that, if you looked at him, you would have never thought he was a bank robber."[42]

Police chased the getaway car as it sped out of town toward Birmingham, but the driver managed to lose the authorities, and no trace of the gangsters could be found.[43]

Like many times before, Kathryn and Kelly sought refuge from their illegal acts at the Shannon farm in Paradise. They spent Christmas with the family and, before New Year's Eve, returned to their home in Fort Worth.

While the Kellys spent their year planning on executing robberies or abductions, Congress had been busy amending and rephrasing the Federal Kidnapping Act to satisfy lawmakers in the House and Senate. On June 17, 1932, Congress passed the act, sometimes referred to as the Lindbergh Law, making kidnapping across state lines a federal felony. President Herbert Hoover signed the act into law on June 25, 1932. The law enacted did not supersede state measures against the offense. It merely allowed the federal government to prosecute the offenders as well, if, in their seizure of persons for ransom or other purposes, the victims were carried across state lines.[44]

An article about the passage of the act in the June 25, 1932, edition of the *Indianapolis News* explained that, "Since kidnappers frequently travel far from the scene of their crime, the federal statute complements the state laws. An interesting feature of the measure is the broad power given federal judges over sentences of persons found guilty. Anyone, the law reads, who knowingly conveys a kidnapped individual from state to state, or to a foreign country, is to be punished by imprisonment for such term of years as the court, in its discretion, shall determine. That is, confinement may be any period up to life. The maximum sentence risked is more severe than that provided for by many states thus far, and is exceeded by only those that permit the death penalty."[45]

Whatever the politicians were doing in Washington, DC, was of no interest to the Kellys. They'd defied the law for several months and intended to continue to do so. Their goal for 1933 was to select a rich somebody to kidnap. By mid-January, they had identified their target. In celebration and preparation for their plan, Kathryn decided to purchase her husband a special gift from the Wolf & Klar Pawn Shop. She bought Machine Gun Kelly a model 1921 tommy gun.[46]

CHAPTER 4

THE ABDUCTION OF CHARLES URSCHEL

KIDNAPPING WAS AN EPIDEMIC in the United States between 1925 and 1934. Few states were exempt from the horrific dilemma. Limited resources and lack of manpower inhibited local law enforcement agencies from effectively tracking criminals who had taken individuals and held them captive. According to the March 3, 1932, edition of the *New York Times*, "Abduction for ransom has become a big money crime taking its place beside the liquor, vice and drug trafficking among the prominent rackets of the country."[1]

The authority of the federal government's Bureau of Investigation had yet to extend into the areas of kidnapping. Their area primarily involved enforcing prohibition and the Mann Act (also known as the White Slave Traffic Act), crimes on the high seas, and identifying Communist activities, to name a few. The Bureau of Investigation was established in 1908 and tasked with examining antitrust cases, such as the ones involving meat packaging plants and factories and oil companies. In less than fifty years, the agency was being investigated by Congress for a myriad of wrongdoings including questionable hiring practices and manufacturing evidence. The troubled Bureau was reorganized in 1924, and President Calvin Coolidge appointed twenty-nine-year-old J. Edgar Hoover as the director.[2]

Among the most notable kidnapping cases in the nation between 1925 and 1932 included the abduction of twenty-nine-year-old Madge Oberholtzer. She was taken by D. C. Stephenson, the Grand Dragon of the Indiana Ku Klux Klan. Oberholtzer was raped and murdered before authorities found her. Twelve-year-old Marion Parker, who was lured from school when she was told that her father, wealthy banker Perry M. Parker, had been injured, was also murdered by her abductor. Mary Agnes Moroney, a two-year-old child taken from her Chicago, Illinois, home, was never found in her parents' lifetimes.

And then there was Charles Augustus Lindbergh Jr. On March 1, 1932, the twenty-month-old boy was taken from his crib at his parents' East Coast home. The child's famous father's accomplishment as a military officer and the pioneer of international commercial aviation and air mail, had elevated him to celebrity status. Because of Lindbergh's notoriety, the governor of New Jersey, Arthur H. Moore, summoned the state's top investigators to handle the case. The Bureau of Investigation was also brought in to help.[3]

Lindbergh felt police involvement would jeopardize his son's life and rejected any assistance from them or government agents. Like most people at the time, he viewed the department as ineffective and incompetent. The Bureau had a reputation for politicized investigations as well, and Bureau agents weren't opposed to spying on members of Congress who disagreed with their policies.[4]

After the Lindbergh baby was found dead, Hoover, who had been hired to transform the Bureau, and his staff proved to be more helpful than the state authorities in finding a suspect. They covered thousands of leads across the United States, handwriting experts examined the ransom notes, and evidence left at the scene was thoroughly scrutinized by specialists.[5]

While the Bureau of Investigation was preoccupied with finding the murderer of the Lindbergh child, the Kellys were planning their next kidnapping.

Kathryn Kelly was reclining on an oversize sofa at the Texas home she shared with her husband. It was the fall of 1932. Magazines and newspapers were scattered about the coffee table in front of her and music from a Philco cabinet radio filled the room. She sang along with the tune "Everything I Have Is Yours" by Art Jarrett while circling items of interest found in issues of the *Fort Worth Star-Telegram*. The story she highlighted in the October 18, 1932, edition of the publication was about the marriage of widow Berenice Slick to widower Charles F. Urschel. Both were reported to be prominent, wealthy oil personalities. According to the article, the couple planned to leave immediately for an extended tour in Europe, then return to the mansion they purchased in Oklahoma on December 15. The article circled in the October 21, 1932, edition of the newspaper pertained to the appraisal of the estate of Berenice's late husband, wildcatter Thomas B. Slick. His Oklahoma holdings alone were worth more than six million dollars.[6]

Throughout November and December, Kathryn collected every newspaper article she could find on the Urschels. She read about the newlyweds' time in France and Italy and sailing to New York after their honeymoon. She learned the exact day they were to arrive in the States and the address of their home in Oklahoma City, 326 NW 18th Street, the names of their teenage children and where they attended school, and the bridge club luncheon scheduled to be held at the Urschel home in early December. The December 15, 1932, edition of the *Oklahoma News*, featured a story inviting readers to visit the Urschel's residence to see the beautiful table settings the bride and groom possessed.[7]

"I want to suggest to you that you drive by the Charles F. Urschel home at 18th Street and Hudson Avenue some night and take a look at the window of the dining room that faces on Hudson," the article read. "Mrs. Urschel has a passion for beautiful china and glass and in this window are shelves upon which stand glasses of various sizes, all in the ruby Venetian glass, through which the lamps of the dining room shine warmly out to the street at night and through which the setting sun pours gorgeous hues into the dining room, near the close of day."[8]

Kathryn discussed the Urschels with Kelly over the holidays and into the new year. She let him know about the newlyweds' busy social calendar and how the couple often attended dances at the country club to which they belonged and concerts at various venues in Oklahoma City. Kathryn learned from newspaper arti-cles how often the pair traveled to Chicago to visit family, that Charles Urschel preferred to walk alone to his office in the morn-ing, and that the two had a standing date on Saturday nights to play bridge with friends.[9]

Although they were uncomfortable with the idea of having a bodyguard around, the Urschels gave in to pressure from Bere-nice's parents and hired one. The man was fired shortly thereafter for sleeping on the job.[10]

According to Kelly's son Bruce Barnes, when his father expressed his concerns about the "big undertaking" to Kathryn, she assured her husband that nothing would go wrong with the kidnapping. "Don't worry," she told him. "We won't move until every last detail is in place." Kathryn suggested recruiting Albert Bates to be a part of the job. She pointed out that the pair had worked together well in the past. Kelly was persuaded that Charles Urschel was the perfect individual to hold for ransom. He specu-lated that Urschel's wife and family could part with two hundred thousand dollars for his release and never miss the funds.[11]

Kelly contacted Bates, and he agreed to meet with George and Kathryn in Oklahoma City. It was there Kathryn explained the job. Bates too was intrigued, and he and Kelly decided to spend time watching the Urschels' home and make notes of their com-ings and goings. When the Kellys weren't monitoring Charles Urschel's every move, they were in Paradise, planning the details of the abduction at the Shannon farm. Kelly informed Bates the farm would be the best place to keep Urschel while they waited for the ransom to be paid. Bates worried that bringing the Shannons in on the job would cause trouble. If Boss, his wife, or his sons decided to talk, the trio might be arrested before they had a chance to get their hands on the money. Kelly told Bates that the Shan-nons were going to be paid for their cooperation and promised his in-laws would be as silent as the grave.[12]

The kidnapping of Charles Urschel was originally scheduled to take place in early February 1933. An article in the *Tulsa World* newspaper noted that Berenice and Charles would be leaving town midmonth, so the Kellys determined that the fourth of February would be the day.[13] Freezing temperatures and a forecast of snow prompted the trio to rethink the timing. They rescheduled the job for some time in the summer. Kathryn monitored the local papers to keep abreast of the Urschels' activities. According to the July 10, 1933, edition of the *Oklahoma News*, the Urschels were planning to spend the remainder of the summer at home, having just returned from an extended vacation at the Edgewater Beach Hotel in Chicago. The couple was looking forward to resuming their usual bridge game and playing golf.[14]

Kelly and Bates kept each other informed as to what was happening with the Urschels via telegram. Many of those telegrams were sent and retrieved by Kathryn. For reasons of secrecy, Bates never sent telegrams to Kelly using George's name. He primarily used Kathryn's stepfather's name. Kelly often used R. G. Shannon as an alias. Just prior to the kidnapping, Bates was watching the Urschels' home and was in a better position to judge the best day for the abduction. Kelly's telegram to Bates, who used the alias George Davis, read, "Write me at same address. Give full particulars if and when drilling is to start." The coded message alluded to Urschel's oil drilling business, leaving no doubt as to whom Kelly was referring. Once the date was decided, Kelly and Kathryn reviewed the details of the job to make sure all was in order.[15]

On Friday, July 21, 1933, the day before the kidnapping, the Kellys and Bates met at the home of T. M. and Mary Coleman near Stratford, Oklahoma. The Colemans were Kathryn's maternal grandparents. The three had lunch with the elderly couple and a few guests the following day, and during the meal Kathryn discussed the failing health of her biological father, James Brooks. She had remained close to him despite her parents' divorce. She told her family that she planned to move her father from the hospital where he was a patient to another facility where he could get better care. Kathryn mentioned she planned to take care of her father as soon as she had the money to do so. Kelly proudly announced to all at the table, "We're going to have plenty of money pretty soon. There's going to be a kidnapping in Oklahoma City tonight."[16]

Before the trio left the Colemans' home around 2 p.m., Bates removed what one of Kathryn's cousins would later recall as an item that looked like a "fiddle case" from his maroon, two-door Chevrolet and placed it in Kelly's Buick. The two men drove off in the Buick. Kathryn stayed behind.[17]

The drive from Stratford to the Urschels' home in Oklahoma City was four hours. Bates pulled into the driveway at the rear of the house at 11:15 p.m. and got out. Kelly followed suit. The armed men proceeded to the back screened porch, opened the door, and marched into the residence with cool conviction. Berenice and Charles were sitting at a table across from their friends, Walter Jarrett and his wife, Clyde, playing bridge, when George Kelly, carrying the machine gun Kathryn had given him, entered the room with Bates at his side. The gangsters had only seen Urschel from afar and didn't readily know which of the two men was the intended victim.

"Everyone keep your seats and no one will get hurt," Kelly announced. "Which one of you is Urschel?" he asked sharply. The four startled card players were too scared to answer. The women instinctively reached out for their husbands.[18]

Clyde Jarrett turned slightly away from the others and started to get up out of her chair. George Kelly leveled his gun at the foursome and Mrs. Jarrett froze. "If you people don't want your brains blown out, you had better not move," he barked at them.

Bates pointed his pistol at Mrs. Urschel and Mrs. Jarrett while Kelly motioned with his gun for the two men to get to their feet. Kelly studied the men's faces, looking for something that would let him know which was Urschel. "We'll take both of them," he finally announced.[19]

Urschel and Jarett reluctantly stood up. Kelly nodded to Bates, who quickly moved to the men's side, his weapon inches from their chests. Bates escorted Urschel and Jarrett out the door. Kelly backed up after them, never letting the tommy gun drop.

"If you try to call the police before you hear our car leave, I won't hesitate to kill them both," he promised the wives. The petrified women stared anxiously at Kelly, afraid to make the slightest move. They held their position for several minutes after the kidnappers had hurried off with their spouses in tow.[20]

Bates forced the abducted men into the back seat of the vehicle. With his gun trained on the pair, they sat quietly with their hands in the air. Kelly leapt into the passenger's side of the vehicle and turned around in his seat, his weapon pointed at Urschel's and Jarrett's heads. Bates backed the car out of the driveway and sped away from the quiet, upscale neighborhood. Soon, the criminals and victims were traveling down dark back roads few regularly ventured.[21]

Kelly tried again to ascertain which of the two men was Urschel. Neither said a word. Frustrated, Kelly demanded they hand him their wallets. Their drivers' licenses told the gun-wielding outlaw what he wanted to know.

"Where there's a will, there's a way." Kelly grinned while glancing at the photos on the licenses. "So, you're Walter Jarrett," he said to the man behind the driver's seat. "We'll make use of this," Kelly told him, removing the money from his wallet and stuffing it in his shirt pocket. "You could have saved your buddy here all this grief if you'd just spoken up," Kelly informed Urschel.[22]

The foursome had gone more than ten miles on the dusty, unfrequented road when Kelly told Bates to pull over. Once the vehicle came to a stop, Kelly ordered Jarrett out of the sedan. He hesitated a bit, but when the barrel of Kelly's machine gun was pressed into Urschel's temple, Jarrett did as commanded. After warning the man to keep his mouth shut about the route they'd taken or where they'd stopped, Bates put the car in gear and rushed away from the scene. Jarrett watched the taillights disappear into the darkness.[23]

Several miles later, the vehicle again slowed to a stop and Kelly ordered Urschel out of the car. Urschel complied. Kelly followed him out of the vehicle carrying a roll of tape and bandages. Bates leaned out of the driver's side window, leveled his weapon at Urschel, and pulled back the hammer on the gun. Kelly placed bandages over Urschel's eyes and cotton in his ears, then ran a few rolls of tape over the man's eyes to secure the bandages. He forced a pair of dark glasses over the bandages and tape, shoved a fedora on his head, and pulled it low over the glasses. Kelly then clamped Urschel's wrists together with handcuffs. "For your sake, don't attempt to remove the bandages," he cautioned his victim. "I don't want to harm you and if you don't see anything, you'll stay alive. If you try to yell for help, they'll be the last words you'll say. And if you try to struggle, I have a hypodermic loaded with something to put you out for at least twenty-four hours." Urschel was guided back to the car and tossed onto the floor of the back seat. The door of the vehicle was slammed and locked behind him. Resigned to his fate, the bound man said nothing as the car hurried to the next destination.[24]

Walter Jarrett began his trek back to town as soon as he was tossed out of the kidnappers' car. Two boys in an old Ford truck picked him up and drove him to the Urschel home. He arrived at the house shortly before one in the morning. By 1:30 a.m. Jarrett was at the police station reporting the crime. He wasn't completely sure but believed one of the fugitives was Charles "Pretty Boy" Floyd. According to the July 23, 1933, edition of the *Oklahoma News*, "All police scouts and deputy sheriffs were thrown into the pursuit, but the kidnappers had about ten minutes' start. The sheriff's office ordered all cars stopped and searched on all highways leading out of the city."[25]

Agents from the Bureau of Investigation joined in the manhunt too. The chief of police and Berenice Urschel had placed calls to J. Edgar Hoover himself. Earlier in the day she'd read an article about the Bureau of Investigation's national emergency phone line created to manage the increased number of high-profile abductions. Berenice's call to the head of the Bureau was the first time the groundbreaking system had been used. J. Edgar Hoover was sympathetic but professional, promising the full cooperation of the department and said they would do all they could to find her husband.[26]

The Urschels' home was a hub of activity. Not only were federal and state police at the scene but many family friends and business associates were on hand to lend their support. The authorities asked Berenice Urschel to send the well-meaning people away. They anticipated hearing from the kidnappers with ransom demands and were worried her husband's life would be in jeopardy if anyone attempted to interfere. The worried wife graciously requested all but the police to leave. After everyone had gone, investigators had a chance to question Berenice and the Jarretts more thoroughly. During their talk, Berenice told the authorities that a few days before the kidnapping, she and her daughter, Betty, had been shopping and noticed they were being followed by two men in a large blue sedan. She also noted that she'd seen the same car, with Missouri plates, passing by their home earlier in the evening.[27]

Bates's hands were tense on the wheel as he drove along the back roads several miles away from Oklahoma City. He and Kelly conversed briefly, both making veiled references about the direction they were going. They were confident Urschel couldn't hear them but didn't want to take any chances. They talked as though they were heading north to Missouri, but in truth they were traveling south toward the Coleman homestead near Stratford, Texas.[28]

An hour so before daylight, Bates informed Kelly they needed gas. Kelly had Bates pull the car to the side of the road and the two men got out. Bates jerked Urschel out of the vehicle and led him into a row of scraggly bushes. The pair hid in the vegetation while Kelly drove to a filling station. On the road again, the kidnappers proceeded on to the Colemans' place. They planned to transfer Urschel to Kelly's Chevrolet and continue on to the Shannon farm in Paradise.[29]

Kathryn was waiting for her husband when he returned to her grandparents' home. She was with him when he and Bates pulled Urschel out of the sedan and watched them reapply the tape holding the bandages over the man's eyes. After replacing the hat on his head and shoving the dark glasses back on his face, Kelly reminded his victim that he could hurt him if he didn't follow orders. He also warned him to forget anything he heard. The cotton didn't totally block out sounds; it only muffled them.[30]

Kathryn's grandmother proved to have excellent hearing. The muffled activity in the driveway of her home woke her up, and she came to the window just as Kelly was siphoning gas from the Buick to the Chevrolet. Kathryn hurried to her. She asked her granddaughter what was going on, and Kathryn quickly motioned for the elderly woman to close her window. Again, the grandmother asked what was going on.[31]

"They've got a man out there," Kathryn explained. "They've kidnapped a man."

"Lord of Mercy," the horrified woman exclaimed. "Tell them to get that man away from here as quick as he can or I'll scream until I arouse the whole settlement!"[32]

Kathryn raced back to Kelly to let him know what had transpired. Her grandmother was out of bed and dressed when she entered the house through the back door. Kathryn told the baffled, upset woman that she had to leave. She told her that she had to get back to Fort Worth to take care of her father because his doctor wanted to operate on him on Monday, July 24, and that she had to be at the hospital that morning. Kathryn's grandmother tried to persuade her to stay long enough to have some breakfast, but she refused. By dawn, Kathryn, Kelly, Bates, and their kidnap victim were gone.[33]

Kathryn left at the same time her husband did, traveling in her Ford Roadster for a while. It was a six-hour drive and she arrived at her parents' farm before Kelly. When she arrived, she packed a bag for Pauline and her stepsister, Ruth, for their stay at her home in Fort Worth. Before leaving Paradise, she stopped by her stepbrother Armon's farm, immediately adjacent to Boss's property, and convinced Armon's wife, Oleta, and her one-year-old son, to join them on their trip. Oleta was more than happy to go. Before Kathryn left Armon's place, she whispered to her stepbrother that Kelly would be stopping by their parents' house soon. Kathryn and her passengers waved to Armon as they headed down the road.[34]

Early Sunday morning on July 23, 1933, more than a dozen newspaper reporters gathered on the front lawn of the Urschel home to meet with Berenice Urschel. The distraught woman was obviously suffering from lack of sleep and struggled to maintain her composure as she read a prepared statement written specifically to address her spouse's kidnappers.

"I am in no way interested in your capture or prosecution," she recited, her voice thick with emotion. "I care only for the safe return of my husband. To facilitate this, I have had police withdraw from my house and there is no one here now except my family.* We are sitting beside the telephone waiting for you to call."[35]

"We, just our family, have made preliminary arrangements to negotiate with you speedily and confidentially. Arthur Seeligson, my husband's closest friend, will be in charge. You can trust him. We want you to get in touch with us as soon as possible. The welfare of my husband and his immediate return, is my only concern."[36]

Standing nearby as Berenice talked to the press was family spokesman, E. E. Kirkpatrick, her mother, and her two brothers. "I want Charles to know, wherever he is, that Arthur will take charge when he arrives in the morning," she told the journalists on hand. "Charles will know that Arthur will handle everything with utmost care so that no harm can come to him, and I believe the abductors, if they know our family at all, will realize Arthur is the best suited person to communicate with them."[37]

When Kelly and Bates reached the Shannon farm, they pulled the Chevrolet into the garage a few yards from the main house. Kelly jumped out of the vehicle and closed the door behind them. He left Bates with Urschel and walked to the Shannons' home. He noticed Ora and Boss in the nearby field as he passed by, and the pair accompanied him inside. Kelly helped himself to the food in the kitchen, telling Ora that he was making a couple of sandwiches for a friend of his who'd had too much to drink the night before and was recuperating in his car.[38]

With food in hand, Kelly returned to the garage and let Bates know he could join the Shannons for supper. Bates hurried off and Kelly turned his attention to Urschel. He ordered the man to get up

---

* Berenice dismissed the local police but, for a time, allowed only a handful of Bureau agents to remain at the home out of sight. She wanted the kidnappers to think she'd sent all the authorities away.

off the floor of the car and sit in the seat. Once Urschel did that, Kelly removed the disheveled, disoriented man's blindfold and untied his hands. Kelly's machine gun was at the ready in case Urschel had any idea other than eating the sandwiches his kidnapper had made for him. When the man was through eating, Kelly tossed a blanket to him so the oil tycoon could go to sleep. Just after dark, Kelly and Bates would move Urschel to another location.[39]

Kathryn arrived at her home in Fort Worth and helped Pauline, Ruth, and Oleta carry their luggage into the house. Kathryn's father and her friend, Louise Donavon, were already there and happily greeted the guests.* A maid prepared a meal for the group, and they all sat down to enjoy supper. When everyone retired to the living room to talk, Kathryn excused herself from the group to make a phone call. She phoned Detective Ed Weatherford and asked him to come over for a chat. Kathryn had no idea the officer and his cohort were the ones who had reported her plans to kidnap Guy Waggoner. She was convinced the detective was corrupt and someone with whom she could confide. If she was wrong about him and indeed he turned out to be an honest policeman, at least she'd have used him to provide an account for her whereabouts should the need arise.[40]

Detective Weatherford was as congenial at their second meeting as he was at their first. Kathryn told him that she had just returned from St. Louis and that Kelly had decided to stay on there a few more days to finish a job. The conversation was friendly, with Kathryn asking what had been happening in town since she'd been gone and if they'd found who killed the Lindbergh baby. Finally, she got around to the subject of the Urschel kidnapping. News of the abduction had made the front page of many newspapers through the nation, and given the businessman's friendship with President Franklin Roosevelt, a high priority had been placed on the authorities finding him. The detective offered general answers to Kathryn's

---

* Louise Donavon had numerous aliases, including Louise Magness, Louise Clark, Louise Seaton, Mrs. H. E. Campbell, and Miss G. Robinson. She had been arrested more than once for offenses ranging from shoplifting to burglary and aggravated assault.

queries but did tell her that the police had no leads in the Urschel case yet.[41]

Before Weatherford left, Kathryn asked him if he and his family would be attending the World's Fair in Chicago. She promised he would enjoy the fair and offered to pay for the trip if he decided to go. She added that Kelly would have money to spare when he got home. Detective Weatherford thanked her and turned to leave as she was heading back into her home. He happened to glance inside her vehicle parked in the driveway as he passed and noticed an Oklahoma newspaper on the seat. The newspaper and the red dirt around the tires of the Roadster aroused his suspicions.[42]

When Weatherford got back to his office, he called the special agent in charge (SAC) of the Dallas office of the Bureau of Investigation and told him about his exchange with Kathryn, and that he believed the Kellys might be involved with the Urschel kidnapping. The Bureau representative dismissed the detective's observations but thanked him for his input.[43]

Under cover of darkness, Kelly moved Urschel from the garage into a room added onto the back of the Shannons' home. After the victim changed into a pair of pajamas Kelly tossed at him, Bates helped Kelly blindfold Urschel again, placed the cotton back in his ears, and handcuffed him.[44]

Charles Urschel was rousted from his restless sleep the next morning by Kelly bringing in a tray of food. The kidnapper removed the cotton from his victim's ears before giving him permission to eat. Kelly sat across from Urschel with a newspaper in his hand. Urschel heard his abductor unfold the paper and flip through the pages.[45]

"I'm going to read the news to you, wise guy," Kelly announced to Urschel. "Your wife has called in the cops, and that's going to make it tough to arrange for the ransom money. Seems Mrs. Urschel thinks more of your money than she does your skin. Well, it may be a little more tricky, but we'll get what we want."[46]

As Urschel ate his breakfast, Kelly studied the Associated Press story about the abduction and how quickly "Mrs. Berenice Slick Urschel reported the crime to the police and the federal authorities." Kelly's eyes widened when he read that Charles Urschel had taken charge of his wife's estate when they married, which was worth more than a hundred million dollars. Kelly was convinced the payoff for Mrs. Urschel's husband was a sure thing and he smiled to himself, imagining what he and Kathryn would do with the money.[47]

Kelly and Bates would have to move Urschel to another location before any ransom note could be sent. The idea that the Bureau of Investigation was now involved frightened the Shannons, and they were too nervous to have Urschel on the farm. Boss was promised ten thousand dollars for his part in the job but knew he'd never see a dime if the authorities found Urschel before the ransom was collected.[48]

Boss watched from his porch as Kelly ushered his victim at gunpoint into his car and drove him to his son Armon's broken down farmhouse fifteen minutes away. There, Urschel was locked in a windowless room. Kelly, Bates, Armon, and Shannon took turns guarding the businessman.[49]

Berenice Urschel desperately tried to remain calm while waiting for word from Charles's abductors. She wanted to believe that Hoover and the Bureau of Investigation were doing all they could but doubted how effective they could be. The newspapers were filled with stories about kidnap victims unaccounted for or killed after the ransom was paid. In Philadelphia, the kidnappers of fifty-six-year-old real estate investor Frank A. McClatchy shot him twice, and he died instantly. The criminals were still on the run. The family of John O'Connell, the nephew of two powerful Democratic party leaders, who was abducted on July 7, 1933, continued their vigil with little to indicate when they might see their loved one again. In addition to those cases, the Bureau was still investigating leads in the Lindbergh matter.[50]

Concerned the men who took her husband hadn't reached out because of the presence of the police, Berenice decided to deal with the kidnappers independent of any official investigators and ordered authorities from the mansion. "We've done everything we can," Mrs. Urschel told reporters. "Now we're just sitting here waiting for them [kidnappers] to make the next move. The officers have given up every cooperation. They have agreed not to spread any net while we deal with the kidnappers."[51]

According to the July 24, 1933, edition of the *Austin American*, "The ransom demand is expected to be one of the greatest ever made."[52]

Two days later that expectation proved to be right.

CHAPTER 5

THE RANSOM

STREAMS OF HOT SUNLIGHT POURED in through the dirty windows of the cluttered one-room shack on Armon Shannon's property. Charles Urschel sat on top of an oil-stained pallet in the corner with his hands cuffed to a well-used child's highchair. He struggled to find a comfortable position and finally settled on resting his head against the wall with his feet outstretched in front of him. Sweat ran down his face like condensation off a winter glass. His hair was lying like a second skin over his forehead and his shirt clung to him in both the front and back.[1]

Armon sat in the room with him, strumming a fiddle. He backhanded salty droplets that formed above his lip and neck. There was nothing timid about the Texas heat, and the tune the sharecropper played was an attempt to keep his mind off the sweltering conditions. Armon had barely slid his bow over the strings when Kelly jerked open the door of the hovel. A blistering breeze assaulted the guard and kidnap victim. Urschel turned his head in the direction of the gust of hot wind just as Kelly reached him and got him on his feet. Kelly motioned for Armon to bring a couple of chairs to him and he quickly followed orders.[2]

A chair was placed behind Urschel and Kelly eased him into the seat. He then removed the covering over his eyes and unlocked the handcuffs from the highchair. Urschel blinked and squinted, trying to focus on his crude surroundings. Kelly laid a notepad in the disoriented man's lap and placed a pencil in his hand. "You're going to write a ransom note to your wife," Kelly told Urschel. As Urschel's eyes struggled to adjust to the light after being blindfolded continuously for two days, he reminded Kelly of the newspaper articles he read to him about the kidnapping. The Bureau of Investigation was now involved, and if Kelly didn't want them to interfere, perhaps a go-between should be used. Kelly agreed, and reasoned that only a trusted confidant could make contact with Berenice Urschel. The proliferation of police at the home would think nothing of a minister visiting the frantic wife. Kelly asked Urschel about the church he attended and the name of the pastor. Urschel gave him his name but noted the man couldn't help because he was on vacation. Urschel suggested his friend John G. Catlett. Catlett was an oilman who lived in Tulsa. He and Urschel had been business associates for years and shared a mutual respect.[3]

Once Catlett was determined to be the one to get the ransom letter to the family, Urschel began writing it as instructed, making sure to keep his eyes on the paper and to never deviate from that view. The kidnap victim explained to his friend that he had been abducted, was fine, but the situation was serious. He shared with him his current financial state, and that it would be necessary to borrow the two hundred thousand dollars being demanded. He didn't know if a loan of that size would be approved and added if it wasn't possible because it was too excessive, to not even try to raise the funds. Kelly and Bates disapproved of Urschel's letter. The outlaws didn't want their victim to be a martyr, and they also didn't believe Urschel would have any trouble getting the sum requested quickly. They thought Urschel was trying to send some sort of a message to his friend by lamenting how difficult it would be to acquire the money demanded.[4]

Kelly tore up the letter Urschel wrote and made him write another one. The two men dictated to Urschel what they wanted him to say. When that was done, they allowed him to write a note to his wife to let her know that he was well and that he loved her. The letter to Berenice was placed in a separate envelope from the ransom letter he had written to Catlett. Also included in the package was a third note addressed to rancher and oil executive E. E.

Kirkpatrick. According to the newspaper articles Kelly had read, Berenice named Kirkpatrick as the go-between for the Urschels and the kidnappers. Kelly used Boss and Ora's typewriter to compose the letter to Kirkpatrick.[5]

Albert Bates left Armon Shannon's home on Tuesday, July 25, 1933, and drove to the Western Union office in Tulsa. The package was to be delivered to John Catlett the following morning. Kelly stayed behind with Urschel. Before handcuffing him to the highchair again, he replaced the bandages on his eyes and taped them shut again. While waiting for Bates to return, the fugitive kept his victim occupied with conversations about cars, bootlegging, time in prison, and how much his in-laws received for allowing bank robbers to hide on this property.[6]

The strain of the three days and four nights of sleeplessness and anxiety was evident on the faces of Charles Urschel's family and friends. Berenice was weary and worried. She'd received no communication of importance regarding her husband's abduction. What had come in were several tips and suggestions from cranks and cruel individuals hoping to make money off a desperate situation. Four unidentified men had even written a misleading ransom note and given it to a newspaper carrier to deliver to the police. The note was written on the back of a blank check from the Exchange National Bank. The ransom requested was ten thousand dollars. Authorities placed little credence on the typewritten note. Mrs. Urschel's name was misspelled and there were many other errors. The note threatened violence if the press or police were called in and was signed, "One who saw you play bridge." Officials later determined the note to be a hoax.[7]

Berenice received several mysterious phone calls from the supposed kidnappers warning her not to ignore their demands. They told her that her children were next on the list to be taken. Frightened the sinister caller could be legitimate, she sent Charles's seventeen-year-old son, her boys, ages sixteen and twelve, and her daughter to an unnamed location in southern Texas.[8]

Mrs. Urschel had asked agents at the Oklahoma City Bureau of Investigation office, and city and county officials to step away from the case to give the kidnappers a chance to establish contact with the family or the family spokesperson. The Bureau had agreed, not only because the grief-stricken wife was adamant—she did not want Charles killed because of their presence, and it was believed that the Lindbergh child was killed for that reason—but because the federal authorities' resources were strained dealing with the abduction of two other millionaires at the time. The authorities were searching for the kidnappers and killers of the Lindbergh baby, the kidnapping of John Factor, brother of Max Factor, and that of William Hamm Jr., president of Hamm's Brewery.[9]

Berenice hoped to receive word from the men who took her husband immediately after the Bureau agents and the police withdrew from the Urschel home, but it didn't happen. Every hour she didn't hear from the kidnappers she became more anxious. Her family was concerned about how long she could endure the wait.[10]

On Wednesday morning, July 26, 1933, Western Union delivered a large brown envelope to John Catlett's home. Albert Bates followed the delivery boy to the Tulsa mansion and witnessed the package being signed for and taken into the house. The curious Catlett opened the parcel and quickly read the letter addressed to him.[11]

"You undoubtedly know my predicament," the letter from Urschel began. "If Arthur has returned, please deliver the enclosed letter to him, otherwise to Kirkpatrick. Deliver in person and do not communicate by telephone. Tell no one else about this letter, not even your wife, and when you deliver it do not go to your residence. Authorities must be kept off case or release impossible and they cannot effect [sic] rescue.[12]

"For my sake, follow these instructions to the letter and do not discuss with anyone other than those mentioned. This is my final letter to any of my friends or family and if this contact is not successful, I fear for my life.

"When in Oklahoma City keep out of sight as much as possible because you will probably be used later on in this capacity. I am putting all my dependence on you regarding this matter and feel sure you will take every precaution possible. Best regards as ever, your friend C. F. Urschel."[13]

The package contained a letter from the kidnappers to Catlett. They reiterated he was to deliver the letters in person and not to telephone anyone about what he'd received. It also noted that Urschel was afraid for his life and not to take what he was tasked to do lightly. And finally, the authorities were to be "kept off the case."[14]

Catlett hurried to Oklahoma City, arriving at a hotel there in the early afternoon of July 26. He got word to Mrs. Urschel, Kirkpatrick, and Arthur Seeligson to meet him in his room and handed them the letters for which they'd been waiting. Berenice was relieved to finally have heard something about her husband. Enclosed with the ransom note and message to her was Urschel's identification card. She verified it was indeed his and that the notes to her and Catlett were in Charles's hand.[15]

Kirkpatrick opened the correspondence addressed to him and read the contents. He then passed the ransom note to the others to read.

"Sir: The enclosed letter from Charles F. Urschel to you and the enclosed identification card will convince you that you are dealing with the abductors.[16]

"Immediately upon receipt of this letter you will proceed to obtain the sum of TWO HUNDRED THOUSAND DOLLARS ($200,000) in GENUINE USED FEDERAL RESERVE CURRENCY in the denomination of TWENTY DOLLARS ($20.00) Bills.

"It will be useless for you to attempt taking notes of SERIAL NUMBERS MAKING UP DUMMY PACKAGE, OR ANYTHING ELSE IN THE LINE OF ATTEMPTED DOUBLE CROSS. Bear THIS IN MIND, CHARLES F. URSCHEL WILL REMAIN IN OUR CUSTODY UNTIL MONEY HAS BEEN INSPECTED AND EXCHANGED AND FURTHERMORE WILL BE AT THE SCENE OF CONTACT FOR PAY-OFF AND IF THERE SHOULD BE ANY ATTEMPT AT ANY DOUBLE XX IT WILL BE HE THAT SUFFERS THE CONSEQUENCE.[17]

"As soon as you have read and RE-READ this carefully and wish to commence negotiations, you will proceed to the DAILY OKLAHOMAN and insert the following BLIND AD under the REAL ESTATE, FARMS FOR SALE, and we will know that you are ready for BUSINESS, and you will receive further instructions AT THE BOX ASSIGNED TO YOU BY THE NEWSPAPER AND NO WHERE ELSE SO BE CERTAIN THAT THIS ARRANGEMENT IS KEPT SECRET AS THIS IS OUR FINAL ATTEMPT TO COM-MUNICATE WITH YOU, on account of our former instructions to JARRETT being DISREGARDED and the LAW being notified, so we have neither the time or patience to carry on any further lengthy correspondence.[18]

"RUN THIS AD FOR ONE WEEK IN DAILY OKLAHOMAN.

"FOR SALE – 160 Acres Land, good five room house, deep well. Also Cows, Tools, Tractor, Corn and Hay. $3750 for quick sale. TERMS Box #_____.

"You will hear from us as soon as convenient after insertion of AD."[19]

Kathryn Kelly's Fort Worth home was crowded with friends and relatives. Her daughter Pauline, stepsister Ruth, sister-in-law Oleta and her baby, father James Brooks, and good friend Louise Donavon were all staying at the house. Kathryn gave Pauline, Ruth, and Oleta money to go to the movies and shopping. When they weren't on the go, they were reading and playing games.[20]

Kathryn came and went after bringing the guests to her house on Sunday, July 23. The Shannons' farm was forty miles away, a short drive for Kathryn in her Roadster. She brought groceries and ice to her mother and stepfather's residence and, on occasion, she and Boss visited Kelly at Armon's home. Kathryn delivered sup-plies to her husband and newspapers. The couple made sure they were out of earshot of the Shannons and Urschel when they spoke to one another. Whether they were conferring on the kidnapping or the wisdom of getting Pauline, Ruth, Oleta, and her infant off the property isn't clear. What is known is that the pair expected a windfall and had big plans for the money.[21]

Kelly, Armon, and Boss took turns guarding Urschel. Kelly decided to change out the handcuffs on the victim in favor of a chain. Urschel would no longer be affixed to a highchair but to an iron bed. During the day Urschel sat on the floor beside the bed and at night he slept, or tried to sleep, in the bed. His captors drew water from a well close to the shack where he was being held and then brought a bucket to him. He drank from a dipper. Kelly alternated between reading the headlines to Urschel or news of the stock market. He kept his machine gun close at hand and shared stories with his victim about using the weapon on various bank robbing jobs. Kelly assured Urschel he was a good shot and, even if he weren't, couldn't miss hitting a target at close range. The veiled threat wasn't lost on Urschel.[22]

Although the long-awaited ransom note had arrived and was deemed legitimate, not only by Charles Urschel's family but by the head of the Task Force of the Texas Bureau of Investigation Agent Gus "Buster" Jones, Berenice continued to suffer through calls from unscrupulous characters claiming to have her husband. She had to treat all the calls as valid possibilities because she couldn't give away the fact that they'd already heard from the real kidnappers. Jones feared what the press would do if they learned the family was in possession of the real ransom note and were making plans to meet the kidnappers' demands. Voracious reporters would most certainly print what they knew and Urschel's life would be in jeopardy.[23]

Not only did Berenice have to talk with counterfeit abductors but also with well-meaning individuals. Concerned citizens offered to serve as go-betweens, to bring packs of bloodhounds to the scene to sniff out the criminals, and to find the kidnappers using a mystic on a radio program. One man offered the use of a gadget he invented and claimed had the "powers of a doodle bug." For the contraption to work, a photograph of Urschel needed to be placed under its powerful lens, which would then be affixed to an electrical device. Wires would be attached to a button on the device and the mechanism then given to the authorities hunting for Urschel. When the gadget was turned on, the lens would look at the photograph and the indicator would point in the direction Urschel could be found.[24]

Berenice took such generous offers good-naturedly, thanking the callers for their kindness. The merits of the many proposals provided interesting conversations between Berenice, Kirkpatrick, Seeligson, and Jones, as did the ad the kidnappers demanded be placed, which appeared in the July 27, 1933, edition of the *Daily Oklahoman*. Several interested parties responded to the attractive ad offering to purchase the land immediately. On July 28, the only offer Urschel's wife and friends cared about was placed in Box H-807. Albert Bates had handwritten the box number on the envelope. The enclosed letter explaining what needed to be done next had been typed.[25]

"In view of the fact that you have had the ad inserted as per our instructions, we gather that you are prepared to meet our ultimatum," the ransom note read. The kidnappers requested that the two hundred thousand dollars be packed in a light-colored bag. Kirkpatrick was instructed to take the MK and T line, known as "The Sooner," leaving Oklahoma City at 1:10 p.m. on Saturday, July 29. The train would be bound for Kansas City, Missouri.[26]

"You'll ride on the OBSERVATION PLATFORM where you may be observed by someone at some Station along the Line between Oklahoma, City and K. C. Mo. If indications are alright, [sic] somewhere along the Right-of-Way you will observe a Fire on the Right Side of Track (Facing direction train is bound). That first Fire will be your Cue to be prepared to throw BAG to Track immediately after passing SECOND FIRE.[27]

"Mr. Urschel will, upon instructions, attend to the fires and secure the bag when you throw it off, he will open it and transfer the contents to a sack that he will be provided with, so, if you comply with our demand and do not attempt any subterfuge, as according to the News reports you have pledged, Mr. Urschel should be home in a very short while.

"If there is the slightest HITCH in these PLANS for any reason what-so-ever, not your fault, you will proceed on into Kansas City, MO. And register at the Muehlebach Hotel under the name of

E. E. Kincaid of Little Rock, Arkansas, and await further instructions there, however, there should not be, If YOU COMPLY WITH THESE SIMPLE DIRECTIONS."[28]

On Friday, July 28, Kelly and Bates left Boss and Armon Shannon to guard Urschel alone. They told the men they would return by Sunday. Neither asked Kelly or Bates where they were going or what they would be doing. The family and friends staying with Kathryn didn't ask her where she was going when she left her Fort Worth home on Friday either. "She was going to see some friends in Dallas," Kathryn's stepsister Ruth recalled later. "She never did come back. . . ."[29]

Unbeknownst to Kathryn, police detective Ed Weatherford was so insistent the gangster's wife needed to be kept under observation, his superiors finally agreed to allow her phone to be monitored. A supervisor from the phone company was put in charge of informing the Bureau if any suspicious calls came through. Kathryn didn't trust the police and anticipated they would be spying on her. Any calls she made from Fort Worth or Paradise were brief and she always spoke in code.[30]

Berenice tasked Seeligson with getting the ransom money together. He had Lyle Barnhart, the comptroller at the First National Bank and Trust Company of Oklahoma City, arrange for two hundred thousand dollars' worth of used federal reserve twenty-dollar bills to be bundled and placed in a sealed package. Before turning over the funds to Seeligson, the serial numbers on the bills were recorded. E. E. Kirkpatrick would be making the trip to Kansas City as per the kidnappers' instructions. John Catlett planned to accompany him and carry the money. When Agent Jones expressed concern for the men and asked Kirkpatrick if he had any misgivings, the Urschel family spokesman admitted to being scared. "But these ransom notes were addressed to me and that makes it a personal affair between them and me," he added. "I've got to be the one who delivers the money."[31]

Prior to Kirkpatrick and Catlett's trek to Missouri with the ransom money, Arthur Seeligson held a press conference at the Urschel home. The family anticipated that the number of newspaper and radio reporters at the residence would have lessened since they had requested the authorities keep their distance, but rumors Urschel had been abducted by vengeful unemployed oil field workers had prompted more members of the media to visit the scene of the crime.[32]

Any movement by Berenice or Urschel's friends and family with her was the subject of an article. Seeligson requested that the continual, detailed reporting of the comings and goings of the family on routine, innocent errands, be minimized so that the kidnappers would not get the impression that the family cannot move without being watched or followed. He told those at the press conference, "We have absolutely nothing new to put out. There has been no contact of any kind."[33]

The lights were snapped off in the Urschel home before midnight on the 27th. Most of the journalists were respectful and left the family alone. but Kirkpatrick and Catlett weren't willing to take a chance some reporters wouldn't be lurking around. On Saturday, July 29, they decided to make their way to the train station under cover of darkness to not arouse suspicion. The men left carrying two bags, one containing two hundred thousand dollars in twenty-dollar bills and the other filled with magazines and newspapers. The bag containing the magazines and newspapers was a precaution in case word got out and someone tried to rob them.[34]

"Our instructions were to remain on the observation platform but there were two Chicago excursion cars," Kirkpatrick later explained. The rail line had added cars to carry the many unexpected passengers heading to Chicago for the World's Fair. "We had to leave our car and go through these two cars and there was no observation platform on the rear of the car, so I stayed on the vestibule." Hoping the kidnappers would see him, Kirkpatrick stood directly under the light of the outer area leading from one car to another, smoking a cigarette. Catlett stayed inside the car.[35]

"We kept one grip [bag] inside the door and one outside in case we got hijacked by some outsider," Kirkpatrick said afterward. "We fixed the brakeman so he would let us stay out there [on the vestibule]. When we would near a town, Catlett would go inside so as not to be seen. After we would leave the lights [from the station] he would come back out with me. We rode the train the entire night and didn't see any flames. . . ."[36]

Kelly and Bates had their eye on the Urschel go-between and knew he'd ignored the instructions. Kirkpatrick was supposed to have made the trip alone. The fugitives raced ahead of the train in their car and were waiting in the shadows each time the vehicle arrived at the stations. Kelly never had any intention of hauling Urschel with them to have him "attend to the fires." The threat was meant to keep Berenice and the others from calling the police, and it had worked.[37]

When Kirkpatrick and Catlett arrived in Kansas City they did as the ransom note told them and made their way to the Muehlebach Hotel. Built in 1915, the twelve-story, five-hundred-room hotel had played host to several celebrities including Helen Keller and Ernest Hemingway. Kirkpatrick registered as E. E. Kincaid and Catlett as E. E. Catwell, both from Little Rock, Arkansas. The men checked into their rooms and settled in to hear from the kidnappers. On Sunday, July 30, 1933, at ten in the morning, a member of the hotel staff delivered a telegram to E. E. Kincaid that read: "Unavoidable incident kept me from seeing you last night. Will communicate about 6:00 o'clock." The message was signed "E. W. Moore."[38]

Kathryn Kelly quickly snapped up the ringing phone at her parents' farmhouse and greeted the caller with an anxious "Hello?" The operator on the other end announced, "Bristow, B-R-I-S-T-O-W calling." The next voice Kathryn heard was her husband's. "Is this Kathryn?" he asked. "Yes," she replied. "Have you been out there all this time?" he inquired. Kathryn told him she had, and asked when she would see him. Kelly explained he'd been delayed on account of the weather and told his wife to deliver a message to her stepfather that he'd return to the farm on Monday, July 31.[39]

Kathryn hung up the phone and hurried to her stepbrother's home where Charles Urschel was being held. Armon and Shannon had been taking turns guarding the kidnap victim during Kelly and Bates's absence. When Shannon wasn't at his son's place, he was doing chores on his farm. which included making sure his guests, bank robber Harvey Bailey and Bailey's associates, Bob Brady and Tom Clark, were comfortable. The criminals had paid Shannon to take refuge on his property until the police search for them had died down. After Kathryn told her stepfather what Kelly had to say, she hurried back to her mother to help prepare a meal for their outlaw guests and Urschel.[40]

Back at the Muehlebach Hotel, Kirkpatrick and Catlett sat waiting in the room for further instructions from the kidnappers. "At twenty minutes to six, someone called and said he was Moore," Kirkpatrick recounted later, "and asked who I was and I told him Kincaid and he said, 'Are you ready to go through with the farm deal?' I said, 'I am, if I knew I was dealing with the proper parties.' He said, 'You ought to know by now you are dealing with the proper parties!'"[41]

George Kelly as E. W. Moore was annoyed. Kirkpatrick had already disregarded the directions and sensed the go-between was deliberately being difficult. "Follow instructions," Kelly told him. "Get a taxi and go to the LaSalle Hotel and get out and walk west with the bag." Kirkpatrick told Kelly that he had ordered dinner and wasn't dressed and it would take some time. Kelly told him he was in a hurry and wanted to complete the deal. Kirkpatrick told Kelly that he too was in a hurry and informed him that he would meet him in thirty minutes.[42]

At the designated time, Kirkpatrick left the hotel alone. Except for the gun tucked out of sight in his belt, he was careful to follow the kidnappers' directives. He took a taxi to the LaSalle Hotel, and when he reached the destination he got out and started walking west along Linwood Boulevard with the bag containing the ransom clutched tightly in his hand. Two-thirds of the way down the block he came face-to-face with George Kelly.[43]

"My adversary had black hair, dark skin, was nearly six feet in height, weighed about one hundred and eight-five pounds," Kirkpatrick noted in his written account of the event. "He was stylishly dressed in a natty summer suit with a turned-down Panama hat. He wore two-toned shoes; his tie was immaculately knotted into the collar of his well-fitting two-toned shirt. Yet his nervous, shifting, swinging stride, his furtive glances screamed at me, like a siren, his mission."[44]

The gangster ordered Kirkpatrick to hand him the case. Kirkpatrick didn't readily obey. "How do I know you're the right party?" he asked Kelly.

"Give me that grip," Kelly barked.[45]

"Well, if I do give you the grip, how soon will you fulfill your part of the contract?"

"Don't argue with me. . . ."

"We have gone through with our part of the trade and you should give me definite information so I can phone. I am going to phone as soon as I get back to the hotel and I would like for you to tell me."

"Don't argue with me. Give me the grip! The boys are over there watching me."

"Tell me definitely what I can tell Mrs. Urschel."

"Urschel will be home within twelve hours. Now, you turn and walk to the LaSalle Hotel and don't look back."[46]

Kirkpatrick set down the grip and Kelly took it. Kirkpatrick turned and started walking toward the hotel. He glanced around and noticed two cars parked close by with sinister-looking characters in the vehicles. Kirkpatrick didn't stop or look back.[47]

Kathryn stood on the front porch of her parents' home at noon on July 31, watching the dust trail behind a vehicle barreling down the dirt road leading to the farm. Kelly drove his Buick onto the barren lawn, kicking up gravel as he brought the car to a furious stop.

Before Kathryn made it down the steps to her husband, Kelly and Bates were out of the vehicle, both grinning from ear to ear. "We pulled it off," Kelly proudly announced to his wife. "Two hundred thousand bucks, baby!" He gave her a quick hug and hurried into the house, with Bates following close behind. The two men were sweaty and disheveled. They needed a shave and a change of clothes before continuing with their business.[48]

Ora watched the three hurry about, filling their luggage with their clothes, Dopp kits, photographs, and other personal items lying about. Glancing outside, Kelly noticed Harvey Bailey in the backyard. He took a break from packing to pay off a five-hundred-dollar debt he owed his fellow bank robber. When he walked back inside the house, Kelly politely but firmly advised his mother-in-law to keep quiet about everything that had transpired.[49]

"Now, for getting rid of Urschel," Kelly told his wife. He exchanged a knowing look with Bates. Bates nodded to his partner in crime, then quickly left the Shannons' place to deal with their victim. Moments later, Kelly and Kathryn dashed out the door as well.[50]

Bates arrived at Armon's property in a flash. Shannon and his son met the gangster at the door, and he pushed past them into the room where Urschel was being held. Urschel had nodded off and Bates shook him awake. The chain was removed from the bed and from around his hands, and Urschel was ordered to shave and change into the clothes purchased for him that had been tossed on the bed. Bates informed Urschel that the ransom was paid and it was time to go.[51]

While an emotionally exhausted Urschel struggled to pull himself together. Bates turned his attention to Armon and his father. He promised they would be paid well for their services. When Urschel was ready, the tape around his eyes was reinforced, dark glasses placed over the blindfold, and a hat positioned low on his head. The kidnap victim was escorted to a Chevrolet sedan and into the passenger's seat in the front. Shannon and his son looked on as Bates started the vehicle and sped away.[52]

Kelly drove his wife out of Paradise in a Cadillac. They met Bates more than two hours later in a secluded location near Oklahoma

City. Bates surrendered the driver's seat to Kelly, moved Urschel to the back seat of the sedan, and took his place in the passenger's seat. Kathryn trailed behind the pair in the Cadillac as they drove to Norman, Oklahoma.[53]

It was nine in the evening when Kelly stopped his car several yards from a gas station and barbeque stand called Classen's on the Oklahoma City Norman Highway. Any idea Urschel had that his abductors would simply let him out of the car and drive away was quickly dispelled. They entertained the idea of chaining the man to a tree in the woods nearby and leaving him at the mercy of some lone individual finding him before he died. Ultimately, the kidnappers decided to let Urschel go in a populated area if he agreed to a list of their conditions. He was not to make any phone calls from Norman, take the cab from the service they told him to contact, and go straight home. He was to refrain from telling the cab driver who he was and to tell the police that the vehicle in which he was released was a light-colored small coupe. After Urschel promised Kelly and Bates to do what they asked, they removed his blindfold and restraints, returned the watch that they had taken from him, shoved ten dollars in his hand, and booted him out of the vehicle.[54]

Kelly and Bates quickly drove away, leaving a traumatized kidnap victim behind in the drizzling rain.[55]

Charles Urschel made his way to Classen's, where he phoned the cab company he was instructed to contact.[56]

Shortly after Kirkpatrick turned the ransom note over to Kelly, he phoned Berenice to let her know he'd "closed the deal for the farm." He told her it would take "twelve hours for the lawyers to examine the abstracts, then the title will pass." Kirkpatrick spoke in code to confound anyone outside of the family who might have been listening in.[57]

If the kidnappers were to be believed, the Urschel family and friends anticipated that Charles would be home the morning of July 31. Kirkpatrick had returned to Oklahoma and the Urschel mansion from Kansas City immediately after he called Berenice with the news. Catlett had accompanied him on the midnight train as far as Tulsa, where he got off. When Kirkpatrick didn't see Urschel upon his arrival at his home, his heart sank.[58]

As the hours slowly passed and day turned to night, the thought that Kelly had killed Urschel consumed the minds of everyone waiting. No one said it aloud, but everyone was thinking it. "We had been fools to believe that they would keep their promise," Kirkpatrick later admitted he was lamenting during that time. "Why hadn't we started out fighting them from the first?" he recalled thinking to himself. "Why hadn't we given the federals full sway?"[59]

It was after eleven in the evening when Urschel, haggard and mussed, appeared at the back door of his house. His brother-in-law and wife rushed to meet him. Berenice wept and hugged his neck. More than a week had passed since his abduction and there were times she doubted she'd ever see him again. He shaded his sensitive eyes from the lights overhead and smiled as he scanned the faces of those around him who had done all they could to assure his safe return.[60]

CHAPTER 6

OUTLAWS IN PARADISE

KATHRYN KELLY STUDIED HER LOOK in a mirror affixed to the visor on the passenger's side of the car George Kelly was driving. She wasn't interested in the Mississippi landscape rushing by or the magnificent sun hanging low in the cherry-red sky, only her reflection. She powdered her nose, freshened her eye makeup, and lipstick, following the current style: pencil-thin eyebrows, rosebud mouth, rouge high on the cheek bone. Satisfied with her work, she flipped back the visor to its original position, then reached for Kelly's neck and gently smoothed down the back of his close-cropped hair. A grin spread across his face, and she caressed his cheek with the back of her hand. She kissed the air in his direction while casting a furtive glance at the back seat and the bundle of money tucked inside a partially opened suitcase.[1] Having split the ransom money with Albert Bates before leaving Paradise, Texas, the Kellys were on their way to St. Paul, Minnesota. St. Paul was one of three safe haven cities for criminals in the 1930s. Cicero, Illinois, and Hot Springs, Arkansas, were the other two. For a small fee, and in exchange for abstaining from crime while in these cities, corrupt politicians and police chiefs turned a blind eye to gangsters and their transgressions in these locations. Bootleggers in particular had spent time in St. Paul hiding from the Bureau of Investigation. Kelly was among those whiskey peddlers who had frequented the area.[2]

Upon their arrival in the city, the Kellys checked themselves into a well-known downtown establishment called Hotel St. Paul. The happy couple registered as R. G. and Ora Shannon. Kelly wanted to celebrate their criminal accomplishments, but in order for them to be able to use their half of the ransom, the money needed to be laundered first. Bates was satisfied paying "money mules" eighty cents on the dollar to exchange the marked bills for unmarked ones. Kelly found that deal unacceptable. He preferred that the money launderer take a portion of the ransom and invest it in liquor sales and distribution. Kelly was personally aware of how much could be made bootlegging and believed he could double his seven-thousand-dollar investment. After completing the liquor deal, he opened an account at a St. Paul bank. Kelly deposited two thousand dollars, then later that same day withdrew some of it, exchanging marked notes for unmarked ones. Flush with clean cash, Kathryn was able to go on a shopping spree, buying clothes and jewelry.[3]

The Kellys and Bates parted company in Minneapolis. Kathryn and Kelly were anxious to move along to Ohio. They took a room at Hotel Cleveland during their brief time there and again registered as R. G. and Ora Shannon. After cleaning up and changing their clothes, the pair visited a car dealership to discuss buying a new vehicle. Later that evening, the Kellys attended a cabaret show with friends.[4]

While perusing the newspaper the following morning, Kelly noticed an article involving the men in St. Paul who he had given money to for the bootlegging venture. The story under the headline, which read, "Federals Trace Part of Ransom Money to City" came as a shock to Kelly. "Four Minneapolis men were apprehended today and placed in the St. Paul city jail in connection with the Department of Justice's investigation of the kidnapping of Charles F. Urschel, millionaire Tulsa oil magnet," the August 8, 1933, edition of the *Minneapolis Star* reported. The article spooked Kelly. On August 9, the couple quickly packed their belongings in preparation to travel to Chicago in their newly purchased Cadillac. Just prior to checking out of their hotel, Kelly received a message from Bates, who was still in St. Paul, completing the job of getting his money laundered. He wrote his partner to warn him that government agents were on their trail.[5]

"Deal has fell through," the telegram read. ". . . Communicate with me at Box 631." The coded message was signed "George." George was Albert Bates's alias. Kelly understood from the message that Bates was leaving St. Paul quickly and traveling to his home in Denver. Box 631 was Bates's Denver house address.[6] The Kellys were in Chicago long enough to acquire another vehicle, one that wouldn't draw attention. After trading in the Cadillac, they headed to Iowa. Kelly had experience outrunning the law. The years he'd spent delivering alcohol to suppliers and smuggling the product across borders provided him with the education needed to thwart authorities. He knew it wasn't enough to get a different car; a different license plate was also necessary. When Kelly and Kathryn reached Davenport, he stole an Iowa license plate and affixed it to their ride. From Davenport, the couple made their way to Des Moines.[7]

Kathryn was content to let her husband take care of the travel arrangements. She had an insatiable love for beautiful possessions and living in luxury. The cars they now drove, the fine dresses and coats she wore, the meals at high-end restaurants, and the classy accommodations they were enjoying had come about because of Kelly's devotion to her. She knew he would do whatever was necessary to give her all she wanted. Kathryn also knew he would sacrifice anything for her, and that truth kept her from being overly concerned about the authorities and the possibility of getting caught. If Kelly had to choose between his freedom or hers, she was confident of his decision. In fact, she was counting on it.[8]

When word got out that the kidnappers had released Charles Urschel and that he was home with his wife and family, the press swarmed the Urschel mansion like ants on a jelly sandwich. They demanded to know all the details of Urschel's confinement, who was behind the abduction, if he was tortured, when the gangsters let him go, and exactly how much money was paid for his ransom.

Family spokesman Arthur Seeligson explained that no statements would be made until Tuesday morning, August 1. In the brief interim, reporters had time to deduce they'd not been told everything with regard to the crime. "His [Urschel's] return indicated that contact had been established with the kidnappers, perhaps two or three days ago," an article in the August 1, 1933, edition of the *Daily Oklahoman* noted, "although the family insisted no word had come and no contact had been made."[9]

Charles Urschel, his wife Berenice, and Seeligson welcomed media representatives at 8 a.m. They thanked them for coming and for their concern. Before reporters had an opportunity to ask questions of Urschel, Berenice told the assembled group that negotiations for her husband's release were kept so quiet he almost had to break into the house when he returned. According to Berenice, almost everybody in the house had gone to bed when Urschel's taxicab pulled into the back driveway at midnight. "I wanted to keep it quiet and make as little noise as possible," Urschel shared. He reached out to his wife, put his arm around her, and gave her a firm squeeze. "This is the girl who did it," he told reporters while beaming approvingly at Berenice.[10]

"At first, I planned to stop at a drugstore and telephone, to make sure no officers were around and I wouldn't have any trouble," Urschel explained to the media. "But I decided to come home at once. I circled the block a couple of times, looking at the house, and could see nobody around. Then I pulled up at the back and went to the back door. It was locked. When I tried to open it, I was met by a federal man and had to do some explaining before I could get in my home."[11]

Urschel laughed at the story, and the press chuckled along with him. Ready with their queries, the reporters' hands shot into the air. Seeligson wouldn't allow Charles and Berenice to be detained further. "Let's have some breakfast," he suggested to the pair. The couple nodded, and Urschel led the way back into the house. The press conference was officially over.[12]

Journalists were left to seek other sources for the details of the release of the kidnap victim and ransom. The papers found information to print in their articles that was verified by persons unknown. *Tulsa World* reported that a two-hundred-thousand-dollar ransom was paid in Kansas City to members of Harvey Bailey's gang. The Department of Justice and the Urschel family both denied the report. Walter Harrison, the managing editor of the *Daily Oklahoman* and the *Oklahoma City Times*, was annoyed by the Urschels' lack of cooperation and subsequent criticism of inaccuracies of the stories. "The Urschel family now is reaping the result of the foolish policy of withholding the amount of the ransom and of not telling frankly and completely all they know about the negotiations," Harrison wrote in an editorial.[13]

"Irresponsible free-lance reporters have engaged in the wildest speculation as to the ransom and the negotiations for the release. Within an hour I heard that the family was embarrassed at the thought that they paid so little as $25,000 and that they were ashamed to publish that fact because they had paid more than $250,000 without haggling.[14]

"But the family need not be surprised at anything that is said or printed about the case. . . . Urschel himself has not been frank and complete in his stories. Arthur Seeligson thought it was quite all right to make definite misstatements to newspaper people who were attempting to cooperate.

"If Urschel would tell all he knows the hideout where he was held prisoner could be located within twenty-four hours.[15]

"If Seeligson is cooperating to the limit of his ability the federal government will have all of the facts with regard to the handling of the money and have a dragnet out before this.

"If that sort of cooperation has been provided, what is the sense in not telling the public about it? The public has an interest in this case. Many a crime has been solved by broad publication of all surrounding circumstances.[16]

"My friends have chided me for suggesting that the Urschels ought to go the limit in helping apprehend the criminals, saying that I would do just what they are doing if the misfortune were to fall on any member of my family. Probably I would try to meet the demands and pledge body and soul necessary for the safe return of a child. But I hope that I would have the courage, the wisdom, and the common sense to see that I should have to devote my every energy to the apprehension of the kidnappers. I hope I would coop-erate with the police, with the public, with the newspapers, by giv-ing every shred of evidence within the possession of myself and my friends. I hope I would make my first and only business after living through such a dreadful experience to do my bit lest such a calamity be visited upon some friend of mine because of my selfish satisfac-tion at the release and safe return of my own flesh and blood."[17]

The Urschel family couldn't have disagreed more with Harri-son's comments about confiding in the press. Arthur Seeligson fired off a letter to the editor explaining why keeping the newspapers out of the mix was crucial for the Urschel family. "The amount of the ransom paid for C. F. Urschel's release and the circumstances in connection therewith are purely personal matters, and no good, except to satisfy morbid curiosity and to give you a chance for addi-tional headlines, can be accomplished by giving this information to you or the other papers.[18]

"You are correct in stating that during the progress of the nego-tiations I did not give the true information to the papers. Absolute secrecy was necessary to ensure the safe return of Charlie Urschel and that was our first consideration. Past experiences have proven to us the inadvisability of giving you, or your papers, any information of a personal nature.[19]

"I feel that the Oklahoma papers, and yours have been among the worst offenders, were responsible for the kidnapping of C. F. Urschel more than any other one factor. The sensational stories, misrepre-sentations and insinuations about the size of the estate that have been printed at various times during the past three years, together with all other personal matters involving the different members of the Slick and Urschel families which you have featured, and head-lines at every opportunity, has so focused attention on both of these families as to make them one of the first targets for those in the kidnapping racket."[20]

Harrison was offended by the notion that newspapers were responsible in any way for the abduction of Urschel, and he told

Seeligson so in his reply. He argued that the press was not only concerned with Urschel's safe return but with the capture of the culprits. He urged the Urschel family to provide them with information to help track and apprehend the kidnappers. What Harrison, and other newspaper editors and reporters, didn't know and wouldn't know for days is that Urschel himself knew everything needed to lead the authorities to the criminals. Assistance from the press would not be required.[21]

The same morning Charles Urschel was enjoying his first breakfast with his wife and family since being held by kidnappers for more than eight days, President Roosevelt and his staff were meeting with one of his top advisers on crime, outlining a strategy against kidnapping and racketeering. The president had been closely following the abduction and release of Urschel and directed J. Edgar Hoover to utilize his newly enlarged Bureau of Investigation to hunt down the men who took the oil tycoon hostage. Hoover assured the commander in chief that the federal, state, and city police were working together to get the job done. The Bureau head had sent two of his top agents to Oklahoma City to meet with Urschel the night he returned home. Gus Jones, a former Texas Ranger who had been investigating the shooting deaths of several police officers in Kansas City, was assigned to take the lead in the case against the kidnappers. (On June 17, 1933, bank robber and murderer Frank Nash was being transported through Kansas City's Union Station Depot on his way to Leavenworth. Charles Arthur "Pretty Boy" Floyd, Verne Miller, and Adam Richetti tried to free their friend during a stop at the station. Four policemen and Frank Nash were killed in the incident known as the Kansas City Massacre.) Ralph Colvin, the agent in charge of Oklahoma City's Bureau office, was in command after Jones. Before giving the authorities what they needed, Urschel told them his captors promised to kill him if he talked. They'd also threatened to torture and kill his family. He decided to ignore the threats if it would prevent anyone else from going through what he had.[22]

Over the next several days, Urschel gave the authorities a comprehensive and accurate account of his captivity. From what he had heard, sounds and conversations, and the movements he had made, he was able to furnish such a precise description of the farm where he was held captive that a diagram could be drawn of it. When describing the room at his imprisonment, he told how he had left his fingerprints on the planks, walls, and windowsills. He had heard airplanes pass over twice daily. Five minutes or so after the plane had flown by, he would inquire about the time, and Boss and Armon Shannon would innocently tell him. By doing this, he learned the exact schedule of those airplanes. One morning the airliner did not come over, and Urschel made a mental note of it. Jones and Colvin checked all southwestern airlines scheduled, matched the time they passed over Urschel, and discovered that an airliner had gone off course that morning to avoid a storm. Its regular path, which it missed, would have taken it over Wise County, Texas, where the Shannons' farm was located.[23]

In total, Urschel had made a mental note of twenty-five essential details to help authorities with their work. He even assisted Jones in drawing a map of the house, the condition of the floors, and the contents of the room. Agents Jones and Colvin began the process of locating the kidnappers' hiding place by contacting airlines to verify schedules and meteorologists to check past weather patterns across Oklahoma and Texas. Using the valuable information provided by Urschel and reviewing the data from the weather service and airline flight paths, it was determined the initial search should take place in Paradise, Texas.[24]

On August 10, 1933, Bureau Agent Edward Dowd, disguised as a land developer, arrived in Paradise and began visiting farm owners in the area. He played his part well, asking the farmers about the crops and livestock they raised and the value of their land. Boss Shannon was more than happy to show the prospective buyer around his five-hundred-acre farm and his son Armon's homestead. He invited the supposed businessman into his home and gave him a tour of the house. Dowd had studied the map Jones and Urschel created and was astounded at how good Urschel's memory had been. Everything was as he had relayed, from a window with a missing pane to a wooden bench at the foot of the iron bed.[25]

After leaving the Shannons' place and promising to return with an offer to purchase their property, Dowd contacted Jones to let him know of his findings. Jones and Colvin organized a raid on the Shannon farm at a designated spot in Denton, Texas. Among the men who would accompany the Bureau investigators were four additional government agents, eight officers from the Dallas and Fort Worth Police Department, and Charles Urschel, who insisted on taking part.[26]

At daybreak on August 12, three cars sped down the road leading to Ora and Boss Shannon's home. The tires of the vehicles spit gravel as they hurried along and then came to a sudden stop. The men inside the cars jumped out with their weapons drawn. It happened so fast, no one inside the house had time to react. The authorities fanned out around the property, ready to defend themselves against the slightest movement. As Agent Jones quickly inched his way to the back of the house, he caught a glimpse of a man sleeping on a cot under a tree. He motioned for Urschel, who was following him, to stay put. Jones then disappeared behind the building.[27]

Armed with a shotgun, Urschel stood out of sight near the front watching the officers take their position. When the front door slowly opened and Boss Shannon quietly walked out onto his porch to see what was going on, Urschel raised his gun and pointed it at the man. No words were exchanged. Shannon simply held up his hands in surrender.[28]

Jones stared down at the face of the man he spotted sleeping on a cot, careful to keep his weapon trained on him. The man looked familiar, and it only took a moment for Jones to determine he had Harvey Bailey in his sights. He'd been searching for months for Bailey in connection with the Kansas City Massacre. Jones poked Bailey, and when he opened his eyes, he said, "Get up, Harvey! Who's here with you?" The outlaw didn't respond. "If a head bobs up around here or a shot is fired, I'll riddle you with machine gun lead," the agent promised.

"I'm alone," the disoriented man replied. "You have me." Jones escorted the fugitive to a nearby fence, handcuffed him to it, then went about the business of searching the property for other suspects.

Ora Shannon, her granddaughter Pauline, and her stepdaughter Ruth were also taken into custody.[29]

Amid the evidence taken from the Shannon home and Harvey Bailey were several hundred dollars, the serial numbers of which matched the money paid as the ransom for Urschel. Both Boss and Ora claimed to have had no idea that the funds in their possession were part of the ransom. The two insisted they'd never seen Urschel before and were innocent. They were handcuffed and led to the fence where Bailey was waiting. Jones left some of the agents behind to guard the suspects and then he and several others extended their search to Armon Shannon's place.[30]

Charles Urschel accompanied Jones and the others to Armon Shannon's rustic home, and there they found Armon and his wife, Oleta. Armon pretended not to know Urschel at first. It wasn't until Urschel identified Armon's house as the spot where he was held captive, and Agent Jones explained to him the benefits of telling the truth, that Armon confessed. He also told the authorities that George Kelly was the man they were after.[31]

Boss, Ora, and Armon Shannon and Harvey Bailey were transported to the Dallas jail and charged with kidnapping Charles Urschel.[32]

As a result of the Urschel family and law enforcement's decision to withhold most of the information about the kidnapping, many people believed the abduction was a hoax. When news of a raid on a farm in Paradise was reported, those same skeptics doubted the veracity of the story. Articles about the arrest of the Shannons and Harvey Bailey appeared in newspapers across the nation. Although George Kelly's name was given as the person who kidnapped Urschel, Bailey was initially blamed for orchestrating the crime.[33]

"After his arrest, the officers laid an elaborate trap about the Wise County farmhouse in hopes that Bailey's associate or associates might be snared," the article in the August 14, 1933, edition of the *Denton Record Chronicle* read. "In addition to the Kansas City rail station massacre and the Urschel kidnapping, Bailey also was wanted in connection with the bank holdup at Lincoln, Nebraska, on September 17, 1930."[34]

Bailey was guilty of a number of crimes, but abducting Urschel wasn't one of them. The outlaw was simply using the Shannons' farm as a place to rest from being pursued by the law. He had stayed at the Shannons' on a couple of other occasions as well, and always in exchange for a fee. Bailey had arrived the night before the raid with two other criminals, Bob Brady and Ed Davis. Brady and Davis had decided not to stay and moved on after dinner. Bailey opted to take a nap in the yard because he found it unbearably hot inside the Shannons' house.[35]

While Boss Shannon and his family were being led to jail in Paradise, Texas, Albert Bates was being taken to jail in Denver, Colorado, having been arrested in a downtown parking lot. While en route from St. Paul to Denver on a train, Bates was recognized by a detective from the American Express Company. He had become a wanted man to them in late 1932 for passing stolen traveler's checks. The detective remained on board with Bates, secretly watching his every move, and when they reached their Colorado destination, he reported the thief to the police.[36]

The Denver police arrested Bates while he was sitting in a car he had stolen prior to the Urschel kidnapping. The officers confiscated the cash he had on him, which turned out to be money from the ransom. A photograph of the captured felon was sent to the Oklahoma Bureau of Investigation to be shown to Urschel. When Agent Colvin presented the picture to the oilman, he exclaimed, "That's him! That's one of the gang that snatched me!"[37]

With the identification of Bates as one of the kidnappers, the federal government began the process of having him transported to Oklahoma. J. Edgar Hoover and the Department of Justice wanted to make an example of Bates as a part of the nationwide campaign it had launched to stamp out racketeering, kidnapping, and organized crime of all kinds.[38]

On August 16, 1933, Denver Chief of Police Albert Clark ordered extra officers armed with machine guns to guard Bates. Clark had received a tip that Kelly was going to try to bust his partner in crime out of jail. Just before Bates was transferred to an isolated cell, he managed to secret out a message to his wife, with whom he had left the bulk of his portion of the ransom, telling her to leave town.

"There's nothing you can do for me," he wrote her.

Bates managed to get a telegram out of jail and on to Fort Worth. Detective Ed Weatherford retrieved the message.

"George L. Davis held in Denver wanted in Ladonia and Blue Ridge bank robberies," the telegram read. "Will waive extradition. Come at once." The message was signed "George L. Davis."

Weatherford turned over the communication to Fort Worth Detective Chief Tom Jackson, who learned that George L. Davis was an alias for Bates. According to an article in the August 16, 1933, edition of the *Fort Collins Express Courier*, "After reviewing the telegram, Jackson sought to determine if Bates is wanted in connection with the Texas bank robberies. The ex-convict is believed to have sent the telegram thinking that, by getting a conviction for a Texas holdup, he might forestall a more severe punishment for other crimes."[39]

The transfer of Bates from Denver to Oklahoma was carried out in great security. Charles Urschel was at the airport in Oklahoma City with Gus Jones and Ralph Colvin when the plane carrying Albert Bates arrived from Denver.

"Hello, Albert," Urschel greeted the accused man as the armed authorities escorted him off the aircraft.

Bates looked quizzically at Urschel and, without a change of expression, replied, "I don't know you."[40]

Bates was taken immediately to the fortified county jail where the Shannons and Harvey Bailey were being held.[41]

After an extensive interrogation, Boss Shannon confessed to knowing Urschel and told Agents Colvin and Jones that if he hadn't done exactly as Kelly and Bates directed, they would have killed him and his family. Ora wasn't as quick to admit she was aware of Urschel and the situation but eventually acknowledged her involvement.

Like her husband, she noted that all their lives were in danger if they dared defy Kelly.[42]

The Kellys were tucked inside their room at the exclusive Fort Des Moines Hotel in Des Moines, Iowa, enjoying one another's company, when Gus Jones and Ralph Colvin were making plans to make a raid on the Shannon farm. Neither had a clue how close they were to being found out. For the moment, Kathryn was concerned only with seeing the town. She wanted a chance to wear the fur coat, diamond bracelet, and ring Kelly purchased for her in Minnesota. The couple decided to go to the movies then to dinner with her friend Louise Donavon. Louise had been in Fort Worth, staying at Kathryn's home, until Kathryn sent her money to buy a plane ticket to travel to Des Moines. Kathryn and Louise had been friends for some time. They had a great deal in common, including a sordid past. Kathryn believed she could trust Louise to help her and Kelly outsmart the law. Kathryn promised to pay Louise something for her trouble. Until Kelly decided exactly what they needed from Louise, Kathryn decided to treat her friend to a night on the town.[43]

When the Kellys awoke the following day and unfurled the newspaper to read while they were eating their breakfast, they were taken aback by the headline. Charles Urschel had helped lead Bureau of Investigation agents to the farm where he had been held captive, the Shannons had been arrested in Texas, Albert Bates had been apprehended in Colorado, and Kelly was being sought by authorities for the Urschel kidnapping. Des Moines Police had been notified by J. Edgar Hoover's agency to be on the lookout for "R. G. Shannon, alias George Kelly."[44]

Kelly was furious with Urschel. He'd warned the wealthy oilman what would happen if he talked. Even if Kelly wanted to make good on his promise to go after Urschel and his family now, he didn't know where they were located. An article in the *Des Moines Tribune* made it clear their whereabouts were known only to the Bureau of Investigation.[45]

Kathryn was livid over her mother's arrest. She wasn't pleased with the news that her stepfather and stepbrother had been taken into custody either but was more upset about her mother because her role in the ordeal was to simply provide meals for the victim. Kathryn knew Ora would need a good lawyer and was frantic to help make that happen. She chastised Kelly for releasing Urschel instead of killing him, an argument she would make during their weeks on the run at least one more time.[46]

The Kellys quickly packed their belongings and prepared to leave Iowa. They'd had the presence of mind to register at the hotel as Mr. and Mrs. Coleman rather than the Shannons, so they had some time to think through their next move. Fortunately, Louise was there to help with what came next. They would all travel to Kathryn's uncle's farm in Coleman, Texas. Kelly needed a place to bury the remaining share of the ransom.[47]

The fugitives stopped first in Brownsville, Texas, and, posing as Kelly's sister, Kathryn checked herself, Kelly, and Louise into the Southern Hotel. On August 16, 1933, Louise was sent to purchase a 1928 Chevrolet sedan using the name Mrs. H. E. Campbell. She was to maintain possession of the vehicle until either Kathryn or Kelly needed it. The Kellys then drove on to Kathryn's uncle, Cass Coleman's home.[48]

When they arrived, Kathryn got out of the car, walked to the door, and knocked. Cass came out onto the porch and happily greeted his niece. She then let him know that Kelly was waiting in the car to talk with him. When Cass approached the car, Kelly was standing on the driver's side of the vehicle removing small bundles from the back seat and placing them in a larger bag. After filling the bag, he closed the car door and asked Cass to follow him to a barn some seventy-five yards away. Once the pair had reached the barn, Kelly informed Cass he had "a bunch of hot money" and wanted to stash it someplace. He asked Cass if he knew where he could bury the money. The perplexed farmer let Kelly know there was a spot close by in one of his fields near a well and a mesquite tree that might work. The two men collected a pair of shovels lying beside the barn, and Cass led the way to the mesquite tree. They buried more than seventy-three thousand dollars at the spot. Cass later told

Texas backroad outlaws George and Kathryn Kelly traveled to Paradise. *Courtesy Fort Worth Star-Telegram Collections, Special Collections, The University of Texas at Arlington Libraries.*

George "Machine Gun" Kelly. *Library of Congress.*

Kathryn Thorne Kelly. *Oklahoma Publishing Company, courtesy of the Oklahoma Historical Society.*

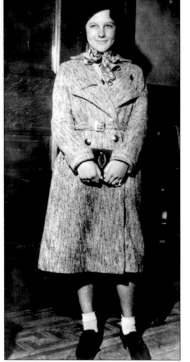

Geralene Arnold.
Author's collection.

A bill for Geralene Arnold's
stage performance recounting her
kidnapping by Machine Gun Kelly
and Kathryn Thorne
Author's collection

George routinely delivered bootleg whiskey
to Memphis nightclubs on Beale Street.
Author's collection.

Kathryn Kelly flashes a smile.
*Courtesy Fort Worth Star-Telegram Collections,
Special Collections, The University of Texas
at Arlington Libraries.*

George Kelly was arrested numerous times in his criminal career. *FBI files.*

Leavenworth Federal Penitentiary, 1933. *Author's collection.*

Shannon family: (left to right) Boss Shannon, Ora Shannon, Kathryn Kelly, sister-in-law Oleta, attorney James Mathers. *Oklahoma Publishing Company, courtesy of the Oklahoma Historical Society.*

Kidnapper Albert Bates.
*Oklahoma Publishing Company,
courtesy of the Oklahoma Historical Society.*

Baby Charles Lindbergh Jr. in his high chair
Library of Congress

Police examining the window from which
Charles A. Lindbergh's baby was kidnapped.
Library of Congress.

Charles Urschel's home
in Oklahoma City.
*Oklahoma Publishing Company,
courtesy of the Oklahoma
Historical Society.*

Kidnap victims Charles Urschel
and Walter Jarrett.
Author's collection.

J. Edgar Hoover, director of
the Bureau of Investigation.
Library of Congress.

Garage on the Shannon property where
Charles Urschel was held for a short time.
Dallas Municipal Archives,
City Secretary's Office, City of Dallas.

Ranch home belonging to
R.G. "Boss" Shannon in Paradise, Texas,
where Oklahoma City oilman
Charles Urschel was held
after being kidnapped.
Oklahoma Publishing Company,
courtesy of the Oklahoma Historical Society.

Room in Armon Shannon's home
where Charles Urschel was held.
Dallas Municipal Archives,
City Secretary's Office, City of Dallas.

The Muehlebach Hotel in Kansas City, Missouri,
was the rendezvous point for the kidnappers
and Charles Urschel's spokesmen.
Author's collection.

E. E. Kirkpatrick, Urschel family friend who acted as negotiator with the oilman's kidnappers.
Oklahoma Publishing Company, courtesy of the Oklahoma Historical Society.

Arthur Seeligson, one of the go-betweens in the Charles Urschel kidnapping case.
Oklahoma Publishing Company, courtesy of the Oklahoma Historical Society.

he Kellys.
Oklahoma Publishing Company, courtesy of the Oklahoma Historical Society.

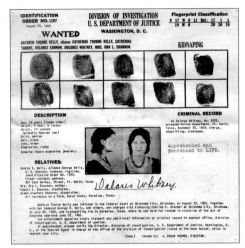

Kathryn Thorne Kelly's arrest record.
Dallas Municipal Archives,
City Secretary's Office, City of Dallas.

The Bureau of Investigation composite
of the location where Urschel was held
and the suspects involved.
Dallas Municipal Archives, City Secretary's
Office, City of Dallas

Aerial view of the Shannon farm.
Charles Urschel was able to help lead
Bureau agents to the location by paying
close attention to the sounds around him
and the airplanes passing overhead.
Oklahoma Publishing Company,
courtesy of the Oklahoma Historical Society.

This map shows the Kellys' various stops
during their flight from justice.
Created by House of Print and Copy, 2023.

Langford Ramsey helped find the gangster
and his wife a place to hide
while they were in Tennessee.
*Oklahoma Publishing Company,
courtesy of the Oklahoma Historical Society.*

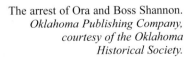

Cass Coleman provided
the Kellys with the location
to hide their portion
of the ransom.
*Oklahoma Publishing Company,
courtesy of the Oklahoma
Historical Society.*

The arrest of Ora and Boss Shannon.
*Oklahoma Publishing Company,
courtesy of the Oklahoma
Historical Society.*

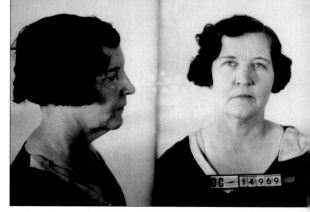

Ora Shannon's mug shot.
*Oklahoma Publishing Company,
courtesy of the Oklahoma
Historical Society.*

Boss Shannon's daughter, Nancy,
and her little girl stand alongside him
in court during his arraignment.
Author's collection.

Kathryn hides her face from news cameras
as she and Kelly are being led out
of the Shelby County jail in Memphis
after their arrest.
AP photo.

Prosecuting attorneys Joseph Keenan (center)
and Herbert Hyde (right of Keenan)
converse with Charles Urschel (left of Keenan)
about the case against the Kellys.
*Oklahoma Publishing Company,
courtesy of the Oklahoma Historical Society.*

George "Machine Gun" Kelly, handcuffed and shackled, is led, under heavy guard, from the Shelby County jail en route to the Memphis airport and Oklahoma City, where he and his wife would be tried for kidnapping.
Library of Congress.

(Left to right) Albert Bates, Harvey Bailey, Armon Shannon, and Boss and Ora Shannon stand and face the judge and jury during their sentencing.
Oklahoma Publishing Company, courtesy of the Oklahoma Historical Society.

Judge Edgar S. Vaught presided over both the Shannons' trial and the Kellys'.
Oklahoma Publishing Company, courtesy of the Oklahoma Historical Society.

Against the advice of their lawyers, the Kellys pled not guilty to the charge of kidnapping. *Library of Congress.*

Prosecuting attorney Herbert Hyde was confident he could prove beyond a doubt that both Kelly and Kathryn violated the Federal Kidnapping Law. *Oklahoma Publishing Company, courtesy of the Oklahoma Historical Society.*

View of the courthouse in Oklahoma City where the Kellys' trial was held. *Oklahoma Publishing Company, courtesy of the Oklahoma Historical Society.*

Law enforcement had to manage the crowds that came to the courthouse in Oklahoma City to see the Kellys escorted into the building. *Oklahoma Publishing Company, courtesy of the Oklahoma Historical Society.*

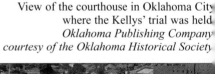

Charles Urschel kidnapping case's jury.
*Oklahoma Publishing Company,
courtesy of the Oklahoma Historical Society.*

Among the spectators in the courtroom during
the Kellys' trial were Charles and Berenice Urschel.
*Oklahoma Publishing Company,
courtesy of the Oklahoma Historical Society.*

George Kelly was suffering from an injury to his head
when he entered the courtroom the first day of the trial.
One of the guards had hit him with his gun.
*Oklahoma Publishing Company,
courtesy of the Oklahoma Historical Society.*

Kathryn's daughter Pauline (on left) and stepsister Ruth (on right) were two of a handful of relatives who testified in the trial against her for kidnapping. *Oklahoma Publishing Company, courtesy of the Oklahoma Historical Society.*

George and Kathryn Kelly sit with their lawyer, James Mathers, waiting for the hearing to begin. *Oklahoma Publishing Company, courtesy of the Oklahoma Historical Society.*

Cass Coleman led authorities to the location of the ransom money buried at his farm and testified against the Kellys at the hearing. *Oklahoma Publishing Company, courtesy of the Oklahoma Historical Society.*

An array of kidnapping equipment and other articles collected by Bureau agents that included the vacuum jug unearthed at the Coleman farm containing $72,950 and the red wig Kathryn wore while on the run.
Oklahoma Publishing Company, courtesy of the Oklahoma Historical Society.

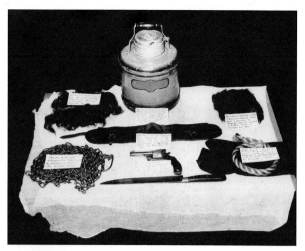

George Kelly would reside at Alcatraz Island for more than a dozen years. He was sure he would die there.
Library of Congress.

Kelly leaving Leavenworth in 1934 to be transferred to Alcatraz.
Oklahoma Publishing Company, courtesy of the Oklahoma Historical Society.

Kathryn Kelly and Ora Shannon
left federal prison in 1954
and settled in Oklahoma.
*Oklahoma Publishing Company,
courtesy of the Oklahoma Historical Society.*

Visitors to George Kelly's grave ne
Paradise, Texas, leave behind coi
to pay their respects to the outla
Author's collectio

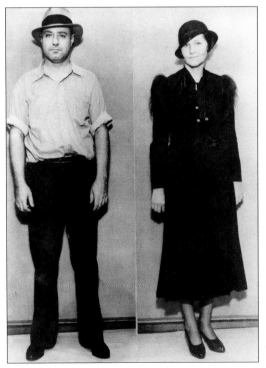

George "Machine Gun" Kelly
and Kathryn Thorne.
AP photo.

authorities that before heading back to the house, Kelly threatened to kill him if he ever told anyone about the money.[49]

Kathryn stayed inside her relative's home, visiting with her aunt and waiting for Kelly and her uncle to return. She claimed later to have had no idea what her uncle and her husband were doing in the field. The couple decided to stay the night at the Colemans.' The Kellys were offered the spare room, but Kelly was nervous about the money and imagined the law would soon swarm the homestead. He slept outside, close to the field where the ransom was buried.[50]

Kelly was disheveled and frustrated when Kathryn saw him the following morning. He looked like he hadn't slept. He had a hard time staying still and smoked one cigarette after another. It was as though he felt the need to move without end. Kathryn was on edge as well. She told her husband she was going to try to find a lawyer for her mother. Had it been just the two of them to deal with the authorities she could have coped more easily, but the thought of her mother behind bars was more than she could bear. "We have got some innocent folks in trouble," she told Kelly. "And we have got to get them out."[51]

Disguised in a red wig, Kathryn left the farm, promising to return soon. Within two hours she was back, driving the vehicle they'd had Louise purchase.

"Come on, George," she urged. "We've got to meet Louise at the end of the dirt road."

Kelly didn't want to leave. Kathryn begged him, but he wouldn't budge. He was formulating a getaway plan and needed time. He pleaded with her not to go, but she couldn't stay. She assured him she wouldn't be gone long. Louise left behind the Chevrolet coupe she was driving for Kelly and got into the 1928 Chevrolet sedan with Kathryn and the two hurried away toward Dallas.[52]

CHAPTER 7

LETTERS FROM GANGSTERS

K ELLY WAS ALONE. UTTERLY and completely alone. No Kathryn, no Albert Bates, no pals from his time in Leavenworth, no one. There wasn't anyone to confide in or anyone with whom to discuss what to do next. Staring out at the cotton field where he'd hidden the ransom, which he'd shoved into a vacuum jug and a molasses can and buried under a tree, he contemplated his circumstances. He didn't regret his actions and doubted the cash would ever be discovered. He'd been careful to rake the ground around the area where he placed the money and anticipated that the impending rainstorm would cover any footprints he might have missed. He questioned the wisdom of staying put and keeping a vigil over the funds. He didn't wait well, especially when he was alone. His wife had told him she'd be back after she'd had a chance to find a lawyer who would take her parents' case, but who knew how long that would take?

The heat was unbearable and kept him from formulating a clear thought. There was no cooling breeze or cloud to block the hot August sun and it played on his nerves. Kelly had never been in this position before. His name and face had never been so prominently featured in newspapers from one part of the country to the next. The only good thing about it was that Kelly could track the authorities' whereabouts through the various articles printed in the press.[1]

The August 19, 1933, edition of the *Fort Worth Star-Telegram* reported that the police were combing the Denver area in search of

Kelly and his partners. Law enforcement had received a tip that he was in Colorado and were reflecting back on a threat he supposedly made when he found out that Bates had been arrested to go to Denver and get his friend "out of that tin-can jail." Kelly felt he had to leave Texas for a time. It seemed the only way he knew to feel he had any power over the situation. Backhanding the perspiration gliding down his face from his hair, which Kathryn had bleached blond as a way to disguise his looks, he penned a note to her, explaining that he was going to Mississippi.[2]

Kelly drove more than 740 miles to Biloxi. He arrived on August 24, 1933, and spent that night at the Hotel Avelez. After a few days there, he moved to the Avon Hotel, where he registered under the alias J. L. Baker. News of the Shannons' trial covered the front page of every newspaper he saw. According to the articles, the courtroom was guarded by men with machine guns as Boss Shannon testified that Albert Bates and Kelly were the ones who brought Charles Urschel to his home for safekeeping. Kelly's picture was also featured on the front page of the papers under the headline "Sought in U. S. Kidnap Roundup." Nervous the law was closing in, Kelly left town and headed for Memphis. It was familiar territory for him. Having been a bootlegger there, he knew all the back roads and hidden spots where he could take refuge if he needed. He also had family in Memphis he could call on, and he did.[3]

Although it had been several years since they had spoken, Geneva Ramsey immediately recognized her ex-husband's voice when he phoned. He was polite but pointed. He was looking for her brother, George. George couldn't be reached and she offered to contact her other brother, Langford, to meet him downtown. Langford, a promising Tennessee lawyer, did so, then drove him to Geneva's home. Geneva hurried out of her house to meet the pair. She didn't want Kelly to come inside. Her second husband and the sons she had with Kelly were there, and she didn't want their lives disrupted. Kelly agreed not to make trouble for them. As Langford drove him away from Geneva's place, Kelly explained to his former brother-in-law that he needed a place to stay for the night and asked him for help. Langford introduced him to his friend Al Tichenor, a disabled gentleman who worked as a parking garage attendant. Tichenor offered Kelly a room.[4]

Kelly's stay with Tichenor lasted a week. During that time, he shared with Langford that "they were putting the heat on him" and that "they were going to kill him with machine guns when he wasn't looking." Kelly refused to answer when Langford inquired as to whom he was referring.[5]

Kelly purchased a Ford coupe on August 31 and left town without letting anyone know he was going.[6]

When Kathryn left Kelly in Coleman, Texas, on or about August 17, 1933, she was bound for Dallas to hire an attorney to represent her parents. She decided to contact Sam R. Sayers. Sayers and his firm, McLean, Scott, and Sayers, had a reputation for being unafraid to represent clients with serious criminal backgrounds. Sayers was also well-known for his stance on repealing prohibition. As Kathryn's name was now linked to Kelly's in connection with the Urschel kidnapping and the pair had been the subject of newspaper articles and radio news reports, the authorities were searching for her. Because of that, she knew she couldn't contact Sayers through traditional means. She decided to travel to Mineral Wells, a small town fifty-six miles away from Fort Worth, and write him a letter. The letter was delivered by a messenger the same day she wrote it.[7]

In Kathryn's correspondence to Sayers, she promised to deliver Kelly to him in exchange for her parents' freedom. Included in the letter was one thousand dollars and the diamond ring Kelly purchased for her in St. Paul. She hoped for a quick response, but that did not happen. She heard nothing about the package she sent him, but a story in the August 18, 1933, edition of the *Fort Worth Star-Telegram* led her to believe the lawyer had taken the case. The story noted that " . . . Sam Sayers, Fort Worth attorney, obtained permission to visit R. G. Shannon and gained permission to seek reduction of the amount of the bond." Kathryn's stepfather, mother, stepbrother, and his wife were being held on bond of fifty thousand dollars each. The Shannons protested that they could not raise two hundred thousand dollars and intimated that they would ask for a hearing before federal authorities for a lower bond. An article in the August 19, 1933, edition of the *Fort Worth Star-Telegram* confirmed that the defense of the Shannons had officially been accepted by Sayers' law firm.[8]

In addition to writing Sayers about her parents, Kathryn also penned a letter to the Oklahoma assistant attorney general, Joseph B. Keenan. The Shannons were to be tried in Oklahoma for their part in the Urschel kidnapping and Keenan was to be leading the prosecution. "The entire Urschel family and friends, and all of you will be exterminated soon," Kathryn wrote Keenan. "There is no way I can prevent it. I will gladly put George Kelly on the spot for you if you will save my mother, who is innocent of any wrongdoing. If you do not comply with this request, there is no way in which I can prevent the most awful tragedy. If you refuse my offer I shall commit some minor offense and be placed in jail so that you will know that I have no connection with the terrible slaughter that will take place in Oklahoma within the next few days."[9]

Kathryn was desperate to intercede on behalf of her mother and other relatives and would do or say anything to bring about their freedom.[10]

While reading the same newspaper that reported Sayers had accepted the Shannons as clients, Kathryn learned that she and Kelly were in worse trouble than she'd imagined. Federal agents were attempting to connect the duo with the abduction and murder of the infant son of Colonel and Mrs. Charles A. Lindbergh. Frantic to see Kelly, discuss the news, and get more money from him, Kathryn hurried back to Coleman, Texas. She was furious when she read the note he'd left her. Not only was she disappointed he didn't wait for her but she let herself believe that he'd taken off to find solace in the arms of one of the molls he had been involved with in the Southeast during his bootlegging days.[11]

When she left Coleman, she considered driving to Biloxi to find Kelly but changed her mind and headed to her housekeeper's home in Temple, Texas. It was September 2, 1933, and Kathryn needed a place to freshen up and collect her thoughts. During her short visit, she ranted about not being able to reach Kelly. She wanted to talk to him about giving himself up so she and her mother could be free from the charges levied against them.[12]

From Temple, Kathryn traveled to Waco. Believing the Chevrolet she was driving was too conspicuous, she decided to trade it in for a used Ford Model A truck. After swapping vehicles, she checked herself into a local hotel to try to get some rest. She couldn't sleep because she was thinking about her mother and the pending trial. After tossing and turning most of the night, she decided to call Sam Sayers to check on her family's case. He wasn't pleased to hear from her, and their short talk ended abruptly. Frustrated that she wasn't able to learn anything about the case, Kathryn loaded her belongings into the truck and headed to Fort Worth. Her mind was racing as she drove along. She needed to find a way to communicate with Sayers without getting caught. How to manage it eluded her until she spotted a family of three hitchhiking near the town of Itasca, Texas.[13]

On September 4, 1933, Kathryn had just passed a gas station when she slowed her truck to a stop beside Luther Arnold, his wife, Flossie, and their eleven-year-old daughter, Geralene. She asked the trio if they wanted a ride, and Luther nodded affirmatively. Kathryn motioned for them to climb aboard and they did. After introducing herself as Mrs. Montgomery, Kathryn asked Luther what he did for a living. He told her he didn't have a job at the present, but he was "looking for anything to do to feed three hungry people." Smoothing down a section of her red wig, she replied, "I live on a ranch near Brownwood, Texas, and might be able to help you."[14]

According to Luther, Kathryn was exceptionally kind. She stopped at a roadside stand to treat her passengers to a cold drink and a snack before continuing on their way toward Waco.

"When we arrived in Cleburne, Texas, we drove through the town on a highway leading south," Luther later recalled. "We crossed a bridge and stopped at a tourist camp a short distance from it. The camp only had four framed cabins and we rented two of them. Myself, my wife, and child occupied one cabin and the woman the other.[15]

"After we drove into the camp the woman gave me some money and told me to go out and register and pay for the cabins. We arrived at this camp about six or seven o'clock. In conversation that night the woman asked me many questions about my past life and my identity and also asked me if there was anything against me or if I was wanted. I told her that there was nothing against me and I was not wanted for any offense. She also asked my wife many questions concerning my identity and past life.[16]

"The next morning, September 5, 1933, this woman took my wife and girl to town and bought them some house dresses. That morning she said: 'I like you people and would like to fix it so you could make a little money.' She then said, 'Can I trust you?' I replied, 'Absolutely.' She then said, 'I have driven three thousand miles to see my lawyer and he failed to meet me. I came all the way from Gulfport, Mississippi.' She then said, 'What would you people think if I told you who I am?' I said, 'Go ahead and tell me, you can trust us.' She then said, 'I am Kathryn Kelly, whom you no doubt have read about in the papers, and am wanted for questioning.'[17]

"She then said, 'Mr. Arnold, I am going to place a big trust in you. I want you to go to Fort Worth and contact my lawyer, Sam Sayers. I want you to ask Sayers for the details of the situation up to date and to specifically ask him what has happened concerning my offer of compromise by surrendering Kelly for the release of my father and mother.' She also asked me to find out how her father and mother were being treated in jail and whether or not they needed anything. She then gave me about $50 in cash. She instructed that I go to Fort Worth and return to Cleburne that day. She gave me an unsigned note to Sam Sayers telling him that I was okay and to give me all details. She instructed me that all I would have to do to identify myself to Sayers was to say that I was 'Ingersoll.'"[18]

Luther Arnold boarded a bus early on September 6, bound for Fort Worth. When he arrived, he checked into the Texas Hotel and called Sam Sayers's office from a nearby coffee shop. As Kathryn instructed, he identified himself to the attorney as Ingersoll. Sayers invited Arnold to meet him at his office on the twelfth floor of the Sinclair Building. Kathryn's spokesperson was greeted warmly and was told to share with her that although his firm, and all the other lawyers connected with the case in Texas, did everything they could, they couldn't get the Shannons released on bond. Sayers also wanted Kathryn to know that he put her proposition [to give up George] to the authorities and talk trade but couldn't get any satisfaction out of the judge or the United States attorney. Luther asked the lawyer to confirm that he'd received the diamond ring and the money and Sayers assured him he had. Sayers then suggested Kathryn seek representation for her parents in Oklahoma, where they would be tried.[19]

Luther returned to the tourist camp in Cleburne after he finished with Sayers and relayed what had transpired to Kathryn. "You're an Oklahoma boy," she reminded Luther. "You ought to know some good lawyer in Oklahoma that I could employ." Luther told her about an attorney named John Roberts in Enid, Oklahoma, whom the governor of the state had employed at one time to prosecute accused murderer Earl Quinn. He believed the ambitious lawyer was more than qualified to take her parents' case and assist in selecting a jury.[20]

After Luther's revelation, Kathryn asked him if he'd be willing to go to Enid and hire Roberts for her. He agreed. She gave him five hundred dollars to pay the lawyer, drove him to the bus depot, and sent him on his way with a letter she had written to Sam Sayers. Sayers was taking care of Kathryn's Chevrolet coupe, and in the letter to him, she asked that he turn the vehicle over to Luther. Luther was then to drive to Oklahoma City, where he was to arrange a meeting with Roberts. Before leaving Kathryn for a second time, she promised him she would take good care of his wife and daughter in his absence. She informed Luther she was going to take them to San Antonio and told him to meet them there after he retained John Roberts. When he arrived in San Antonio, he was to go to the post office and ask for a letter in general delivery addressed to L. W. Arnold. The letter would contain the address where Kathryn, his wife, and his daughter would be.[21]

Confident that Luther would secure Roberts's services, Kathryn decided to return to Coleman with Flossie and Geralene in tow. She hoped Kelly would be at the farm when she arrived, but if he wasn't, she wanted to leave a note behind telling him where she would be. It had been several days since Kathryn had seen Kelly. She could only imagine where he was and what he was doing, and she was worried about him. She was sure he would eventually come back to the farm to check on the money, and when he did, he'd find her message. Like most men, Kathryn reasoned, Kelly could be tempted by other women, but she also knew he was devoted to her. She was sure he'd follow her to San Antonio and anywhere else she asked him to go.[22]

Luther wasn't alone when he reached Oklahoma. During his travels, he had picked up two professional women who agreed to keep him company on his trip. Using the money Kathryn had given him for the journey, he acquired a room for himself and his guests at the upscale Skirvin Hotel. Luther and friends hosted a party in his suite that, at times, was so loud other guests complained to management.[23]

The following morning, on September 9, 1933, John Roberts and a handful of other lawyers from his office arrived at the hotel for a scheduled meeting with Luther. Members of Oklahoma's Bureau of Investigation, scattered at hotels throughout Oklahoma City, were instructed to be on the alert for any suspicious activity or behavior from patrons. Luther's actions, the women with him, and the presence of high-powered attorneys at the Skirvin asking for his room number were suspect. By the time the agents were directed to intervene, Luther had left town.[24]

Kathryn wasted no time in finding a house to rent in San Antonio. Calling herself Mrs. Montgomery, she paid cash for a month's use of the residence at 160 Mahneke Court to the landlord. She then took Flossie and Geralene on a shopping trip, purchasing clothes and shoes for the pair as well as household items and food for the duration of their stay.[25]

Kelly did indeed return to Cass Coleman's place. He had put on more than ten pounds since he'd been gone and was sporting the same close-cropped hairstyle, now dyed a dull yellow. Shortly after his arrival, Cass sent a telegram to Kathryn to let her know her husband was there. Kelly desperately wanted to be with his wife but was fearful the law might recognize his car. If he were to get to San Antonio, Kathryn would have to get him. She decided to take Geralene along with her to retrieve Kelly.[26]

When the pair reached Coleman, Texas, Kathryn didn't try to hide her frustration with Kelly. She cursed him for taking off like he had and leaving her in the lurch. She let him know she thought he was selfish and a womanizer. Not only had he left her without adequate funds but he cared about little else than chasing old girlfriends. The pair argued about the best place to go next. Kathryn explained she had rented a house in San Antonio where they could lay low while she tried to make legal arrangements for her parents. Kelly wanted to hide out in Chicago or New York. Kathryn won the argument.[27]

Luther Arnold was reunited with his family on Tuesday, September 12. As Kathryn promised, the letter waiting for him at the post office told him where they'd be. In addition to his wife and daughter, Luther shared the house Kathryn had rented with her husband. According to Luther, the Kellys were affectionate with each other and seemed genuinely happy to be together. In the beginning, the Kellys spoke only in generalities about kidnapping Charles Urschel. Kelly did mention that if he had to do it over again, he would have stuck Urschel's head in a barrel of lye rather than let him go after the ransom was paid. Kathryn too commented on the wisdom of releasing Urschel. "I would have killed him myself, if I'd had a chance," she remarked to her housemates.[28]

Kathryn was anxious to hear from Luther about what had transpired during the meeting with John Roberts, Sayers, and the other attorneys at the law firm. She was relieved to learn that Roberts had accepted the case and agreed to be paid after the hearing. She reiterated that her mother and father were innocent and deserved fair legal representation. Kelly wasn't as quick to champion the Shannons as their daughter. He boasted of the plan to abduct Urschel and the work that went into the job. He didn't defend the Shannons like

his wife but instead pointed out the trusted help needed to successfully pull off a kidnapping.[29]

Kathryn regretted involving her family in the crime and was
preoccupied with making things right. She asked Luther to meet
with Roberts again and let him know if he could get her mother
and the rest of the Shannons out of jail, it would be worth five thousand dollars. Luther agreed and left San Antonio with three hundred dollars Kathryn had given him. He didn't hurry to Oklahoma
as he'd promised. He got as far as Fort Worth, where he stopped to
enjoy the evening drinking at a tavern with two prostitutes. Again,
he checked into the Skirvin Hotel in Oklahoma City with the two
women late in the morning on September 14. John Roberts arrived
at the hotel in the early afternoon of that same day, stopping at the
front desk first to ask for Luther's room number.[30]

An employee of the hotel, who knew of the Bureau of Investigation's previous interest in Luther, phoned the Oklahoma office
and let them know that Luther had returned to the business and of
his afternoon visitor. Agents invaded the establishment and apprehended Luther. He wasn't willing to talk to the authorities until
they arrested him for violating the Mann Act, which involved
transporting the women in his room over state lines for the purposes of sexual favors.[31]

Kathryn and Kelly left San Antonio the same day Luther departed for
Oklahoma. Kelly planned to retrieve the vehicle he had left behind
at Cass Coleman's place and drive to Chicago. Kathryn promised to
meet him there once John Roberts had negotiated the release of her
mother. Geralene was allowed to ride with the outlaws to Coleman,
Texas. Kathryn felt the young girl would be the perfect cover. She
reasoned that the police would be searching automobiles only for
couples and not a family of three. Flossie permitted her daughter to
go, believing she would be back in a day or two. She had no idea then
that the Kellys wouldn't return to San Antonio.[32]

The Kellys' time at the Coleman farm was brief. They stopped
long enough to learn that the police had been there looking for

Kathryn. After trading vehicles with her cousin, Gray Coleman, the trio hurried off to Illinois.[33]

Bureau of Investigation agents learned the location of the Kellys' San Antonio home from Luther, but by the time they reached the residence, the fugitives had fled. Flossie was taken into custody, and both she and her husband made a deal with the authorities to help capture the kidnappers.[34]

Driving into downtown Chicago on September 17, 1933, Kelly's grip on the steering wheel loosened a bit. Newspapers across Texas reported on possible sightings of him and Kathryn in San Angelo and Abilene. Calling themselves the Johnson family, the outlaws rented an apartment, and Kelly then contacted fellow bootleggers and bank robbers he knew in the area he hoped would help them dodge authorities. J. Edgar Hoover and his agents at the Bureau had cast a wide net in their efforts to capture the pair and, because of the publicity, Kelly's associates refused to lend a hand.[35]

Kelly panicked and his imagination ran wild. He got it into his head that everyone recognized him and Kathryn, and that at any moment the police were going to overtake them. They left an eatery before finishing their evening meal when he noticed a couple at a nearby table staring at them. Kelly was convinced they wouldn't be safe in the apartment they had just moved into and strongly suggested they relocate. Kathryn took charge of the situation. She sent Kelly to a movie to calm his nerves and drove Geralene to the apartment to retrieve their luggage. By the time the double feature ended, Kathryn had rented another apartment for the three on the north side of the city. The change did little to settle Kelly's nerves.[36]

The following morning it was Kelly's turn to help deal with Kathryn's anxiety and fears. The front page of the Chicago and Oklahoma newspapers featured articles about the trials of her parents, Harvey Bailey, and Albert Bates. Included in the articles was news that on the previous evening, US District Attorney Herbert K. Hyde had turned down John Roberts's offer for "the surrender of George [Machine Gun] Kelly who has escaped a nation-wide man hunt in the case, conditioned on the release of R. G. (Boss) Shannon, his wife, and their son Armon."

Kathryn was furious. Even if she could persuade Kelly to give himself up so her family could go free, such a deal would not be accepted. The picture of her mother that accompanied the story further enraged her. The headline above her photograph read, "Mrs. Shannon, 'Mail Order Bride' and Sunday School Teacher to Mark Wedding Anniversary in Cell." Kathryn cursed Charles Urschel and the lawyers and swore she would get her revenge.[37]

Kelly was equally as angry at Urschel as Kathryn and issued his own threats against the kidnap victim. He wasn't content to simply tell his wife what he'd like to do to the man; he wrote a letter to Urschel explaining what his vile intentions were toward him and his loved ones.[38]

"Just a few lines to let you know that I am getting my plans made to destroy your so-called mansion, and you and your family immediately after this trial. And young fellow, I guess you've begun to realize your serious mistake. Are you ignorant enough to think the government can guard you forever? I gave you credit for more sense than that, and figured you thought too much of your family to jeopardize them as you have, but if you don't look out for them, why should we? I dislike hurting the innocent, but I told you exactly what would happen and you can bet $200,000 more, everything I said will be true.[39]

"You are living on borrowed time now. You know that the Shannon family are victims of circumstances the same as you was [sic]. You don't seem to mind prosecuting the innocent, neither will I have any conscious qualms over brutally murdering your family. The Shannons have put the heat on, but I don't desire to see them prosecuted as they are innocent and I have a much better method of settling with them. As far as the guilty being punished you would probably have lived the rest of your life in peace had you tried only the guilty, but if the Shannons are convicted look out, and God help you for he is the only one that will be able to do you any good.[40]

"In the event of my arrest I've already formed an outfit to take care of and destroy you and yours the same as if I was there. I am spending your money to have you and your family killed—nice—eh? You are bucking people who have cash, planes, bombs, and unlimited connections both here and abroad. I have friends in Oklahoma City that know every move and every plan you make and you are still too dumb to figure out the finger man there.[41]

"If my brain was no larger than yours, the government would have had me long ago, as it is I am drinking good beer and will yet see you and your family like I should have left you at first—stone dead.

"I don't worry about Bates and Bailey. They will be out for the ceremonies—your slaughter.[42]

"Now, say, it is up to you. If the Shannons are convicted, you can get another rich wife in hell, because that will be the only place you can use one. Adios, smart one. Your Worst Enemy, Geo. R. Kelly."[43]

Kathryn wrote a couple of letters of her own while Kelly was writing his letter to Urschel. One of those was to Flossie. She had written to her prior to leaving Coleman to let her know that she and Kelly would not be coming back to San Antonio anytime soon, and that they were taking Geralene with them. Kathryn promised Flossie that her daughter would be well taken care of and told her to make her way to Oklahoma City with Kathryn's clothes, furs, and other valuable belongings, and check into a boardinghouse on Reno Street. Bureau of Investigation agents seized Kathryn's letter to Flossie when they raided the San Antonio home after Luther's arrest.[44]

The letter Kathryn wrote to Flossie from Chicago explained that she could reach her via special delivery mail at the Michigan Tavern on the south side of Chicago. "I am taking care of the baby, honey," Kathryn noted, referring to Geralene. Before Kathryn finished the letter, she reminded Flossie to take care of the things she asked her to bring with her to Oklahoma and to make sure they never left her sight.[45]

Bureau of Investigation agents escorted Flossie to the Oklahoma boardinghouse where Kathryn instructed her to go and were there with her and Luther when the letter Kathryn had written to her in Chicago arrived.[46]

Another letter Kathryn penned from Illinois was to prosecuting attorney Joseph Keenan, pleading again for her parents' release and standing firm on her repeated statement that they were innocent. She placed the blame for all that had happened on Kelly and claimed that she had left her husband because of the trouble he had brought to her and her family. She offered to lead the authorities to wanted criminals she knew the Bureau of Investigation were after and concluded her tirade casting aspersions on Urschel's friend and business associate Walter Jarrett. Kathryn accused Jarrett of helping to arrange Urschel's kidnapping.[47]

The Kellys sent Geralene to buy stamps for the letters they had written and she brought them back to Kathryn. The young girl watched Kathryn affix the postage on the envelopes, which were placed in the mail when they left the apartment. While the Kellys were stuffing the letters into the envelopes they continued to blame Urschel for their predicament and mentioned again how much they wanted to kill him. They admitted in retrospect that they should have taken Urschel to the desert in Arizona to do away with him and bury him there.[48]

In addition to the letter Kelly wrote Charles Urschel, he also wrote one to the editor of the *Daily Oklahoman*.[49]

"Dear Sirs, you will please publish the enclosed in your paper as I want the Shannons to be sure to read it. Yours truly, G. Kelly.

"Gentlemen: I desire the public to know that the Shannon family are innocent victims in the Charles F. Urschel case the same as Urschel was.[50]

"I understand that they are now government witnesses also defendants, and I don't want them convicted, for I desire to settle with them in my own way and with no assistance from the government.

"Mr. Urschel and the government prosecution know that the Shannons had no part or no intention of aiding in the matter and were forced to do so the same as Urschel was forced to leave his home.[51]

"Why didn't Urschel call the law in Norman when he was released instead of riding a cab peacefully into the city and waiting a given time to call them? Fear, gentlemen, fear, the same that dominated the Shannons.

"I hate and despise the government for their crooked dealings and do not wish them to convict people as innocent of that crime and guilty of one thing—talking to me. I can take care of my end and will the way I want to. You might state for Mr. Keenan's benefit that he never came anywhere near to catching me, although I have even been in Oklahoma City four nights and uptown each day.[52]

"We will see how the trial progresses and can adjust our end accordingly. I am putting my prints on this so you will know it is genuine. Yours Truly, Geo. R. Kelly."[53]

Kelly didn't believe he and his wife were safe in Chicago. Not only would none of the lawbreakers he knew in the area lift a finger to help him but he believed they would lead the police to his door to help themselves. Too nervous to attempt to leave town in the vehicle he drove to Chicago, Kelly made arrangements to buy a car from a contact at the Michigan Tavern. As he planned to get out of the city as soon as the transaction was completed, it was necessary that Kathryn and Geralene go along with him to the bar. Seated between Kelly and Kathryn, Geralene stared wide-eyed at the loud patrons filtering in and out of the beer joint, some with prostitutes on their arms and bottles of booze in their hands. Once the keys to the new car had been exchanged for the roll of cash Kelly offered for the automobile, the trio left the seedy establishment.[54]

Melvin Purvis, one of the Bureau of Investigation's top agents, was notified by Bureau agents in Oklahoma City that the letter Kathryn had sent Flossie indicated that the Kellys' mail was being delivered to the Michigan Tavern. If Purvis hadn't been preoccupied with tracking one of Al Capone's henchmen, an armed robber and murderer named Gus Winkler, the detail might not have slipped his mind. He would have been at the saloon when Kathryn and Kelly arrived to collect the getaway car. The blunder allowed the pair to escape undetected.[55]

CHAPTER 8

CAPTURING THE KELLYS

THE LETTER GEORGE KELLY SENT to the editor of the *Daily Oklahoman* appeared on the front page of that paper on September 20, 1933, as well as the front page of several other newspapers across the state. Federal authorities verified that the fingerprints on the letter were Kelly's, and they did the same for the threatening letter sent to Charles Urschel. Bureau of Investigation agents took the outlaw's threats seriously and, following a directive from J. Edgar Hoover, increased security around the oil tycoon to make sure nothing happened to him before he took the witness stand to tell the story of his nine days in captivity at the hands of the kidnap ring. Federal prosecutor Joseph Keenan called Kelly's warnings "cheap threats from a human rat." He further noted to the press that Kelly was a marked man. "It may be a month, or it may be a year, but he cannot escape the government forces. . . . He is a brutal, boasting, immoral derelict."[1]

Kathryn's character was also called into question in various newspaper articles, which reported that she goaded her husband into the desperate acts committed. According to the September 23, 1933, edition of the *Muskogee Daily Phoenix*, "Kelly's infatuation for his wife made him a willing tool of the dominating mother love of Kathryn."[2]

The Kellys left Chicago in the early morning hours of September 22, 1933, with Geralene in tow. The pair were on edge, constantly snapping at each other, their heads swiveling every time they heard a siren. Geralene wanted to know where they were going and why they lied about their plans. They explained that a problem had come up and they needed to get to Tennessee to have the vehicle that was given to them the day before licensed. The answer seemed to satisfy the young girl, and she sat quietly in the back seat, enjoying the sights en route to Memphis.[3]

Kathryn spent the drive poring over newspaper stories about her parents' trial and that of Bates and Bailey. The picture of her grandmother, Mary Coleman, being pushed into the courtroom in a wheelchair was particularly upsetting to her. In his opening statement, US District Attorney Herbert Hyde described Kathryn's entire family, including her grandmother, as individuals who had questionable morals. He described the Shannon farm as a "post office" and hideout for the worst criminals in gangland and attacked the supposed churchgoing country folks as "harborers of desperados." Kathryn was angry and insulted.[4]

Kelly tried to calm his wife's anxiety over what was being said about Mary Coleman and her family as a whole by telling her that the jury would be able to clearly see that her parents were innocent. He also told Kathryn that only a handful of people would actually attend the court proceedings anyway, and that few would even know what was said about the Colemans or the Shannons. The September 22, 1933, edition of the *Daily Oklahoman* noted just the opposite of Kelly's assessment. The courtroom was filled to overflowing with curious individuals. In fact, the crowd proved to be so problematic, the judge ordered everyone out with the exception of the officers, reporters, and witnesses.[5]

Fortunately for the Kellys, law enforcement agents in the Midwest were so busy chasing down erroneous leads, they weren't as careful about monitoring the traffic in and out of George's hometown. Numerous crimes, from bank robbery in Wilmot, Arkansas, to kidnapping in Edwardsville, Illinois, were being attributed to Kelly. Among the many sought-after gangsters of the time including Ma Barker and her sons, John Dillinger, and Pretty Boy Floyd, the manhunt for Machine Gun Kelly was the most extensive. Police and regional Bureau investigators were tracking down every known sighting of the fugitive and his wife. Kathryn believed the continued presence of Geralene was what kept them from being caught.[6]

Shortly after the Kellys arrived in Memphis, George contacted Al Tichenor. Tichenor had allowed Kelly to hideout at his home before and hoped he would again. The garage attendant did not disappoint. Not only did he agree to rent a room to the fugitives but he sold Kelly a gun. After purchasing the Colt 1911, the Kellys had little money left to see them through. They were struggling when they left Chicago but managed to persuade the man who sold them the car before they fled the city to give them two hundred dollars. With barely enough of those funds to get by, the pair decided it was time to retrieve the ransom money.

Both Kathryn and Kelly knew they'd need help getting the cash. Kelly called his ex-brother-in-law, Langford Ramsey, to ask for his assistance. Ramsey had proved himself trustworthy, and when Kelly called requesting he meet him at Tichenor's home, he didn't hesitate.[7]

"I did not again see or hear from George Barnes until Saturday, September 23," Ramsey recalled later. "On this occasion, he was accompanied by a woman whom he said was his wife and by a young girl whom they called Gerry. During our conversation he asked me to drive to Texas to see a man. I told him that if it was a matter of life and death I would do it, but otherwise not. George told me that if he was caught he would get the chair and I was then practically convinced that he was Machine Gun Kelly. Prior to this time, I didn't think he was Machine Gun Kelly, thinking that he was merely bragging as was his custom when I knew him several years ago."[8]

Kelly told Ramsey that it was imperative for him to contact Cass Coleman because he would be able to clear up all the charges against him and he'd be a free man. Ramsey believed him, and for the sake of Kelly's sons, who were Ramsey's nephews, he agreed to help him in his time of trouble. Kelly's instructions to his former brother-in-law were specific. He was to make the trip to Coleman, Texas, with Geralene, who would direct him to the Coleman farm. He would then arrange a meeting between Kelly and Cass at a point five miles west of McGregor, Texas, on highway number seven at midnight on Thursday, September 28, 1933.[9]

Kathryn had her own request for Ramsey. She wanted him to ask Cass's wife to turn over the furs she'd left at the home to him. After contacting Cass Coleman, Ramsey was to go to Oklahoma City and call Luther Arnold at the Skirvin Hotel to collect more of Kathryn's things. Kelly warned the gullible courier to "be very careful and don't let anyone trail you back." Kathryn stressed the importance of watching out for Geralene. The Kellys were clear that the young girl was to return to Memphis with Ramsey. They wanted to have her with them later in case they needed her to aid in their getaway.[10]

Ramsey and Geralene left Memphis at six in the morning on September 24, 1933, driving Kelly's Chevrolet sedan. Kathryn watched them go, frantically contemplating the outcome. Newspapers circulating in Chicago, Tulsa, and Dallas the same day Ramsey departed, reported on the fifteen-thousand-dollar reward being offered for the Kellys. The capture of George was ten thousand dollars and for Kathryn it was five thousand.[11]

John Roberts, the attorney Kathryn hired to represent her parents, had shared with the press his speculation that Kathryn might make a dramatic appearance at the court proceedings against her mother and father when they resumed on Monday, September 25. Federal prosecutor Joseph Keenan made an appeal to Kathryn through various newspapers imploring her to come in. Journalists who read the six-page letter Kathryn wrote to Keenan pleading for mercy for her parents noted that "though authentic reports are that her mind has been wracked, her health broken by relentless pursuit of the marshaled forces of the United States government, there is still fire left in the twenty-nine-year-old Kathryn Kelly."

Both the press and federal officials doubted Kathryn would surrender in an effort to save her parents. J. Edgar Hoover and other Bureau of Investigation agents branded Roberts's prediction as "absurd" and made it clear that even if she did "come in," their duty was to capture not to compromise with criminals.[12]

Whatever was to happen next, Kathryn wanted to look her

best. Toward that end, she paid a visit to a salon to have her hair done. According to the manager of the salon and the stylist who worked on Kathryn, the "titan-haired" woman asked for a cut and dye job. The two ladies contacted the local authorities about Kathryn after seeing a photograph of her in the paper and identifying her as Machine Gun Kelly's wife. They told the police Kathryn was extremely nervous and reportedly told them, "You'll see my name in all the papers tomorrow" and "You'd be surprised to know who I am." Kathryn reportedly entered the shop wearing a blond wig. She had both the wig and her natural hair dyed auburn. She wouldn't give her name and claimed her husband worked in the oil industry, and that she was traveling the following day to meet him.[13]

Langford Ramsey and Geralene Arnold pulled onto the dirt road leading to the Coleman's farm on Monday, September 25, 1933, at five in the morning. Ramsey waited in the car while Geralene got out to meet Cass Coleman as he stepped onto the porch. He followed the young girl back to the vehicle, and she introduced Cass to Ramsey. Ramsey recalled later that the farmer appeared frightened and in a hurry to dismiss the callers. Ramsey tried to explain why he was there, but Cass held up his hand as a gesture to stop him from talking. "I think I know what you came after," he told Ramsey. In a low voice, he admitted that the authorities were watching the farm. Ramsey informed him that the Kellys wanted him to arrange a meeting between the three of them. Cass politely but steadfastly refused to be at the spot Kelly suggested. He didn't want to get any further involved with the Kellys.

"Kathryn has some furs here. I can take them, can't I?" Ramsey asked Cass. Cass refused, adding that the police had machine guns leveled at the place and he didn't want his home shot up. "I have to protect my family," he told Ramsey.[14]

Cass strongly suggested Ramsey and Geralene leave, and Ramsey quickly complied. When he reached Fort Worth, he sent a telegram to Al Tichenor in Memphis. The message, intended for Kelly, read "Had several tough breaks. Ran into several rainstorms caused brake trouble. Tried to get a later appointment, but prospect was afraid. Impossible to change his mind. Don't want to bring home a sad tale. Can go on if advisable. Wire instructions here."[15]

Ramsey had every intention of taking Geralene with him to Oklahoma City as instructed, but he wanted to wait until after he received a reply from Kelly to his telegram. Geralene, however, was anxious to see her mother and asked if she could travel by train ahead of him to get to her sooner. After explaining how long it had been since she had seen her mother, Ramsey agreed. By the time Kelly responded to Ramsey's message, he'd already escorted the young girl to the train station, purchased a ticket for her, and allowed her to send a telegram to her father to let him know when she would arrive. Kelly's orders to Ramsey were to proceed as planned. Ramsey thought about sending another telegram to let Kelly know Geralene would be traveling by train to Oklahoma City instead of with him but decided the detail wasn't important enough to mention.[16]

Neither the Kellys nor Ramsey knew that Luther and Flossie Arnold were collaborating with the authorities. As far as the Kellys were aware, Luther and Flossie were at separate locations in Oklahoma City. Luther was at the Skirvin Hotel and Flossie was at a boardinghouse. Both were supposedly waiting for Kathryn to contact them.[17]

Bureau agents accompanied Luther to the depot when he met Geralene but kept out of sight. From the train station, Luther took his daughter to the home of Agent Ralph Colvin. Colvin was the head of the Bureau of Investigation's Oklahoma City office. He was a part of the case since Charles Urschel was kidnapped. He and another agent, Harold "Pop" Nathan, introduced themselves to Geralene and then asked her to tell them about her time with the Kellys. She was eager to share everything she knew including where the pair was hiding in Memphis.[18]

When Ramsey arrived in Oklahoma City, he met with Luther Arnold at the Skirvin Hotel to discuss the matter of Kathryn's clothing. Flossie and Geralene were also at the hotel. Colvin, Nathan, and a handful of other Bureau of Investigation agents watched the four from a safe distance away. The Arnolds had been instructed by authorities to say nothing that would make Ramsey suspicious. Luther told Ramsey that his wife no longer had Kathryn's things and confessed to having to sell the clothes to pay their debt to the hotel.

"It will take about two hundred dollars to pay the hotel bill," he admitted to Ramsey. Luther asked Ramsey where he could find Kathryn to ask for more money, and Ramsey lied and told him he didn't know. Ramsey advised Luther that if he and his family changed their address, they could notify him in Memphis, and if the Kellys wanted the changed address, they could get it from him. Ramsey was more frustrated than suspicious when Geralene declined to leave with him to travel to Memphis. Both Kathryn and Kelly were adamant that she return with him to Tennessee. The young girl didn't want to leave her mother and Ramsey didn't argue.[19]

The Kellys made the most of their time while waiting for Ramsey to make his way back. They dined out at Memphis's most respectable cafés and spent an evening celebrating their third anniversary at the Loewe's State Theatre watching a film starring Will Rogers entitled *Doctor Bull*. After the meals and movie, when the pair was tucked away inside Tichenor's home with nothing but the radio to keep them company, Kathryn and Kelly drank. Glasses of whiskey and gin eased their anxiety. Neither slept well. Kathryn continued to worry about her family, Kelly worried about the authorities discovering their location, and both fretted over the ransom money. Life beyond Tichenor's address at 140 S. Raynor Street would be difficult without it.[20]

Between drinks and chain-smoking, the fugitives scrutinized the pages of the newspapers delivered daily. An article on the front page of the September 25, 1933, edition of the *Knoxville News Sentinel* was particularly upsetting to Kathryn. The headline read "Shannons Lay Kidnap Blame on Daughter and Her Husband." The story under the headline noted that, "In a desperate move to save themselves from prison, the three Texas Shannons placed the blame in the $200,000 Urschel kidnapping case today on their daughter and sister, Kathryn, George (Machine Gun) Kelly, and Albert Bates. The surrender of Kathryn Kelly to save her parents, which was hinted at in a letter she wrote never happened."[21]

The five-thousand-dollar reward being offered for Kathryn's capture, dead or alive, factored into her decision to stay away from the court proceedings. She was frightened she would be shot before she could give herself up and come to her family's aid. She went to bed alone that night after reading more newspaper reports. She hoped the jury would believe her parents' story and let them go. She didn't really think they would, but imagining their release helped her fall asleep.[22]

Thinking about the Shannons and the Kellys kept J. Edgar Hoover awake the evening of September 25, 1933. He and other top members of his staff were reviewing the developments in the hunt for the kidnappers that had spanned from Chicago to the Rio Grande. Now that the authorities knew the exact location of the pair, Hoover was supervising the Bureau of Investigation's next move. He was determined not to let the Kellys slip out of the Bureau's grasp again, and it was with that in mind that at two in the morning he phoned William Rohrer, special agent in charge of the Bureau of Investigation office in Birmingham, Alabama. Hoover ordered Rohrer and agent B. F. Fitzsimmons to fly to Memphis at once. They were to meet with authorities there who would take part in the raid on Tichenor's home. In addition to agents from Birmingham, there were representatives from the Chicago and St. Louis offices. A squad of officers from the Memphis Police Department were also on hand.[23]

The force was instructed to move in before dawn. By sunrise at five-fifty in the morning, the home was completely surrounded. SAC Rohrer, Detective Sergeant Floyd Wiebenga, and two Memphis police patrolmen took up a position at the back door of the home. Detective Sergeants Bill Raney and Anthony Clark and two Memphis Bureau of Investigation agents stood at the ready at the front door. Detective Raney had a tight grip on the shotgun in his left hand as he gently turned the latch on the screen with his right. To his surprise, the screen door wasn't locked. Slowly and quietly, he swung the screen open, then carefully tried the knob on the front door. It wasn't locked either.[24]

Detective Raney stepped into the home, both hands now on his weapon, ready to aim and fire when the time came. Detective Clark and two other armed officers were prepared to shoot if needed as well. They moved through the living room without making a sound, passing to a half-open bedroom door on the right of a long hallway. Al Tichenor and his brother-in-law, Seymour Travis, were lying in twin beds in a deep sleep. Movement from one of the bedrooms at the end of the hall prompted Detective Raney to stop in his tracks, and he motioned for the men behind him to do the same. Raney raised his shotgun and waited. A man clad only in his underwear staggered sleepily into the hall. It was Kelly, and he had his pistol in his hand, dangling at his side.*[25]

"Drop that gun, Kelly," Detective Raney forcefully demanded. The outlaw did as he was told, then jerked his hands skyward.

"Okay, boys," Kelly said, grinning. "I've been waiting for you all night."[26]

Detective Raney snapped handcuffs on the desperado and Detective Clark kept his gun trained on him during the process. While Kelly was being marched to the living room, two other officers rousted Tichenor and Travis out of bed and led them to the same area, along with Kelly.[27]

Detective Sergeant Wiebenga and SAC Rohrer entered the home through the back door and charged into the bedroom where Kathryn was sleeping. The rude awakening made her cranky, and she let the police know how she felt about the intrusion. Bureau agents gave the Kellys, Tichenor, and Travis fifteen minutes to get dressed before the group was to be transported to jail. After the outlaws had made themselves presentable and just before they were restrained, Kathryn burst into tears and threw her arms around Kelly. "Honey,

---

* Detectives at the scene would later note in their written reports that Kelly was not armed when they approached him. That particular detail was erroneously added to make the arrest that much more compelling.

I guess it's all up for us," she cried. "The G-men won't ever give us a break. I've been living in dread of this."*

Rohrer pulled the pair apart and motioned for the other officers to handcuff them and escort them outside.[28]

Kelly was placed in a vehicle with Detectives Raney and Clark. Kathryn, Tichenor, and Travis rode in a car with Detective Wiebenga, agent R. E. Peterson, and patrolman A. B. Randle.[29]

News that the kidnapping couple had been caught and were being brought to the Memphis police station created a stir at the department. Law enforcement officers from all over the city poured into the booking center to watch the pair arrive, get fingerprinted, and photographed. No one said a word while Desk Sergeant Lee Quianthy questioned Kelly to process him into the system.

"What's your name?" Sergeant Quianthy began.

"George R. Kelly," the gangster replied.

"What's your age and where do you live?" was the next query.

"I'm thirty-seven-years of age and I live everywhere," Kelly stated.[30]

Once the preliminaries were completed, officers flanked the outlaw on both sides as he was hustled into the jail quarters. "Hey, Chief," Kelly called out to Detective Raney, who was carefully eyeing his every move. "Looks like there might be a war going on around here," Kelly joked. "Tell the world I'll be out of this jail before long," he said lightheartedly as the guards locked him in a small cell alone. Kelly laughed as the officers filtered out of the area and back into the booking center to watch Kathryn be questioned.[31]

Wearing a black satin dress with a chic black hat, the striking figure was all smiles while being led to the desk sergeant. 'I am Mrs. George Kelly," Kathryn told Sergeant Quianthy. "I am nearly twenty-nine and I live most every place." The police and agents clamored behind Kathryn as she was escorted to the lockup and waited for her to make a remark as her cell door was being locked. "I was going back tomorrow to give myself up," she announced to

---

* G-men is short for government men.

no one in particular. "Kelly told me he would kill me if I did, but I was going anyway."[32]

The capture of Machine Gun Kelly and his wife was plastered across the front page of special edition newspapers throughout Tennessee. Most accounts reported that the pair was taken by surprise but peacefully. Some articles claimed that Kelly was so frightened when Bureau agents burst into the home where he and Kathryn were sleeping that he dropped to his knees in the cover of the bedroom and pleaded, "Don't shoot me, G-man! I'll give up." When Kelly learned what was being reported he was annoyed. "Say, Chief," he said to Police Chief Will D. Lee and the other authorities as he was being taken from his cell for additional questioning, "where do you boys get the idea that I was afraid or had a gun on me? I sat up all night expecting you cops. Then I decided to take a nap. I just got up to see what the noise was when that chap [Detective Raney] shoved a gun in my stomach. The .45 I was supposed to have was in the bathroom."[33]

Kelly chain-smoked his way through the initial interrogation, ultimately refusing to offer any statement about the kidnapping or the more than fifty days he and his wife spent on the run from the law.[34]

Kathryn was just as tight-lipped. By late afternoon on September 26, 1933, she was exasperated with authorities allowing her arrest, and the arrest of her husband, to become a media circus. Hundreds of curious spectators had gathered at the police station. Along with members of the press, they had come hoping to get a glimpse of the notorious couple. Newspaper photographers tried to snap a picture of Kathryn on her way to the interrogation room, but she put up her hand and hid her face. She didn't want her photograph printed in the newspaper because she didn't want her daughter to suffer any embarrassment from it. She disregarded arguments from reporters pointing out that her teenage daughter had probably suffered her share of embarrassment with the frequent appearance of her grandparents' pictures in the papers as well as the articles about her mother's involvement with Charles Urschel's kidnapping.[35]

Kathryn's answers to the investigators' additional queries about her background and alleged crimes were brief at first.

"How long have you been married to Kelly?" she was asked.

"Three years," was the response.

"Where were you married?"

"In Minneapolis," she offered.

"Where is your home?" agents probed.

"Fort Worth, Texas," she replied.

"And where do your parents live?" the authorities questioned.

"My mother and father live in the country on a farm near Fort Worth," she said. "My own father lives in Fort Worth."

"Is R. G. Shannon related to you?" the agent continued.

"Yes, Mr. Shannon is my stepfather and Mrs. Shannon is my mother," Kathryn admitted.[36]

"What do you know about Kelly as a gangster and what do you know of the Urschel kidnapping?"[37]

"I know nothing about it except what I am going to tell my lawyer."

"Do you deny having a part in the kidnapping or knowing about it?

"I'll answer that question after I've talked to my lawyer."[38]

Kathryn refused to answer any further questions and was returned to her cell. Although smoking wasn't permitted in lockup, she managed to sweet-talk the police chief into making her an exception. And when the jailhouse meals proved distasteful, the chief gave his staff instructions to let Kathryn order food from a nearby eatery.[39]

"That Kelly woman isn't talking," Memphis Bureau Investigator John Keith noted about Kathryn after her questioning. "She's stubborn and she's clever."[40]

Langford Ramsey learned of the Kellys' arrest when he returned to Memphis in the early hours of September 27, 1933. He read about the raid on Tichenor's home and that police were looking for him in connection with the capture of the outlaw and his wife in the newspaper the *Commercial Appeal*. Ramsey turned himself in to the Shelby County jail at five-thirty in the morning on the 27th. He was held at the facility until Department of Justice agents arrived at the station to question him. Ramsey made a full confession, detailing his part in the quest for the ransom money and confessing to knowing Kelly's identity for more than a month and of knowing Kathryn's identity as well.[41]

At the same time Langford Ramsey was traveling to Memphis from Coleman, Texas, Bureau of Investigation agents Gus Jones and Ralph Colvin were traveling to Coleman from Oklahoma City. Geralene Arnold had told authorities where the Kellys had buried the ransom and about the farmer who helped them, and the agents were directed to retrieve the money and apprehend the accomplices. They wired the county police while en route and ordered that Coleman be placed under arrest but not taken from the farm. The men arrived at Cass Coleman's place early on the morning of September 27, 1933. The homestead was buzzing with activity. Coleman's daughter, who was expecting a child, had gone into labor, and the local doctor and several relatives were on hand for the event.[42]

The investigators were focused on the ransom and informed Coleman that he needed to make that a priority regardless of what was happening with his family. Carrying a crowbar he would use in lieu of a shovel, the farmer led the agents to a mesquite tree standing in the cotton field. After counting out a handful of steps from the tree, he gestured at the ground and told the men the money was buried at the spot to which he was pointing. The agents ordered him to start digging and Coleman did as he was told. A molasses can was eventually unearthed, and the container was filled with bundles of twenty-dollar bills. Coleman led the agents to an additional spot in the field where more money was buried. Once he dug up the ransom and all of it was counted, the total was $73,250.[43]

Shortly after the funds were reclaimed and bundled, Colvin and Jones left with the cargo tucked safely inside their vehicle and proceeded back to Oklahoma City. Cass Coleman was escorted to jail.[44]

Bureau agents assigned to the Kelly investigation kept in constant contact with Director Hoover. Hoover was pleased to learn his men had not only apprehended the gangster and his wife but had recovered the money as well. Hoover told reporters hoping to get a statement from him that his agents were never far behind the Kellys as the manhunt for the outlaws spanned the Midwest. The Bureau director noted that the desperados narrowly missed being captured in Chicago shortly after mailing threatening letters to Charles Urschel and the federal prosecutor handling the Oklahoma City trial of the Shannons, Albert Bates, and Harvey Bailey. Hoover boasted about his determined and dedicated department and of the far-reaching implications that placing the wanted criminals in custody would have on the apprehension of other high-profile hoodlums.[45]

"Kelly's capture means something to the underworld that the average person doesn't understand," Hoover explained to reporters. "The criminal fears death more than anything else. At heart they are all rats, dirty, yellow rats. A gangster will kill you, oh sure, if he has a machine gun and you are absolutely helpless. They like to think they are above the law. But they actually operate most of the time with one eye on the electric chair. You see, the underworld doesn't like to feel that our men or the police can reach in at a moment's notice and pluck its kings out of bed—and that is just what we've been doing. Doesn't it seem strange to you that most of these bold, bad killers are taken when they are enjoying a little nap?"[46]

At five-thirty in the evening on September 27, 1933, Memphis police officers and Department of Justice agents swarmed around George and Kathryn Kelly as they were quickly led from the city jail and ushered across the street to the Shelby County courthouse. Kelly was hustled to a cell on the ground floor and Kathryn was taken to the women's quarters on the third floor. Curious onlookers were barred from the grounds surrounding the building and officers armed with machine guns patrolled the corridors inside. Reporters and photographers who were approved to be present at the Kellys' arraignment jockeyed for a position to see the pair first as they were escorted into the courtroom.[47]

Kelly exchanged joking comments with officers he knew from his younger days. "Watch those popguns," he warned. "It would be a shame if one of them went off and killed someone." Kelly nodded at the press as he passed by on his way to see US Commissioner

Lester Brenner. Brenner had been hired to help with the sitting judge's overwhelming caseload. Kathryn's demeanor was different from her husband's. She tilted her hat low over her eyes and held a handkerchief over the bottom part of her face as she followed in step behind him.[48]

The courtroom was packed. The walls were lined with deputies holding rifles. Bureau of Investigation agents milled about, their guns holstered but at the ready. Reporters busily scribbled on pads and talked among themselves. The Kellys stood before Commissioner Brenner's desk and his gavel quieted the murmuring crowd. US Deputy Marshal Elman Jester glanced over the warrants in his hand, then began reading them aloud. Kelly complained that he couldn't hear the deputy marshal and Commissioner Brenner took over the reading. His voice was clear and distinctive. The warrant charged Kelly and his wife jointly with kidnapping Charles Urschel, transporting him to Paradise, Texas, and holding him for ransom in violation of the Federal Kidnapping Law.[49]

Not only did Kelly plead not guilty after the reading but he told the court he wouldn't sign the warrant. "You don't have to sign it. That's the charge against you," Department of Justice Investigating Agent John M. Keith told Kelly. Smiling proudly, Kathryn also pleaded not guilty. A one-hundred-thousand-dollar bond was set for each of the accused. Kathryn and Kelly exchanged a look, and she leaned in to talk with him, but the guards intervened and hurried her out of the courtroom. She kept her eyes on her husband the entire time she was being led away. As Kelly was being escorted out, shortly after his wife, he commented to the press, "They got me, but keeping me is another matter."[50]

Kelly's parting threat prompted Agent Keith to order all officers connected with the case to keep quiet about the inevitable extradition of the gangsters to Oklahoma. "Not long back," Keith noted, "we had a massacre of officers in Kansas City in broad daylight. That was the result of too much talking. We don't intend to let anything like that happen in Memphis."[51]

Right after the Kellys were charged, the government discussed rushing the pair to Oklahoma by plane, but Oklahoma authorities requested the removal of the couple be postponed until the other trials involving the Urschel kidnapping were concluded. Kathryn was furious when she learned officials were going to wait to move her and Kelly. The state was seeking the death penalty in her parents' case, and she was overwrought. She wanted to be in Oklahoma to testify on their behalf and, possibly, save them. The situation loosened her tongue a bit about her husband. She told Agent Keith that Kelly was intimidating and that she knew she could not defy him. According to Kathryn, she bought machine guns for him on his orders, automobiles, tires, clothes, ran his errands, sent his telegrams, made his telephone calls, and anything else he needed done.

"She's afraid of him," Keith told reporters. "Kelly hit her in the face with a pistol once. She still has a scar on her forehead and another one on her arm from the blows."[52]

US District Attorney Herbert Hyde, who was to help prosecute the case against the Kellys, didn't believe Kathryn was a victim. "Her whole life has been one of deception," he told the lawyers in his office. "Soon she'll tell that her husband forced her into the kidnapping. It's a convenient defense. One I hope the jury sees right through."[53]

CHAPTER 9

LEAVING MEMPHIS

A S DARKNESS SURRENDERED TO DAWN on October 1, 1933, a caravan of police cars and paddy wagons assembled in front of the Shelby County jail in Memphis, Tennessee. Officers and federal agents carrying pistols, sawed-off shotguns, and submachine guns emerged from the vehicles and raced inside, leaving behind an army of deputies and investigators to guard the area.[1]

Photographers and newspaper reporters overwhelmed the lobby of the facility, their writing tablets and cameras at the ready. Special Agents in Charge John Keith and William Rohrer, Detective Bill Raney, and the other law enforcement agents who took part in the arrest of the Kellys serpentined their way through the throng of men and women with the press, toward the jail cells. A few daring reporters followed after the men as far as they were allowed, then peered through the window of the steel door that had been shut in their faces, which led to the lockup. After a few moments, one of the reporters shouted, "Here they come!" The crowd galvanized into tense expectation.[2]

A quartet of police officers led a handcuffed Kathryn Kelly down the corridor into the reception area. She was wearing a black formfitting dress adorned with monkey fur and a matching hat. She smiled as the authorities whisked her past the onlookers outside to an awaiting car. Photographers took pictures of the attractive felon interacting with the officers and showing off her legs as she took her place in the back seat of a Plymouth sedan.[3]

Spectators across the street from the jail called out Kathryn's name and tried to push past a line of uniformed officers who had created a barrier between themselves and the inmates scheduled to be flown from Tennessee to Oklahoma that morning.[4]

Moments after Kathryn was removed from the jail, Kelly was led out of the building. Agent Keith kept his machine gun trained on the handcuffed and shackled convict as he shuffled through the main doors of the station house. Once outside, Kelly was instantly surrounded with heavily armed Department of Justice agents. Newsreel photographers filmed the bootlegger-turned-kidnapper's slow walk down the flight of stairs leading to his transportation to the airport. Newspaper photographers snapped numerous shots of Kelly being loaded into a Packard wagon. Agent Keith waited outside the vehicle until everything was set, then gave the signal for the convoy to be on its way. Motorcycles manned by half a dozen members of the Memphis Police Department roared, taking positions in the front and back of the vehicles carrying Kathryn and Kelly.

"We have no fear of gangsters or of any pals of Kelly's making an effort to free him," Keith told journalists prior to Kelly's trip. "However, we aren't taking any chances."[5]

Memphis law enforcement managed the traffic along the route the Bureau of Investigation used to haul the Kellys to the municipal airport. The automobiles all traveled at a safe steady speed, ignoring red traffic lights at the direction of the motorcycle officers. Once they reached their destination, the drivers of the cars steered the vehicles onto the landing field right to the plane. In anticipation of the cargo, the engines on the Curtiss Wright Condor were running and ready to taxi. Reporters, photographers, and newsreel producers present at that location all maneuvered for a prime position to record the transfer of the outlaw couple from one mode of transportation to another.[6]

Kelly was the first to be brought on board the plane. He stopped and turned toward the press when he reached the top of the steps leading to the cabin door. He grinned and nodded to the cameras pointed at him. Department of Justice agents ended the show after a bit, gruffly urging him to move along.[7]

Once Kelly was done posing for the reporters, Kathryn was escorted up the stairs. With the exception of the handcuffs, there was nothing about her presence that would lead anyone to think she was a prisoner on her way to trial. She climbed onto the plane without hesitating and took the seat she was appointed without saying a word. By 8:32 a.m., the Kellys were in the air, along with their heavily armed escort.[8]

The same media frenzy generated by the Kellys' departure from Memphis was replicated in Oklahoma City with their arrival. Both Kathryn and Machine Gun Kelly were all smiles when they alighted from the plane. They responded to the publicity as though they were Hollywood celebrities instead of felons. "Hello, boys," Kathryn announced, looking out over the sea of reporters and photographers before being ushered into a police vehicle. Kelly greeted the crowd with a simple, "Hello, gang," as he was hurried down the steep stairway and was hustled into a car by armed guards. The pair was rushed to the Oklahoma County jail, and several journalists followed after them in their automobiles, fearful something might happen to the couple en route that they might miss.[9]

One taxpayer present at the Oklahoma City airport when the criminals landed was so moved by the spectacle, he authored a poem about it that appeared in all the local newspapers the following day.

> Kelly hovers o'er the airport and Kitty hovers at his side
> As the men of Uncle Samuel take the couple for a ride.
> The fans begin to murmur as Kelly plays the pilot's role,
> Call him Ace because he's flyin? No, because he's in the hole.
> Hello, boys, says Kitty Kelly. Look me over, I'm feeling fine.
> I'll be at the County's jail. Come up to see me—anytime.
> The multitude starts hissing as downtown the actors go,
> They see far better gangsters in a motion picture show.
> So, the Shannons and the Kellys, Bates and others of the troupe,
> Now they're holding a reunion in a dilapidated coop.[10]

The trial against Boss and Ora Shannon, Albert Bates, Harvey Bailey, and six others involved with the Urschel kidnapping, individuals who either aided in the abduction or laundered some of the ransom money, was concluded by the time the Kellys reached the jail in Oklahoma City. The trial spanned eleven days, and all the participants were found guilty after the jury spent less than three hours deliberating. Their sentencing was scheduled for October 7, 1933.[11]

US District Attorney Herbert Hyde was pleased with the outcome and claimed a victory for the government in its war against racketeering with the new Federal Kidnapping Act as the chief weapon. Also known as the Lindbergh Law, the act made kidnapping a federal offense and allowed federal investigators the authority to pursue kidnappers across state lines. The case was prosecuted as the first major test of the Act.[12]

According to the October 1, 1933, edition of the *Daily Journal Capital*, "Bailey was accused as the master mind of the plot, until the end of the trial. Bates was identified as the man who accompanied George (Machine Gun) Kelly into the Urschel mansion here July 22 and kidnapped the oilman.

"The Shannons', testimony showed they guarded Urschel on their ranch near Paradise, Texas, while the nation's largest ransom ever was demanded and paid in Kansas City."[13]

Kelly was delivered to the fourth floor of the heavily guarded jail and placed in a cell next to Albert Bates and Harvey Bailey. Unbeknownst to the hulking ex-bootlegger, Charles Urschel's wife, Berenice, was present when his plane landed at the Oklahoma airport and he was escorted off by the police. She positively identified Kelly as one of the kidnappers. DA Herbert Hyde added that bit of information to the list of items to be shared with the accused when the justice of the peace visited him in lockup shortly after he was processed. In addition to letting Kelly know he'd been identified by one of the victims, he was also informed that he and Bates were being charged by the state with robbery for stealing money from Charles Urschel and Walter Jarrett. Both men pled not guilty to the charge and their preliminary hearing was set for October 5, 1933.[14]

Kelly couldn't resist hurling another threat at Urschel after the justice of the peace had delivered Hyde's message. "He hasn't got long to live," Elman Jester, one of the US deputy marshals standing guard over the outlaw reported he heard him say. "That's right," Kelly continued. "I wouldn't sell Urschel any insurance."[15]

Bureau of Investigation Director Hoover gave jailers and his agents specific instructions that Kelly and his wife were not allowed to see anyone except their lawyers. Herbert Hyde agreed with Hoover's directive. Of the two, Hyde believed Kathryn was the most dangerous. He thought she was smart, cunning, manipulative, and capable of masterminding a series of brutal crimes. "She is a vicious woman," he told the press, "and should be placed securely in prison where she can do no harm." Regardless of the directive, the federal agents allowed her to visit her mother, who was at the same jail as Kathryn, awaiting sentencing.[16]

Ora Shannon's lawyers, John Roberts and Sam Sayers, were present when she and her daughter met. Both women wept when they saw each other and commiserated over their desperate situation. Kathryn apologized to her mother and promised she was going to make it right. Her first attempt at doing so came when she heard from the authorities that Albert Bates refused to tell them where part of the ransom money he took was located. Kathryn wanted to make a deal with the government, and told officers at the jail that she could get Bates to tell her what they wanted to know if mercy was shown to her parents. According to her, Bates had ninety thousand of the two-hundred-thousand-dollar ransom. Less than 10 percent of that amount had been recovered. Bates was brought to her cell, but once he realized why he was summoned, he wouldn't talk. Kathryn pleaded with him, but to no avail.[17]

Unwilling to give up on trying to find a way to help her parents avoid a long prison sentence, Kathryn again appealed to the officers at the jail to please get a message to the prosecution team. "Tell them I'll plead guilty and even go to the electric chair if the Shannons would be given suspended sentences," she announced. The government had no interest in making a trade with the accused and suggested she focus on her and her husband's pending trial.

Unless the pair pled guilty to the kidnapping charges, the hearing was scheduled to begin on October 9, 1933.[18]

Newspapers from New York City to San Francisco and all points in between reported daily on the Urschel kidnapping case and the husband-and-wife team behind the crime. Readers were fascinated with the particulars and newspaper articles about the pair's married life and profiles on Kathryn Kelly proved to be popular editions of the publications. The attractive gangster's wife's involvement with the abduction of the respected Oklahoma oil tycoon had cemented her place in the public's consciousness and they demanded to know more.[19]

Female reporters such as Frances Corry with the *Oklahoma News* were eager to supply detailed stories about the "kidnap trial fugitive." She was the first to provide an in-depth look at Kathryn Kelly's life in print. According to Corry, "Had she loved less the bright lights of the city, the sheen of the diamonds, the soft luxury of beautiful clothes, and the purr of expensive autos, she herself might not be a fugitive from justice and her mother and stepfather perhaps would still be living their quiet lives at home on the farm." The article revealed that Kathryn's background was sordid, and she was no stranger to encounters with the law. "She can't be painted as a lily, but rather as some gilded flower that grows rank and boldly beautiful, then withers into ugliness," Corry wrote.[20]

Some members of the public were moved by the desperate attempts Kathryn made to intervene on behalf of her Paradise family. She repeatedly proclaimed their innocence along with her own, and begged the court to set aside the verdict and allow that she alone be made to pay the price for having married Kelly. The majority of law-abiding citizens found her statements disingenuous. Few believed her life was ever in danger or that Kelly (whom she claimed "worships me. . . . I'm his whole life") at any time threatened to harm her.

"Before she conspired to hold Charles Urschel captive for ransom on her father's farm in Texas, would have been a better time for Kathryn Kelly to 'offer her life for her parents' who now face life sentences for their part in the kidnapping," one individual noted in the October 3, 1933, edition of the *Tulsa Tribune*. "If this is a fore-runner of the sob-stuff the Kelly woman is going to try to pull on a jury, the real thing will probably be nauseating."[21]

Despite the low opinion some had of her, Kathryn's attorney, John Roberts, recognized his client did possess a generous degree of charm and planned to capitalize on that in court. Leading up to the trial he hoped to be able to change the public's view of her and see her more as a sympathetic character rather than a vicious tigress. He spoke out to the press criticizing the strong-arm tactics used by the government to try to get Kathryn to plead guilty to save them the expense of going to trial. "If she lays out her case before a jury she will at least escape with a light sentence," Roberts declared.[22]

Federal authorities disagreed with the lawyer's belief that Kathryn would escape serious punishment. New developments in the case against the Kellys unfolded daily and were subsequently leaked to the press. On October 3, 1933, the headline across an article in the *Bartlesville Daily Enterprise* announced that Kathryn was the one who wrote the threatening letter sent to Charles Urschel after her parents were arrested. Handwriting experts examined the letter, comparing it with correspondence penned by Kathryn and determined the writing was the same. Officials went as far as to claim she admitted to writing the letter. Roberts denied Kathryn did so and chastised investigators for making the accusation.[23]

A visit from Kathryn's father did little to improve the public's perception of her. Indeed, it made it worse. James Brooks told reporters after leaving the jail that he was ready to assist his daughter in her fight against the kidnapping charge. He was adamant that any part she had in the plot was involuntary. "Kelly was responsible for everything that happened," he insisted.[24]

A columnist with the *Shawnee Morning News* didn't see it that way. "Kathryn Kelly is about to desert Mr. Machine Gun," he wrote. "George's friends reminiscent of those marriage vows . . . love, honor, obey, protect, defend . . . are whispering 'she lied, Kelly, she lied.'"[25]

George Kelly's attorney, James Mathers, wasn't interested in improving his client's image. Planning his defense was going to be challenging, and the comments Kathryn made to investigative reporters about her husband being the sole reason they were in trouble just made it more difficult. Mathers, a respected Coal County, Oklahoma, lawyer, had advised Kelly of his rights and outlined the case he anticipated the government would build against him and his wife. Kelly elected to force the government to prove its case. "I'm going to fight them all the way," he told his attorney. Federal and state officials were discussing seeking the death penalty for Kelly and Albert Bates, but Kelly didn't believe the threat was serious. Kelly told his lawyer it was a bluff to get him to talk. Mathers assured him they weren't bluffing and that they meant business.[26]

While Mathers was working on Kelly's case, Kelly read the various articles about himself in the newspapers the attorney made sure he received. Reporters had uncovered that his nickname in high school had been "Jellybean" and noted he was a favorite with the girls. They wrote about the trouble he had with his first wife, his time in prison, and how his second wife plotted the kidnapping of Urschel that he boldly executed with Bates. He didn't mind being recognized as being popular with the opposite sex but took offense to the idea that he wasn't smart enough to plan his own crimes. He read interviews Kathryn gave where she stated she was done with him and could prove he forced her to go along with him on the felonies he committed. Kelly knew she was trying to save her own skin and found reason to believe she loved him in comments she made, such as "I'd still do almost anything I could for him."[27]

After reviewing the evidence, the government had against Kelly, James Mathers was hard-pressed to think of a defense for his client and told him so. If and when they went to court, the lawyer believed the best strategy was to say nothing. Mathers preferred to avoid any perjured testimony. He would let the matter play out in court and determine how to proceed then. Attorney John Roberts, on the other hand, was convinced Kelly would change his plea to guilty and take the stand to support Kathryn's claim that she was innocent.[28]

In anticipation of Kelly's guilty plea, Roberts planned to seek a delay in his client's case. Kathryn's father, James Brooks, agreed to pay Roberts's fee, and Kathryn promised to pay the remainder of the balance with the reward money she believed she would receive from Kelly. She vowed to file a lawsuit to prevent anyone from getting the funds for his capture. Kathryn told Roberts she had every intention of surrendering herself and her husband to the police before they surrounded the Memphis home where they were staying. It was on that basis she felt she was entitled to the reward.[29]

Kathryn sent a message to Roberts through Mathers for Kelly. She begged him to help her make things right and testify before her parents' sentencing that he was the original and chief plotter of the crime. The sentencing of the Shannons, Bates, Bailey, and the others was scheduled to take place on Saturday, October 7.[30]

On Friday, October 6, John Roberts was elated to learn from James Mathers that Kelly had indeed agreed to plead guilty. Mathers had spent a great deal of time with the fugitive at the county jail discussing his options. He had provided an incentive for Kelly to plead guilty by letting him know that a deal could then potentially be worked out with Judge Edgar Vaught on the armed robbery charge. Vaught had been appointed to the federal bench in 1928 by President Calvin Coolidge and before presiding over the Urschel kidnapping case dealt primarily with civil cases. Kelly's armed robbery charge, which carried a possible death penalty, would be dismissed with a guilty plea. If Judge Vaught agreed, Kelly would be sentenced along with the Shannons, Bates, and Bailey.[31]

If Kathryn changed her plea to guilty, Roberts promised to try to arrange for her to be in the same facility with her mother. If she couldn't get her mother free, Kathryn at least wanted to be with Ora to help take care of her. Roberts wasn't entirely convinced pleading guilty was best for his client. He and his cocounsel members, Prince Freeling and Edward Box, believed if they went to trial there was a possibility they could get the court to declare the federal kidnapping statute unconstitutional. If that happened, Kathryn's sentence would be less severe. None of that would be possible with a guilty plea. Roberts strongly advised Kathryn against pleading guilty.[32]

When news that Judge Vaught denied a motion for a new trial

for Boss and Ora Shannon, Albert Bates, and the others convicted for their involvement in the Urschel kidnapping, Kelly decided to change his plea. But he kept the news to himself.[33]

The Kellys were all smiles when they entered the crowded Oklahoma County courthouse to hear the federal government's charge against them in the Urschel kidnapping. Kathryn was adorned in a new black dress, smoking a cigarette and chatting happily with the guards as they escorted her to the bullpen area in front of Judge Vaught's bench. She exchanged hopeful looks with her parents and stepbrother, who were there awaiting sentencing. Kelly filed in after his wife and nodded to the press seated in the galley. Their attorneys took their places beside their clients and in low voices explained the court formalities to them.[34]

All conversation stopped when Judge Vaught exited his chambers and proceeded to his chair. As soon as the court was called to order and the judge made his opening remarks, Mathers and Roberts argued for a change of venue. Their petitions were denied. The accused were then asked to enter their pleas. After a long pause, Kathryn announced to Judge Vaught, "I plead not guilty." Kelly followed suit and mumbled, "Not guilty." Spectators, courtroom officials, and attorneys were stunned. The Kellys had solidified their deal with the court in exchange for a guilty plea thirty minutes prior to their reversal. The Kellys' response prompted loud chatter in the courtroom. The judge instructed Roberts and Mathers to consult with their clients again. The lawyers huddled together with Kathryn and Kelly. The outlaws refused to change their plea again.[35]

Mathers quietly explained to Roberts the need now for the two to get together to try to "harmonize defense plans" for the pair. Roberts reiterated to Mathers that his client maintained she did not know Urschel was to be kidnapped and that her husband coerced her into joining the conspiracy after it was underway. Roberts made it clear to Mathers that he would base Kathryn's defense around that story.[36]

Once Judge Vaught regained control of the courtroom audience members, who were conversing with one another about the Kellys' statements, he turned his attention to the sentencing of the Shannons, Bates, and Bailey.

"The court is of the opinion this verdict of guilty is fully sustained by the evidence," he began.[37]

"While it is not a pleasant duty for a court, even in the face of a verdict of guilty, to impose a sentence that deprives a person of his liberty, there are times when duty requires a court to exercise the full responsibility of his office.[38]

"There is something more at stake in this trial than the mere punishment for the crime committed. The question before the American people today is whether crime will be recognized as an occupation or profession, or whether the public will enforce the laws of this nation as they are written. So far as this court is concerned, it is his purpose to enforce these laws as they are written!"[39]

With this ultimatum, the veteran jurist who "'put the teeth into the Lindbergh kidnap law'" began pronouncing sentence on the convicted. "Albert Bates, it is therefore the judgment of this court that you be sentenced to the federal penitentiary for the remainder of your natural life."[40]

Bates, who had been standing during the sentencing, sat down glumly. Bailey received the same life sentence. He didn't blink an eye when the judge made the announcement. Boss and Ora Shannon also received life sentences. Both were stunned. Ora struggled to keep from crying, and Shannon draped his arm around her shoulders to comfort her. Armon Shannon gave the judge a look of startled surprise and began muttering to himself like a schoolboy receiving a lecture when Judge Vaught sentenced him to ten years in federal prison and then suspended the sentence and paroled him for ten years.[41]

Kathryn glared at the judge as he addressed the court and simultaneously fought back tears as she considered the stiff penalty he handed down to her parents. Her anger, pain, and sadness were intertwined, and she stifled a scream from deep within. Newsreel photographers captured the torment from behind their continually running cameras. Before the convicted had a chance to fully grasp the severity of the sentence, guards hurried them out of the setting into vehicles that would transport them to holding cells.[42]

Prior to the Kellys being forced to move along, Judge Vaught scheduled their trial to begin on October 9, 1933. Kathryn blinked away a tear as an officer gently took her by her arm and walked her to the exit past the scrutinizing taxpayers present. Kelly was gruffly escorted to the door by armed authorities who shackled his legs and attached a lead chain to the shackles around Bailey's and Bates's legs. While the guards fumbled with handcuffing the felons, Kelly caught Charles Urschel's eye. The kidnap victim was among the spectators sitting in the front row who came to witness the proceedings.

"You'll get yours yet, you sap," Kelly told him. Kelly then drew his index finger across his own neck in a throat-cutting gesture. Urschel didn't react. Kelly was hustled away with the others.[43]

Kelly's actions had not gone unnoticed by officials and there were consequences for his defiant behavior. Jailers placed the outlaw on a strict bread-and-water diet and the convict wasn't pleased with the discipline. So frustrated by the treatment was he that after a few scant meals, he stomped on the tray of food served to him and threw the meager rations on the wall of his cell.[44]

Kelly was in trouble not only for dumping his food and stomping on the tray but the guards found a note in his cell from Kathryn that she had managed to pass to him while they were in court together. Both were deprived of jail privileges including electric lights and newspapers.[45]

The public's obsession with Kathryn and how she was holding up while awaiting her day in court prompted media outlets such as the International News Service to provide readers with more stories about her. They sent reporters to interview anyone who had any connection with the woman outlaw, including her father. "She was always an easy girl to handle," James Brooks boasted of his daughter. "She was kind and affectionate . . . and up to this never caused any trouble. Kelly was her downfall. You know a man can usually pull a woman one way or the other. The woman usually does what the husband says." When asked if Kathryn was depressed about her circumstances, Brooks assured the press that she was "in good spirits" and confident that a jury could not find her guilty after they heard the full story.[46]

Distant members of Kathryn's family described her as cold, calculating, and frequently "up to no good." They shared a tale about her attempt to avoid being apprehended after she assisted in a robbery. To keep from being caught with the stolen items in her possession she flushed "ten thousand dollars' worth of diamonds through the toilet of a hotel room."[47]

In the few interviews Kathryn gave to hungry journalists, she always painted Kelly as a ruthless criminal and herself as a woman craving the quiet life. She described her early days as Mrs. Kelly as lonely, fearful, and frustrated. "I wouldn't go through it again, not for any man," she told Pulitzer Prize–winning reporter Lee Hills. "The longest and most lonesome hours of my life were spent in apartments in Chicago waiting for Kelly to come home. I'd sit at home and read and then go for a walk in the park. Sometimes he'd be gone for two or three days, sometimes for a week or two. When he'd come back I'd beg him to settle down. I wanted to buy a farm, just any place of our own near town. He'd say, 'Well, Precious,' he always called me Precious, 'We'll do that.' But he never got around to it.[48]

"He never would own up to doing anything except gambling. He always told me that's how he got his money. When I'd accuse him of something just to try and find out what he'd be doing, he would say, 'Now, baby, let's not talk about that. You take care of your affairs and I'll take care of mine, and we'll get along swell.'"[49]

James Mathers grew increasingly concerned for his client after reading the articles written about Kathryn. Not only was he representing Kelly in the kidnapping charges but defending him in the armed robbery case as well. "Kathryn wants George to take all the blame for the kidnapping, clearing her, but if he takes the stand and does that, he would have no defense to the state charges," he told

John Roberts in one of their meetings. "Kelly continues to toy with the idea of taking the stand for her, but it would surely lead to the electric chair. I'm advising him to not do it."[50]

The Kellys' attorneys planned to spend an entire day questioning potential jurors with one of the questions centering around what they already knew or had read about the case and the accused couple and if they'd already formed any opinions. Another question the defense was set to ask was "Would the result of the other trial [involving the Shannons, Bates, or Bailey] tend to influence your verdict in any way?" The prosecution posed the following queries: "Would the fact that one of the defendants is a woman make any difference to you in returning a verdict of guilty if the evidence proved her guilt? And, if it should develop that the woman is the mother of a child, would it make any difference to you in returning a verdict in accordance with the law and the evidence?"[51]

District Attorney Herbert Hyde guaranteed the public that he would speed the case along and be just as tough on Kathryn if she testified as he would Kelly if he took the stand. "The woman's plea that she was forced to aid in the conspiracy through fear of her husband would be fought at every turn with the contention she was a willing conspirator," Hyde told Oklahoma newspaper reporters. "If Kathryn were a man instead of a woman she probably would have figured in the crime more than Kelly."[52]

Hyde estimated that he'd only need twelve witnesses to try the case and among those to be summoned were Luther Arnold, his wife, and daughter Geralene, Kathryn's grandmother, mother, and teenage daughter.[53]

Kelly never imagined a positive outcome for himself from the trial, but Kathryn vacillated between believing she'd be set free and receiving a harsh sentence. "Wouldn't it surprise you if I was acquitted?" Kathryn asked a journalist with the *Miami Daily News*. "It would me. I think I'd drop dead from surprise. If I am convicted all I hope is they put me in the same prison with [my] mother. If they do, I'll be a good prisoner."[54]

Twelve businessmen and farmers who swore they'd not formed an opinion about the Kellys were selected to serve on the jury. One of the veniremen asked to speak to Judge Vaught moments after he was picked as an alternate.

"I just got one eye, judge, and I don't have much education," he admitted.

"Lots of us in the courtroom here haven't had much education, but if you can hear all right, we'll keep you," Judge Vaught replied.[55]

The men chosen to determine the guilt or innocence of the Kellys were reminded of the accusations made against them. George Kelly was charged with "helping plan the crime, being co-abductor of Charles F. Urschel, violating the Lindbergh Law by taking Urschel to Texas, negotiating for a collection of a $200,000 ransom in Kansas City, and writing death-threat letters to Urschel since the kidnapping." Kathryn Kelly was charged with "buying the machine gun used in the kidnapping that was later found in Harvey Bailey's possession, being present when Kelly and Bates predicted there would be a kidnapping and of saying, 'Yes, we'll be in the big money soon,' driving speedily ahead of the kidnap party to remove young children from the Texas ranch hideaway, being at the hideout during most of Urschel's captivity, and remaining a fugitive after violating the Lindbergh Law."[56]

Bureau of Investigation agents kept Director Hoover abreast of what transpired in the courtroom. Hoover was particularly pleased the court mentioned the Kellys had been charged with violating the Lindbergh Law because it helped promote the role the Bureau had played in capturing the first criminals to break the law since it had been passed. A national campaign highlighting the accomplishments of the Bureau and their efforts to solve kidnapping cases since the enactment of the law under Hoover's direction appeared alongside many newspaper articles about the Kellys' trial. In addition to noting that Bureau agents had solved fifteen kidnapping cases reported to them, it urged families of kidnapping victims in future cases to cooperate by telephone to the Justice Department in Washington. The phone number, plastered across the advertisement, was National 7111.[57]

Hoover was confident the phone number would be recited by every man, woman, and child by the conclusion of the Kellys' hearing, and if the pair was convicted, his agency would be celebrated for making the law a success in less than a year. Hoover had no doubt the Kellys would be found guilty.[58]

CHAPTER 10

THE KELLYS ON TRIAL

A N ENORMOUS CROWD GATHERED at the Oklahoma County courthouse on October 9, 1933. It was the first day of the trial against George and Kathryn Kelly. The mass of curious spectators spilled out from beyond the front steps of the building into the street. The police pushed the group back to the sidewalks until the people lining the concrete path to the government building stretched more than a mile on either side. Some overexuberant individuals climbed streetlights to watch the parade of cars soon to be proceeding down the thoroughfare. More officers arrived on the scene and were given the job of holding back the surging mob threatening to move past the walkways onto the paved road. Twenty guards with riot guns, sawed-off shotguns, automatic rifles, and machine guns took posts in the street and around the federal building.[1]

Dozens of photographers skipped, squatted, and darted about like water bugs, taking pictures of the organized commotion. When vehicles carrying the attorneys for both sides, the witnesses, and the accused slowly made their approach, the crowd became even more excited. Many waved magazines and newspapers featuring the Kellys' images at the cars and paddy wagons as they passed.[2]

Among the first to arrive were Joseph Keenan, special assistant to the attorney general, and Herbert Hyde, US district attorney for the government, James Mathers and James Mathers Jr. for the defendant George Kelly, and John Roberts for the defendant Kathryn Kelly. Charles and Berenice Urschel and Walter and Clyde Jarrett arrived together for the hearing. E. E. Kirkpatrick, John Catlett, and Arthur Seeligson were some of the key witnesses for the prosecution, who were greeted by those waiting outside the courthouse. Bureau agents Ralph Colvin and James White were so focused on the business at hand they barely acknowledged the welcoming crowd as they hurried from the cars that brought them to the location.[3]

Kathryn's father, James Brooks, and her daughter, Pauline Fry, were among those called to speak on her behalf. They walked hand in hand and kept their heads down as they made their way into the building.[4]

The shrill screech of sirens heralded the approach of a cavalcade of eight armed cars. When the vehicles carrying George and Kathryn slowed to a stop and gun-toting guards alighted from the wagon with their weapons drawn, the spectators pressed in as close as the law would allow in order to get a good look at the outlaw couple. Both were fashionably attired and smiled pleasantly at the sea of faces studying their every move.[5]

Photographers circled the pair, taking as many pictures as they could before impatient police officers hustled the accused away. Even after the Kellys had disappeared into the courthouse, flashbulbs popped and popped and popped.[6]

The interior of the courthouse was another hub of activity. Government employees, from bailiffs to court reporters, crammed into the lobby area outside the courtroom. They were joined by community members fascinated with the case who had been able to get a coveted position inside the building. An obscene collection of representatives of the press from all over the country stood shoulder to shoulder with the others. Photojournalists competed for the best position to photograph the Kellys being escorted to the chambers.[7]

Kathryn glanced at the people parting like the Red Sea as she was led along and stopped when she caught a glimpse of her father. He offered a reassuring smile, and she stepped toward him to give him a kiss on the cheek. Agent James White stopped Kathryn from making contact with her father, then gave her a firm push in the direction of the courtroom. Kathryn stumbled, regained her footing, then turned and slapped the agent hard across the face. Kelly then took a swing at him. White caught Kelly's hands and struck the gangster with his fist, but Kelly wouldn't back down. Before he could throw another punch, White drew his gun and struck him in the head with the butt of the weapon. Guards rushed in to control the panicked swarm of people frightened by the unexpected brawl.[8]

The back of Kelly's head was bleeding and a knot the size of an egg rose on the left side of his forehead. Newsreel camera operators present in the courtroom trained their lens on Kelly and his injury as he and his wife were escorted to the defendants' seating area. They observed the guards speaking sternly to the couple but couldn't specifically hear what was being said. Reporters flanked the couple to find out what had transpired, and Kathryn was happy to share.

"The officer knocked me down," she said. "George told him not to hit me again and the officer started beating George with his pistol." She admitted that she slapped White and said she would like to "do it again."

Kelly backed his wife's story. He denied swinging at Agent White. "I simply told the officer not to hit Kathryn again and he hit me with his pistol three times."[9]

The violent encounter set the tone for the day's proceedings. "We're not running any pink tea party," Secret Service agent Harold Nathan announced to the agents overseeing the conduct in the courtroom. "Kelly learned there is going to be a lot more than that if he doesn't act right."[10]

The courtroom was still buzzing from the surprise exchange between the defendants and law enforcement when a bailiff instructed everyone in attendance to stand as Judge Vaught entered. The seasoned magistrate was forced to weave around guards and lighting equipment as he made his way to his seat. Six newsreel cameras with microphones and other sound effect devices lined the side and front of the judge's bench. Some cameras had even been mounted on high-hat racks behind the bench. Apart from the whir of the cameras, all was quiet as Judge Vaught took his place.[11]

Moments after the court was called to order and the accused, witnesses, lawyers, and spectators were seated, the judge addressed the jury. "There are some things that I might call your attention to this morning," he began. "Something that's more at stake than the mere punishment for the crime that's been committed in this case. The question before the American people today is whether or not crime will be recognized as an occupation or a profession. Or whether the people will enforce the laws of this nation as they are written. So far as this court is concerned, it's their purpose to enforce the laws as they are written."[12]

Judge Vaught's remarks were interrupted once by Kelly when he attempted to light a cigarette. When he was told there would be no smoking in the courtroom, the gangster shoved a stick of gum in his mouth. Throughout the proceedings, he alternated between holding an unlit butt in his teeth and vigorously chewing gum.*[13]

After explaining the rules for conduct in his courtroom, Judge Vaught invited the attorneys to give their opening statements. District Attorney Herbert Hyde was first to offer remarks. He delivered a scathing indictment of both George and Kathryn as "major conspirators" in the Charles Urschel ransom plot. He promised the court that speed would be his objective in presenting the open-and-shut case to the jury.[14]

Turning his attention to Kelly first, Hyde announced that "The evidence [presented to the jury] will show that two men went into the home of Mr. Urschel under the cover of darkness, that they kidnapped him and sped into the night, out of Oklahoma County and into Pottawatomie County, to the home of a relative of George Kelly, one of the defendants, and then to Texas.[15]

"This proof will show that the defendant Kelly was, on or about July 15th or 16th in Dallas, Texas, that he sent a wire to his friend Bates, who was in Denver, and that wire said, 'When and where will I meet you in Oklahoma City?'

"It will show that Bates wired back to Kelly under the name of R. G. Shannon, and that he said, 'I'll meet you on July 19th at the Biltmore Hotel' which was just three days before the kidnapping.[16]

---

* At some point later in the hearing, the judge gave permission for the accused to smoke.

"The proof will show that they met in Oklahoma City, and that Bates at that time had the car they hauled Urschel away in. It was a Chevrolet, 1933, with an Indiana tag."

Kelly smirked at the jury as Hyde was laying the groundwork for his case. Kathryn occasionally leaned over to whisper something to her husband and her attorney. Hyde was aware of the defendant's behavior but stayed focused on his prepared remarks.[17]

"The proof will disclose," Hyde continued, "that while Urschel was held prisoner down on the farm, Kelly was present until Friday and that Kelly warmed up and got kind of chummy. We'll show that Kelly said, 'This place is as safe as it can be. We used it in the old days as a hangout when we were running liquor from Mexico to Chicago. All the boys used it. After they pull a bank job or something, they'd come down here to '"cool off."'[18]

Hyde told the jury about the Kellys' travels after the kidnapping, the ransom that was paid, where some of the money was laundered, and the amount given to Kathryn's parents for their help in the crime. Hyde spoke of the day the authorities overtook the Shannon farm and what their investigation revealed.

"Shannon walked out and was met with an order to hold up his hands. Outside a building—the same building where Urschel was kept—we found Harvey Bailey sleeping. And, lo, at the same time we find a machine gun that Kathryn Kelly had bought in a pawn shop in Fort Worth for $250. And, lo, gentlemen, we find it was the same gun that was used in the kidnapping of Mr. Urschel. We find it, gentlemen, on the Shannon farm."[19]

Hyde didn't limit his accusations of criminal acts to just the Kellys, Bates, or the Shannons; he also threw a scandalous charge at Kathryn's lawyer, John Roberts. He claimed that Roberts told his client that bank gunmen and robbers Verne Miller and Wilbur Underhill "would take care of Luther Arnold if he attempted to testify at the hearing." Hyde told the jury that evidence would be introduced to prove that the Arnolds' daughter, Geralene, was taken with George and Kathryn as a disguise in their mad race from justice. He also declared that while Geralene was with them in Chicago, it was Kathryn who wrote the vicious letters threatening the lives of Charles Urschel and Joseph Keenan, assistant US attorney general.[20]

John Roberts spoke to the court on behalf of both George and Kathryn. Kelly was advised by his lawyer, James Mathers, that he did not need to seek severance, which is a legal term for separating two defendants or charges that have joined them in the same criminal case. Both Roberts and Mathers were certain Kelly would be convicted and sent to prison for life, but that strategy would give him the opportunity to take the full blame away from his wife. The defense planned to concentrate its entire effort on saving Kathryn from conviction. Roberts told the jury of his client's desire to take the stand in her own defense and insisted she was desperate all the time to keep Kelly from hurting her or her family.

"Her story will be that of a woman who loved a man and acted accordingly to keep that love," Roberts stated. He went on to explain that Kathryn's family would help support her claim that Kelly was a brute who threatened his wife and in-laws if they went against him.[21]

The government planned to use Kathryn's relatives to prove she wasn't a frail, naïve, unintelligent woman who was bullied into being an accessory to a crime. They also planned to show, using those same relatives, that Kelly was a ruthless felon, skilled in the use of a machine gun, and that given his criminal history, he didn't think twice about abducting Urschel.[22]

The prosecution took center stage after Judge Vaught directed District Attorney Hyde to start the proceedings. The lawyer began by reading the ransom note delivered to the Urschel family, as well as the letters Urschel himself was forced to write to John Catlett and E. E. Kirkpatrick. Charles Urschel took the stand and was asked to describe what happened on July 22, 1933.

"About 11:20, two men came in armed with a machine gun and a revolver," he told the jury. When asked if he could identify either of those men in the courtroom, Urschel said he could. "Between the two Mathers," he responded, referring to Kelly, "with that red hair, yellow hair." Kelly smiled proudly and leaned far back in the swivel chair in which he was seated.[23]

"That is the boy that is smiling over there, isn't it?" Hyde asked.

"That's right," Urschel confirmed.

"He is the man who had the gun in his hand," Hyde continued.

"That is right," said Urschel.

"The man that said he was going to blow your head off?"

"Yes, sir."[24]

"He is the same man that threatened to blow your wife's head off?"

"Yes, sir."

"The one who is smiling over there now?"

"Yes, sir."[25]

Kelly was brash and chuckled a bit as all eyes turned to him. He behaved much the same way when Mrs. Urschel, the Jarretts, and E. E. Kirkpatrick identified him.[26]

Kelly's attorney didn't cross-examine any of the witnesses who testified against him, which included the federal agents, but Kathryn's lawyers were on their feet objecting to any statements made that didn't support their client's insistence that she knew nothing about the kidnapping until after the fact. They vigorously questioned each person on the stand in an attempt to absolve Kathryn of any wrongdoing. The prosecution was relentless, however, and Roberts and Kathryn's other attorneys had to be at the top of their game when their focus shifted to her. Bureau Director Hoover pushed for Hyde and Keenan to be as tough as they could to bring about Kathryn's conviction. He never wavered in his belief that she was the mastermind behind the abduction and wanted her to be punished to the full extent of the law.[27]

The government's lawyers were effective, not only tracing the purchase of the machine gun used in the kidnapping to Kathryn but bringing to the stand family members, such as her grandmother, Mary Coleman, who told the court her granddaughter delivered the news to her that Kelly and Bates had brought a kidnapped man to her home. The jury also heard from Kathryn's stepbrother, Armon Shannon, who testified that the morning after the kidnapping, when Kathryn came to take his wife and child, sister, and niece to Fort Worth, she whispered to him to stay in his home in Paradise "because George Kelly might be here this week." Stepsister Ruth Shannon shared from the witness chair that Kathryn unexpectedly took her and two other girls in her family from the Shannon farm to her home the day Urschel was brought to Paradise.[28]

While Kelly's expression went back and forth from a smug grin to cold glares, Kathryn's ranged from friendly smiles, crying eyes, and an angry, clenched jaw. She wept profusely when her invalid grandmother was brought into the courtroom, blew kisses to her daughter Pauline sitting behind the defense attorney, snapped at the district attorney at times, and loudly whispered to her husband about one of the reluctant witnesses that testified against them that "they'll [federal agents] probably take him out and whip him and bring him back."[29]

Kathryn was relieved when she learned that Herbert Hyde was considering leaving Pauline out of the witnesses he was to call. She didn't want her child to have to go through such an ordeal. Hyde later changed his mind about calling Pauline to the stand.[30]

Geralene Arnold, who was close to Kathryn's daughter's age and whose life was placed in jeopardy by the Kellys, would testify to the experience she was forced to endure. Hyde wasted no time in pointing out to the jury before the teenager took the stand how willing Kathryn was to place another woman's child in harm's way.

"Why did Kathryn want you to come with her and her husband?" Hyde asked the star witness after she was sworn in.

"Mostly as a shield for them," Geralene answered. "They said I was a good shield."[31]

The young Arnold girl was self-assured sitting on the stand wearing the red woolen dress Kathryn purchased for her during their time together. Her parents, Luther and Flossie, had already told the court how they met Kathryn and, later, Kelly. Both had shared details of Kathryn's employment of Luther to act as a contact man for the Kellys. Both testified that the Kellys talked about the Urschel kidnapping in their presence. Flossie recounted the day the Kellys left San Antonio with her daughter. She explained to the court that they were to have the child back home no later than four in the afternoon the same day. Flossie confessed that when they didn't return with her child she was frantic.[32]

"Did you give them permission to take your baby to Chicago, or to Tennessee, or anywhere else?" Hyde asked her.

"No, sir," Flossie replied.

"Did you receive a letter from Mrs. Kelly mailed in Chicago, Illinois, after you came to Oklahoma City?"

Flossie confirmed that she had, and the letter containing instructions on where to communicate with the Kellys in Chicago was then introduced in evidence and read by the prosecutor. The letter included a brief note about Geralene and let the girl's mother know she was "fine."[33]

The cross-examination of Flossie Arnold by James Mathers was at times combative. "When you were helping the Kellys, you knew they were fugitives from justice?" Mathers asked.[34]

"Yes," said Flossie.

"How much money did the Kellys give your husband?" asked Mathers.

"Three hundred dollars," she said.

"When did he get the $1,500 they gave him?"

"Never, to my knowledge."

"Where are Mrs. Kelly's clothes?"

"I have them in my room at the hotel. I supposed she would return for them but never did."[35]

Hyde rose to address the court and told the judge that if Mathers wanted the clothes, the government would be glad to turn them over to him. Mathers accepted the prosecution's offer and turned his attention back to Flossie.[36]

"Now, Mrs. Arnold, you had read the papers and knew the Kellys were sought when you concealed them in your home until the reward was offered, did you not?" Hyde continued.[37]

"Yes, I knew they were wanted for questioning," Florrie said.

"That's all."

Herbert Hyde then questioned Flossie again. "It was not your home, was it? Mrs. Kelly rented it in her name and paid for it, didn't she?"

"Yes," Flossie nodded.

"And I'll ask you if you weren't arrested several days ago and had been cooperating with the federal authorities during that time before you even knew there was a reward offered?"[38]

Flossie nodded and told the court that she cooperated with the government because she wanted to get her daughter back.

"What was said about the Urschel kidnapping in your home in San Antonio?" Judge Vaught asked her.

"Mrs. Kelly said she ought to have killed the son-of-a-bitch. She said she was at her peoples' farm after he was kidnapped. Mrs. Kelly's father told me the kidnapping was planned three months before it happened, but this was not until I came to Oklahoma City."[39]

Mathers was again allowed to cross-examine Flossie. "Did they discuss giving up while they were at the house in San Antonio?" he probed.[40]

"No. Mrs. Kelly said George ought not to have got in all that trouble."

"When you came to Oklahoma City and talked to Mr. Roberts after he was employed as attorney for Mrs. Kelly by your husband, did you say that you would trust your baby anywhere with Mrs. Kelly?"

"No."

"Did Roberts suggest you ought to get your baby back?"

"No."

"Did you ever hear the Kellys talking about surrender?"

"No."[41]

When Flossie stepped down from the stand, Geralene took her place again. She smiled at her mother from the witness box and Flossie nodded proudly. After stating her name and age for the prosecution, the twelve-year-old girl was then asked to point out Kathryn and George Kelly and she did so. From there, she described for the court the harrowing summer trip the outlaw couple took her on. She told of the Kellys' disguises and of their travels from Cleveland to Chicago, and explained that while in Chicago, Kelly talked about killing Judge Vaught, Joseph Keenan, Herbert Hyde, and Charles Urschel. She testified that Kathryn said she also wanted Urschel dead. Geralene shared details about the apartment where her captors prepared the death threat letter sent to Urschel during Kathryn's parents' trial. "We stayed at an apartment house," the little girl said. " . . . George wrote some letters. Kathryn wrote some too. I saw George put his fingerprints on them. I bought the stamps at a substation."[42]

When Herbert Hyde handed her the two letters she mentioned were sent, she confirmed those were indeed the ones. "I saw Kathryn put the stamps on the letters and saw her mail them," Geralene told the court. "I saw George put his prints on them and when he did, he said, 'That ought to knock them over.' Kathryn said she hoped it would do good but if it didn't it would do bad." Detailing the fingerprints, Geralene said Kelly poured ink out on the sheet of paper, stuck each finger into the little pool separately, and then placed them on the letters.[43]

Geralene's testimony concluded with her telling the jury about the Kellys sending her to Cass Coleman's farm with Langford Ramsey. She said that Kathryn wanted her to return to her and told her they would eventually go to Memphis.[44]

On cross-examination, the girl told James Mathers that she couldn't say for sure who the threatening letters she saw the Kellys write were addressed to, only that she mailed them. She also couldn't confirm what exact letter she saw Kathryn writing, only that she saw her writing two[45] letters. Mathers questioned Geralene about what she knew of the fifteen-thousand-dollar reward for the Kellys. She testified that she learned of the reward two or three days after the federal officers met her in Oklahoma City.[46]

"And are you claiming a part of that reward?" Mathers queried.

"No, sir," she responded. "If they want to give it to me, they can."

"You are claiming it for the information and now you are testifying for the government," Mathers pressed. "Is that right?"

"Yes, sir," Geralene answered.[47]

Defense attorney Mathers's attempt to portray Geralene as embellishing her testimony in order to get a reward wasn't well received by the jury. The disapproving looks on their faces weren't lost on the members of the prosecution team. They were satisfied that Geralene had proved to be a credible witness and pleased that Kathryn had been pictured through the child's story as a hard, profane woman who said Urschel should have been killed after the ransom was collected.[48]

Luther Arnold took the stand after his daughter concluded her testimony. He corroborated Geralene's story of the family hitch-hiking trip from Carter County, Oklahoma, to Temple, Texas, and back to Itasca, where Kathryn Kelly found them. He told of her befriending them and caring for them at a Texas tourist camp. He told the court about the trip he made to Fort Worth to see Sam Sayers, the lawyer who defended the Shannons, and of the two hundred fifty dollars Kathryn gave him to give to John Roberts to help with the case. Prosecutor Keenan questioned Luther about all the money Kathryn gave him to do her bidding, which totaled five hundred fifty dollars. The lawyer then asked whether Luther told the authorities about the Kellys before he knew a reward was offered. He confirmed the statement.[49]

"Besides telling the government or its representatives what you knew about Kelly and his wife and their whereabouts, did you make any agreement with them as to your future conduct, whether you would disclose to them anything you would learn?" Keenan asked Luther.[50]

"I told them I would," Luther answered.

"You kept your agreement?"

"Yes, sir."

"For the purpose of bringing to justice two criminals that were at large?"

"Yes, sir, because I didn't know anything about it when I got into it, and after I found out what I was into I wanted to get out of it."[51]

Luther went on to explain that he was arraigned in court under a fictious name because he was afraid Kelly's friends or Kathryn's attorney would have him killed before he could take the stand against them.[52]

James Mathers cross-examined Luther and challenged the veracity of his claim that he didn't know the law was looking for the Kellys. He accused Luther of being a confidence man, a person who tricks people in order to get their money, and questioned him again on the amount of money Kathryn actually gave him. Mathers tried to get Luther to admit to taking fifteen hundred dollars from the Kellys. He denied ever receiving such a sum. He also denied he only decided to testify against the Kellys when the government agreed to drop the charge against him for violating the Mann Act. "I went to them because I thought my own kid had got kidnapped and I wanted her back," Luther strongly insisted.[53]

Kathryn's frustration with Luther's testimony was clear. She shook her head through much of what he told the court and every so often whispered to John Roberts that he was lying.[54]

"Luther said he never knew me until I picked them up while they were hitchhiking through Texas," Kathryn later told a reporter with the *Oklahoma News*. "That isn't true. I knew them before. I'd met them in El Paso five years ago. They forgot that. It was a brief encounter, but. . . . I gave them the only break they'd ever had, and look what they did to me. Arnold had only three cents in his pocket when I found them. They didn't have any decent clothes and said they hadn't had much to eat for days. I bought them good clothes and fed them. I took them to San Antonio.[55]

"I took good care of Geralene while she was with me. Jerry's a swell kid. She's crazy about me. She told me she wanted to come with me and live. She's just the opposite from my baby. Polly has been petted and pampered all her life. Everybody loves her so they make over her all the time. She's just a baby.[56]

"Jerry's only twelve, but she has had some hard knocks. You could drop her down in New York and she'd get along somehow. She knows how to take care of herself."[57]

Among some of the other witnesses the prosecution presented to the jury whose testimony caused a stir were the Bureau of Investigation's Special Agent in Charge William Rohrer and handwriting expert D. C. Patterson. Rohrer told the court the details of the capture of the Kellys in Memphis on September 26, 1933. Kelly shared with the agent the names of the other men he and Albert Bates considered kidnapping before Urschel was selected as their victim.[58]

"They considered Frank Johnson, president of the First National Bank, John A. Brown, department store owner, and M. K. Goetz, St. Joseph brewer," Rohrer stated. He said Kelly told him these men had been passed up because they felt there would be difficulty in raising a considerable ransom quickly.[59]

Rohrer also said that Kelly told him he tried to arrange for a meeting with Chicago gangster Gus Winkler to exchange some of the "hot" money for ready cash, but that Winkler told him over the phone, "I wouldn't be seen with you for $10,000." Rohrer also testified that Kelly confessed that five days before he and Kathryn were arrested, he'd made arrangements with Verne Miller to kill Charles Urschel.[60]

When John Roberts had a chance to question SAC Rohrer, he asked him if Kelly mentioned who specifically took part in the kidnapping of Urschel. Rohrer said Kelly told him, "Nobody was connected with it except himself and Mr. Bates."

Roberts continued, "Did he tell you that his wife knew nothing about it?" Rohrer nodded. "He said all along that his wife knew nothing about it and he wanted to do everything he could to keep his wife and the Shannons out of the case."[61]

"You also had an interview with Mrs. Kelly?" Roberts continued with his questioning.

"Yes, sir," Rohrer said.

"And she stated to you that she knew nothing about it?"

"She said she knew nothing about the kidnapping prior to the kidnapping, yes, sir."

"That she didn't know anything about it until after the kidnapping occurred?"[62]

"Yes, sir."

"How long did you interview Mrs. Kelly?"

"I talked to her each day from the time of her arrest until she arrived in Oklahoma, six days."

"Was anything said by Mr. or Mrs. Kelly about who wrote the threatening letters to Mr. Urschel?"

"Kathryn Kelly said that George Kelly wrote the letters."[63] Attorneys Hyde and Keenan put handwriting expert D. C.

Patterson on the stand to refute Kathryn's claim that her husband penned the letters. Patterson showed the jury that Kathryn Kelly wrote the terrorizing letters in which Kelly threatened to slaughter Mr. Urschel, the prosecutors, and other principals involved in the case against the Shannons. Furious over the allegation, Kathryn leaned over to John Roberts and loudly whispered that she had nothing to do with writing the letters.[64]

The national publicity generated by the trial prompted individuals who had lost touch with the Kellys to come forward with their thoughts about the couple. One of those people was Kathryn's ex-father-in-law, J. F. Thorne. His son Charles had been married to her for a short while. "I've been looking for her for a long time," the elderly man told a reporter with the *Waco News*, "and now I'm reading about her in the paper. Well, I don't wish her any luck."[65]

Kelly's ex-wife, Geneva Ramsey, didn't wish any better for her former spouse when reporters for the Memphis newspaper the *Commercial Appeal* sought her out for a quote about him. "I hope he gets three hundred years," she stated. "Then we'll be rid of him." A classmate of George Kelly who hadn't seen him since high school told a staff writer for the *Memphis Press Scimitar*, that Kelly grew up in a good section of Memphis. "There are always people who say it was an environment or heredity that were to blame for boys going wrong," the former friend noted. "That wasn't true in the case of George. He had just as good a start as anyone, maybe better than the average law-abiding citizen."[66]

The public's perception of the Kellys was abysmal. Neither Defense Attorney Roberts nor Mathers had any hope of improving George's public view, but they did believe Kathryn's had a chance. She objected to the prosecution's initial plan to call her daughter to the stand to testify against her, and she was skeptical when her lawyer suggested they have Pauline tell the court about their time together in Fort Worth. The lawyers told her that it would help her case to show the loving relationship she had with her only child. Kathryn reluctantly agreed. Roberts and Mathers also wanted to demonstrate through Pauline that taking her daughter, her step-sister, her sister-in-law, and her sister-in-law's child away from the Shannon farm was not a planned part of the Urschel kidnapping conspiracy.[67]

Fourteen-year-old Pauline wasn't on the stand long. Her take on the short trip was consistent with Kathryn's stepsister, Ruth.

"Now, from the time your mother came to your grandmother's home to get you until your mother left, did you hear anything said about kidnapping or a man being kidnapped?" Roberts asked the teenager before giving the prosecution an opportunity to question her.

"No, sir," Pauline answered.

The cross-examination of the witness was brief. It consisted of two questions. District Attorney Hyde asked the young girl if she was the daughter of Kathryn Kelly, who was being tried for conspiracy to kidnap Charles Urschel. Pauline answered, "Yes, sir" to both queries and was then dismissed.[68]

Throughout the course of the trial there were occasional breaks taken by both the defense and prosecution. It was during those times that spectators sitting in the gallery would leave to use the restroom or to go outside to smoke a cigarette. People who had been standing in the aisles at the back of the courtroom quickly scrambled to fill the open seats.[69]

More than two hundred perfumed Oklahoma society women held meetings in the lobby to discuss the case. They broke into small groups, and every time someone left the courtroom they flocked around them to get information about the witnesses and their testimony. There were some who dared to peek in on the proceedings and then reported back on the appearance of the accused.

"Kathryn looks pale, doesn't she?" one of the women could be heard saying.

"Yes. She's lost ten pounds since she's been in jail," another commented.

"I wouldn't take her for a criminal. Look at Kelly. Doesn't his hair look terrible?" someone else remarked.[70]

According to Prosecuting Attorney Keenan, Kelly looked and

behaved like a "punk" in court. In discussions with Cocounsel Hyde, the two considered some of his conduct to be a good act. They worried that the more he behaved like a thug, the more likely the jury might be to accept Kathryn's claim that he intimidated her into going along with the crime. The two lawyers tried to combat the problem and show that Kathryn was no victim by calling Bureau Agent Ralph Colvin to the stand.

"Mrs. Kelly told me she understood that Mr. Urschel had filed a suit to seize from her certain jewelry that had been found, I believe in a safe deposit box in Fort Worth, and she wanted me to ask Mr. Urschel to come and see her," the agent told the jury. "She said she couldn't afford to lose that jewelry because it was all she had left to provide for her daughter and she thought Mr. Urschel was a heartless man, and she went on to remark that if he won the suit, it would not do him much good because he wouldn't have long to live anyway."[71]

While court was in recess, the Kellys' defense team decided it would be best if Kelly didn't testify to bear out his wife's story that he threatened and forced her to take part in the abduction. After hearing from family, friends, and Hoover's Bureau agents, the only one left to take the stand was Kathryn herself. Her life depended on being able to prove to the jury that all the simple country girl was guilty of was falling for the wiles of a city-bred gangster.[72]

Chapter 11

DEFENDING KATHRYN

A WAVE OF MUTED EXCITEMENT traveled through the Oklahoma City courtroom when the stern-faced bailiff called Kathryn Kelly to the stand on October 11, 1933. Before leaving the chair where she'd been sitting next to her husband and her attorneys, she glanced around the large, impressive vaulted room. It was a room that reflected its great and grave function, and as she got to her feet the full weight of what was about to transpire washed over her. She had to force herself to keep moving or give way to anxiety. She nodded politely to the jury as she passed. Their eyes followed her progress. After being sworn in, she adjusted the stylish black hat covering her red tresses underneath. Her lips wore a tremulous, childish smile that could be interpreted as apologetic, inviting, or secretly pleased at the effect she obviously had on men.[1]

Defense Attorney John Roberts waited for Kathryn to sit down before he began his work. She smoothed her dress over her knees while crossing her sheer clad legs. Roberts gave the members of the jury a moment for their gaze to linger. He started with preliminary questions: her name, where she lived, how long she and Kelly had been married. Once the basics were out of the way, he asked her what she knew her husband did for money when they wed.

"He told me he was gambling and playing the races," she replied.

Roberts then asked Kathryn to tell the jury what happened the morning of July 23, while she was staying with her grandmother.[2]

"I maintained a bedroom there and I was sleeping in my

bedroom, and Mr. Kelly woke me up about 4:30 in the morning by shining a flashlight in my face and asked me to get up and get him a quilt and pillow and a full thermos jug, and he went back out and I got up and began doing that, and he went out at the back," Kathryn answered.

"I noticed a car at the back, and Mr. Kelly came back into the house, and my grandmother had started to get up. She wasn't feeling well. She asked me what was going on, who that was in the back and what all the racket was and I said, 'I don't know.' I said, 'It is Mr. Kelly and I will find out,' and he came back on the back porch where I was filling the thermos jug.[3]

"I asked him what he wanted with these things and where he was going and why he came in. Well, we had a little argument because I accused him of being out at a party because he was out so late. He didn't give me any clear answers but I insisted, but he went back out to the car again. When he came back, I insisted on knowing where he was going. He said he would see me in two weeks or call me. He told me he and Mr. Bates were delivering a man over near the Arkansas line. I wanted to know what he meant. He said, 'You will read it in the newspapers.' He said it was a man kidnapped but he didn't tell me who."[4]

According to Kathryn, she never went out to see the kidnapped man and had no idea who it might be. Within an hour after Kelly came and went from the farm, she testified that she left for Fort Worth, stopping by the Shannon farm first to get her daughter and the Shannon children "for a visit." Choking back tears, she said that Kelly threatened her a day or so later when she returned to her parents' home. It was then she explained that she learned that Kelly and Bates had a man in her stepbrother Armon's tenant house.[5]

"I went into the [Shannons'] house and mother was acting a little funny," Kathryn shared with the jury. "There was another man staying at the house, Mr. Bailey, whom I knew as Mr. Brennan. I sat there and talked for a while. When I got mother alone, she told me George and Bates had a man there and had told her he was drunk. My stepfather told me the same thing. They were greatly worried. I told them I would stay overnight and find out what was going on."[6]

Kathryn said that the following day she did go to her stepbrother's home to get to the bottom of things.

"George Kelly was sitting outside on the doorstep," she noted. "I called him and told him I had some ice water. He came down to the barn. I told him he was going to get my people in trouble and asked him to release this man, but he refused. He threatened me. He said it was none of my business."[7]

"Was anything further said that night?" Roberts inquired.

"Kelly said they were going to kill Mr. Urschel," Kathryn stated.[8]

Prosecuting Attorneys Joseph Keenan and Herbert Hyde leaned forward in their seats as Kathryn was talking and made notes about her testimony on the pads of paper in front of them. When necessary, the lawyers made objections regarding her retelling of the happenings. She tended to interject what she believed Kelly meant to say or do. Often, Roberts would lead Kathryn to make the statements he thought would best benefit her case. She smiled continuously at the jury and whenever she was interrupted by the prosecution, turned to Judge Vaught and respectfully waited for his decision to sustain or overrule the protest.[9]

During Defense Attorney Roberts's questioning, Kathryn was focused, unruffled, and solemn. When she wasn't sure of the day or hour of the incident, she calmly admitted it.

"How long were you at your parents' house after you knew about Charles Urschel?" Roberts asked.

"I don't remember the exact day," she responded. "I had so much on my mind, I can't remember the exact date, but I stayed there until Mr. Kelly came and got me."[10]

She told the jury that once they left Paradise, her husband took her to Minneapolis. They briefly stayed in a St. Paul hotel before going to the other Twin City. She then recounted quick visits to Cleveland, Chicago, and Des Moines. They had dinner with friends and went to nightclub shows.

"From Des Moines we went on down to Texas to my uncle's farm, Cass Coleman's," she explained.

"Is that the Coleman that was here on the witness stand who testified that the money was hid on his farm?" Roberts probed.

Kathryn confirmed it was the same man.

"You made that trip to Coleman's with George Kelly with the money?" the lawyer continued.

"I was with him," she offered. She told the court she didn't know the money was in the car and that she didn't see him take the money out of the vehicle.[11]

Kathryn dabbed a tear from her eye with a handkerchief as she told the jury that the first time she saw any substantial amount of money was in Minneapolis. She didn't know where Kelly got the money, only that he had it. The cash was spread out on the bed in the place they were staying when she returned from a shopping trip. Kelly asked her if she'd ever seen a hundred thousand dollars before. Roberts asked her if she saw the money taken out of the car at the Coleman farm and buried. She swore she had not.[12]

It was around the same time Kelly hid the money that Kathryn learned her parents, Albert Bates, and Harvey Bailey had been arrested. Kathryn testified she then left her husband and traveled to Dallas with her girlfriend, Louise Donavon. Both stayed in Dallas for two days. While Kathryn was there she contacted a lawyer to represent her parents. Louise left for Brownsville. Kathryn went to Mineral Wells. She told the court she was in Mineral Wells for several days waiting for Kelly, but he never showed. Two weeks passed before she saw her husband again in San Antonio.[13]

Between the time she left the Coleman farm and met Kelly in San Antonio, she encountered the hitchhiking Arnold family. Kathryn described meeting the trio and the immediate bond she had with Geralene. She testified to the jury that the child was "with me constantly."[14]

"Where did you leave her father and mother when you took Geralene?" Roberts asked his witness.

"Her mother was in San Antonio and her father was there too, but he was leaving for Oklahoma City," Kathryn replied.

"Did they consent for the little girl to go with you?" Roberts continued.

"Oh, yes," Kathryn assured him.

"Did they ever write you or wire you at any time that if Geralene was with you to send her home?"

"No, sir, they trusted her with me."

"When you left down there did you tell them you would be back and bring the little girl back in a few hours?"

"I told them I would be back that afternoon because I thought I would be back."[15]

Several women spectators in the gallery tittered and whispered during Kathryn's testimony about Geralene. They were appalled that she had taken the little girl from her parents and didn't believe the Arnolds consented to let their child go off with the outlaws for an undisclosed amount of time. The courtroom audience members mumbled disapproving remarks and disrupted the proceedings so that Judge Vaught threatened to have all observers removed. When Kathryn was allowed to resume, she told the jury that Kelly took her and Geralene from San Antonio to Coleman, Texas, to try and get some of the money. From there they continued on to Chicago, where they rented an apartment and stayed five or six days.[16]

"Now, while you were in Chicago, I will ask you if you heard from anybody in Oklahoma or elsewhere except Geralene's mother?" Defense Attorney Roberts inquired.

"Yes, sir," Kathryn responded.

"Whom did you write to?" Roberts pressed.

"Mr. Keenan," the witness confessed.

Roberts had his client review the two letters, which were now in evidence, that she admitted to writing—one to Flossie Arnold and the other to Joseph Keenan. She was also asked to review the threatening letter sent to Charles Urschel during her parents' trial. She testified that Kelly signed the letter but denied writing it herself. She told the court she saw her husband write the letter and put his fingerprints on it. Roberts reminded her what Geralene had told the jury about seeing her and Kelly writing letters, and about Kathryn putting the stamps on them. He also reminded her what Geralene said she heard Kathryn say about Urschel. "I made no threats against Urschel or any of the officials in the presence of Geralene or

Mrs. Arnold," she stated calmly and emphatically. "I had no reason to threaten them. They had done nothing to me."[17]

Before the defense attorneys finished taking Kathryn through their questioning, she told the court about going to Memphis, where she and Kelly were captured because of the information given to the authorities from Geralene after she was dismissed from duty as a "shield." Kathryn said she told Agent Rohrer, while in jail in Memphis, that she was innocent in the kidnapping.

She wiped a tear from her eye before exiting the witness stand. She smiled pleasantly at the jury as she walked back to the empty chair between her husband and their attorneys. James Mathers handed both Kelly and Kathryn a cigarette and took one for himself. Kelly lit the three smokes with one match. The trio then huddled together with Roberts to review her testimony.[18]

Charles Urschel's close friend E. E. Kirkpatrick, who was in the courtroom during Kathryn's initial testimony, noted in his memoirs how duplicitous he found Kathryn to be. He questioned how she expected the jury to believe she and Kelly were through as a couple, a statement she made to the press and the authorities more than once, when they could observe how they treated each other. "She's a consummate actress. She assumed the role during the trial of a country girl who had fallen for the wiles of the city-bred gangster, George Kelly, and she made fair progress under the questioning of her attorneys."[19]

When Kathryn was recalled to the stand and Prosecuting Attorney Joseph Keenan approached her to begin the cross-examination, her demeanor changed slightly. The smile she so generously offered the court prior to that moment was replaced with a serious, clenched-jaw expression and she fixed a contemptuous glare on the counselor as he walked toward her. Her posture, which had been relaxed while her lawyer was questioning her, became stiff as she braced herself for an assault. John Roberts was afraid that would happen. He'd had reservations about Kathryn testifying and tried to warn her about what was in store, but she assured the concerned legal adviser that she could handle herself.

As he watched his client stare Keenan down, Roberts knew it had been a mistake that Kathryn testified.[20]

The prosecution wasted no time diving into her marital background. Keenan and Attorney Herbert Hyde's goal was to show the jury the flippancy with which she managed her many marriages and live-in relationships. Kathryn had difficulty remembering the dates of her various nuptials, divorces, and other key events associated with the men she had wed and left. She couldn't remember the date of her daughter's birth but said she was premature and came seven months after she married Lonnie Fry when she was fourteen years old. Frustrated that the prosecution was hounding her about the specifics of her child's birth and the baby's father, she snapped at Keenan, telling him his questions had nothing to do with the current predicament.

"I'm testing the credibility of the witness," the lawyer informed her and the court.

"You answer the questions, young lady," Judge Vaught admonished her.

"Yes, sir," she replied meekly.[21]

Keenan continued, asking her about her marriage to Charles Thorne. She testified they exchanged vows in Fort Worth and that they lived together until he died. The prosecution then pointed out that Thorne had shot himself and left behind a note. Kathryn could barely hide her annoyance at being asked if she wrote the note. "No, sir," she responded sharply.[22]

"Have you ever been convicted of an offense?" Keenan probed.

"I haven't been in the penitentiary," Kathryn snapped.

"I didn't ask you that," Keenan shot back. "I want to know if you've ever been convicted of an offense."

Kathryn admitted to a robbery conviction in Oklahoma City. She was given a five-year sentence, but the case was dismissed on appeal.

"Now, is that all?" she snarled.

"If Your Honor, please," Keenan appealed to the judge.

"Just answer the question and eliminate any comment," Judge Vaught instructed the clearly frustrated witness.[23]

John Roberts gave his client a pleading look. Kelly tried to catch her eye to give her a smile, but she looked past him at her daughter, Pauline, sitting behind the defense attorney's table.

"Yes, sir," Kathryn told the judge after finding the motivation to curtail her aggravation by looking at the teenager's face.[24]

The prosecution continued their line of questioning, eventually revealing to the jury that in addition to Kathryn's arrest, she'd used multiple aliases throughout her life and could possibly have been apprehended for several crimes, but they couldn't be sure because of the different names. When asked if she could recall the various handles she used, she said she couldn't.[25]

After grilling Kathryn about her relationships, some of which included affairs with men who were thieves and bootleggers, Keenan started on her female friends, specifically Louise Donavon. She too had used many aliases and had a questionable background.

"She is a common prostitute and you know it," Keenan told Kathryn. "Didn't you give her some money? Some of the Urschel money?" he pressed.

Kathryn shifted uneasily in her seat before denying the claim. Roberts objected to Keenan's line of questioning, but the judge overruled his objection.[26]

The prosecution then turned his attention to Kathryn's romance with Kelly and challenged her statement that she didn't know what he did to make money. She swore she didn't find out he was a gambler and bootlegger until after they were married.

"George deceived you in the beginning?" Keenan asked.

"Yes," Kathryn answered.

"Cruelly, about his occupations?" he continued.

"He deceived me," Kathryn repeated.[27]

She admitted that life with Kelly wasn't lacking. The pair lived a life of luxury and ease with fine homes, expensive cars, and high-priced jewelry. Anything Kathryn wanted, Kelly made sure she had.

"And you never knew any way he made a living except he was out at night, is that right?" Keenan queried.

"No, I didn't study anything about it," Kathryn noted.

"Were you interested?" the lawyer continued.

"Not especially," Kathryn snapped.

"So, as long as you got pretty clothes and a nice place to live and plenty of food, you were not interested in how your husband got his money, were you?" Keenan pressed. The witness confirmed his assessment.[28]

Kathryn insisted the six thousand dollars in jewelry he gave her "didn't come out of a robbery." She told the jury that Kelly won a lot of money gambling and shared a story of once watching her husband win twenty-eight hundred dollars at the Arlington Park track in Chicago. According to a reporter with the *Oklahoma News* who was in the courtroom listening to Kathryn's testimony, "That one sentence [about Arlington Park] spoke volumes," he wrote in the October 11, 1933, edition of the paper. "It was at the Arlington track that Al Capone and other gangsters whiled away their time."[29]

Keenan persisted with his questioning. Kathryn's face was pale but composed, her eyes wide with a secret fear or knowledge.

"When did you learn that George Kelly was a dangerous character or have you learned that yet?" the lawyer asked.

"Not for sure," Kathryn stated. "I think he is."

Even after Keenan listed Kelly's crimes, including kidnapping Charles Urschel with a machine gun, threatening to kill a prosecutor, and the men he abducted, Kathryn would not allow herself to state emphatically that he was dangerous. She couldn't deny when asked that she still loved him. Keenan wondered aloud that if Kathryn couldn't wholeheartedly agree if Kelly were dangerous, why was she afraid of what he would do if she went to the police and turned him in? The aggressive prosecutor grilled Kathryn about her parents', grandmother's, and stepbrother's testimonies, which indicated she knew from the start her husband kidnapped Charles Urschel. She denied any involvement in Kelly's wrongdoing, and when Keenan asked her if her family was lying, she told him they were.[30]

Keenan took Kathryn through every step of the kidnapping, from the selection of Urschel as the victim to the abduction, the days leading up to the ransom being paid, collecting the money, and the getaway. At times she was evasive and combative. Keenan occasionally raised his voice. but only when he believed she was being disingenuous.

"All the time you were with your father at your home in Fort Worth [after the kidnapping]. . . . You could have given yourself up to the police a dozen times, couldn't you?" the prosecutor asked.[31]

"I could probably have walked in and done that but I didn't know they wanted me," Kathryn said.

"Were you suspicious of the fact they wanted your husband?" Keenan continued.

"No, sir. I didn't know it," she responded.

"The whole country knew that George Kelly was being looked for and you knew nothing about it?" the lawyer quipped.

"Not up to that time," Kathryn said.

The spectators mumbled to one another. They too found the statement hard to accept. Judge Vaught rapped the gavel on his desk to silence the courtroom.[32]

The prosecutor soldiered on until his questioning centered on the Arnold family. Kathryn told the jury that when she left Kelly at Cass Coleman's so she could go to Dallas to find a lawyer for her parents, she didn't think George was running away from the police.

"And that's when you met these Arnold people along the road?" Keenan asked. "Was there anything to stop you from giving yourself up to the police or seeking protection from the law agencies of the country?" he asked again, still disbelieving Kathryn's previous statement.

John Roberts leapt to his feet to object to the question. "The proof does not show she knew she was wanted," Roberts explained to the judge. Frustrated, Keenan withdrew the question.[33]

Moving on to Geralene, Keenan wanted to know when Kathryn and Kelly took off with the little girl and if Kathryn knew then they were wanted by the police? She admitted she did know. He questioned her about exposing the young girl to danger and putting the child's life at risk. Kathryn assured the court she wouldn't have let anything happen to Geralene.

When she was asked why she didn't send the child home to her parents, Kathryn replied, "She didn't seem to want to return."[34]

When Keenan asked Kathryn about Geralene's testimony regarding money given to her and Kelly from a gangster in Chicago, Kathryn denied such an incident occurred. "Is she telling a falsehood?" Keenan quizzed the witness.[35]

"She's just telling what she was told to tell, I think," Kathryn retorted sharply.

Taken aback, Keenan responded, "You believe the government tried to get that little girl to come up here and swear falsely against you?"

"I know she hasn't told the truth," Kathryn quickly offered.[36]

During the four hours of Keenan's questioning, Kathryn had dissolved into a bundle of nerves and temper. The implication that the prosecution had called witnesses to fake their testimony infuriated Keenan and he struggled to keep himself from losing his self-control.

Kathryn had insisted during the trial that she planned to get away from Kelly and surrender and Keenan's last two questions challenged her claim. "You never did give up until you were apprehended with your husband in Memphis?" he asked her.

"No, sir, but I intended to," Kathryn told him.

"You never had given up before you were apprehended and you were then living with your husband?" Keenan pressed.

"Yes, sir," was all she could say.[37]

The Kellys were sitting together at the defense table when John Roberts offered his closing statements to the court. He told the attentive jury that Kathryn Kelly was drawn unwittingly into the two-hundred-thousand-dollar abduction of Charles Urschel because her notorious husband had deceived and threatened her. He pleaded with the jury to not hold her past against her as it had nothing to do with being manipulated by Kelly. Roberts explained how Kelly coerced his wife into going along with the crime and noted again that George Kelly admitted Kathryn had nothing to do with planning or executing the kidnapping. The attorney affirmed that her actions were born out of fear of her husband and what he would do to her or her family if she went against him.

Roberts promised the court that Kelly was prepared to take full responsibility for the kidnapping.[38]

Joseph Keenan's summation recalled the amazing mass of incriminating evidence against Kathryn the government had presented, which included that she herself had purchased the Thompson submachine gun used by Kelly in the abduction of Urschel that was later found in the possession of Harvey Bailey at the Shannon farm. In spite of Roberts's objection, Keenan did call attention to Kathryn's past, noting that from an early age she'd been initiated into criminal ways. He reminded the court that she had been convicted of putting a victim on the spot for her male robber-partner in Oklahoma City, had been married three times, and became a rich widow of a third husband who was found shot to death in their luxurious Fort Worth home when she met George Kelly.[39]

Keenan concluded his closing remarks by stating that government witnesses had successfully portrayed George Kelly's wife as the "arch-conspirator in the whole case." The prosecutor referred to her as a profane and vicious woman who drove her husband to commit crimes to make sure she had the luxuries she demanded. "She's just as guilty as her husband," Keenan declared. "I hesitate to say which of the two is more guilty. The evidence is overwhelming against both of them."[40]

Before sending the jury away to render their verdict on the case, Judge Vaught had final instructions to offer the men. He explained the serious nature of the charges against the Kellys as well as the important and crucial responsibility that rested with them. The judge then added his own personal take on the accused. Regarding Kelly, he noted that if the jury believed the testimony of those who identified him as one of the actual kidnappers and the man who received the two-hundred-thousand-dollar ransom in Kansas City, he should be found guilty.[41]

"The court would feel cowardly and derelict in its duty if it did not point out its conviction that the defendant, Kathryn Kelly, was not wholly truthful," Judge Vaught added. "This court will not hesitate to tell you that Kathryn Kelly's testimony concerning the removal of the little girls from the Shannon farm near Paradise,

Texas, the day Mr. Urschel was brought there, did not sound convincing. Her conduct at the Coleman farm not only is a strong circumstantial point, but is convincing to the court that Kathryn knew about the kidnapping and knowingly participated. Other testimony from this defendant is utterly convincing to the court that Kathryn Kelly had criminal knowledge of the abduction conspiracy."[42]

The judge pointed out that the jury, however, must be the sole judge of the guilt or innocence of the defendants and that his remarks might be ignored altogether.[43]

The Kellys' defense attorneys objected to the judge's remarks, stating, "There is no doubt about the verdict after those instructions." Judge Vaught dismissed the jurymen for deliberation at 5:45 p.m.[44]

Reporters and spectators both in the courtroom and in the lobby outside the hall of justice openly discussed the intricacies of the case. They didn't find it unusual that the criminals in both cases sold one another out but speculated on the reasons behind the cutthroat tactics. According to an article in the October 12, 1933, edition of the *Oklahoma News*, most of those who flocked to see the proceedings in person were familiar with the details of the trial and the defense lawyer's strategy.[45]

Mathers and Roberts spoke quietly about the case with each other. They knew Kelly was done for. He'd been identified positively by the Urschels, the Jarretts, E. E. Kirkpatrick, and Armon Shannon as one of the actual abductors. Kelly himself had confessed to the details of the kidnapping and hiding the ransom money. Kelly's lawyers refused to let their client take the stand to answer for the crime because it would be the same as pleading guilty and his right to an appeal would have been forfeited.[46]

"But why did Kathryn on cross examination say that her parents were liars in most of their testimony, when she has been protesting all along that they were innocent?" the article in the October 12, 1933, edition of the *Oklahoma News* pointed out.

"Her protests that her parents were innocent were entirely unofficial, that is, not made before the jury. Her parents were already convicted. She couldn't help them. And it wouldn't hurt them now to throw a little blame their way it if increased her chance for liberty. The Shannons will understand must have been the only reasoning."[47]

If all had gone well, John Roberts believed Kathryn had a remote chance of being set free if she took the stand. The case against her was more circumstantial. She wasn't one of the actual abductors, Urschel never saw her face or heard her voice, and she wasn't present when the ransom was paid. If not for her cousin, eighteen-year-old Gray Coleman, or her grandmother's testimony or that of the Shannons that Kathryn had knowledge that a kidnapping was going on, the court might have been persuaded that she was forced into the situation by her brutal husband.[48]

Less than an hour after the jury left the courtroom to resolve the fate of the Kellys, they returned with their verdict. Kathryn and George stood beside their lawyers as the decision was read. Neither showed any emotion when they heard the court clerk utter the word "guilty." Both Roberts and Mathers immediately filed motions for new trials. They based their grounds of appeal on the Federal Kidnapping Law itself, claiming it was "indefinite, uncertain, and unconstitutional."

The appeals were promptly denied. The Kellys declined to say anything when Judge Vaught extended to them the opportunity before he rendered sentencing them. Kathryn stared at the ground in front of her and Kelly scanned the faces of the jurymen while chewing a wad of gum.[49]

"The jury has found you guilty and the court fully concurs," the judge told the pair. "It is the judgment and sentence of this court that each of you be taken to the federal penitentiary, there to remain for the rest of your lives."

The Kellys took their seats again after the sentencing. Both were solemn but not surprised. A wave of quiet excitement traveled through the courtroom. A flash of photographers' bulbs lit up the scene as cameramen hurried to take pictures of the convicted felons' reaction to the court's ruling.[50]

Several armed agents escorted the glum husband and wife toward the exit of the courtroom. Just before they left the hall of justice, Kathryn could be heard saying, "My Pekingese dog would have got a life sentence in this court."[51]

A crush of spectators pushed in on officers as the Kellys were led out of the building into awaiting paddy wagons. The thoroughfare the pair traveled was lined with onlookers hoping to catch a glimpse of the couple being hurried away to jail. Newsreel camera operators recorded the authorities escorting Kelly and Kathryn along their way. Broadcast announcers, who recorded their description of the scene over the newsreel footage, called the action harried and satisfying.[52]

"Now it's all over," the commentator noted. "These people who became famous, or rather infamous, overnight will soon be forgotten by the world. And will spend the rest of their lives within the grim, gray walls of prison. Sirens scream and armored cars speed past the crowds. The passengers are going for a ride, and with the federal government at the wheel. And here's the end of the road, federal prison, and oblivion. The inevitable destination of easy money."

Some of the jurors who convicted the Kellys eagerly shared their thoughts about the verdict with the press. "We reached a verdict on the first ballot," Foreman J. H. Verlty told a reporter with the *Enid Daily Eagle*. "After we sealed it, we debated a while on whether Kathryn should be turned loose."[53]

J. M. Branson said, "I believe all kidnappers ought to get life. I'm not strong for capital punishment."

Jury member Clark Jones noted that, "There wasn't any argument. I voted wholeheartedly for the guilty verdict."

W. D. Kyle agreed. "The law must be strictly enforced. I'm heartily opposed to the criminal wave that's over the country, kidnapping in particular.

Z. R. Bullard commented that, "The Kellys ought to be behind bars the rest of their lives."[54]

Prior to the conviction and sentencing of George and Kathryn Kelly, the authorities had already begun to plan to move the pair to the federal facilities where they would be permanently housed. Kelly would serve his time at Leavenworth and Kathryn would be taken to a women's institution in West Virginia. In the interim, the two were transferred from the courthouse back to the county jail.[55]

A reporter with the International News Service managed to get an interview with Kathryn shortly after she was returned to the county lockup. She was aggravated by the events of the day and distressed by the news that her mother wouldn't be allowed to go to the same prison where she would be.

"They couldn't be so cruel as to separate us," she told the journalist. "If they sent us to the same place where I can watch after my mother and know that she is near me, I'll be a good prisoner. If they don't, I'll go stark, raving crazy.[56]

"I do know they're going to put me into a good strong place that will be hard to get out of. They know I have plenty of friends who will come and get me if I say the word. But if I can be with my mother I don't want to escape.

"My heart got me into this jam. If I'd let myself be ruled by my head instead of my heart, I'd never have been in this mess. Funny thing about a woman if she loves a man she'll do anything for him.[57]

"Men. I ought to be through with men forever. If I ever get out of this pickle, I'll steer clear of them. I'll paddle my own canoe."[58]

On the morning of October 13, 1933, guards at the Oklahoma County jail led Kelly to Kathryn's cell so the couple could say goodbye to each other. With tears standing in her eyes, Kathryn stretched out her hand through the bars and stroked Kelly's cheek. They kissed each other and she told him to be a "good boy." Armed police officers and federal agents hurried Kelly out of the building and transported him to an armored train with barred windows that was bound for Kansas.[59]

Judge Vaught gave Kathryn permission for a supervised meeting between her mother, stepfather, and daughter. The purpose of the meeting was to discuss the disposal of their property and decide where Pauline would live. Kathryn deeded her home in Fort Worth to the teenager and turned over all the possessions in the house to her as well. Pauline wanted to return to the farm in Paradise, but Ora and Kathryn believed it would be best if she moved in with her aunt, Pearl Hopkins, whose home was in Asher, Oklahoma.

Kathryn gave her daughter a hug and told her to "be sweet." Kathryn then grabbed her mother and held her close for a long moment. She was filled with remorse over what she'd allowed to happen to her parents and fought to keep from crying hysterically.[60]

Kathryn and Ora were escorted from the common room where they had all met to their jail cells. Boss Shannon was given time to get his outside affairs in order before his incarceration began. He made sure Pauline was taken care of during that time. Kathryn turned to look back at her daughter as she was being led away from the young girl. "Goodbye, darling," she offered before disappearing from sight.[61]

Alone in her holding cell later that evening, Kathryn sat on her cot writing a letter to her husband about all that had transpired and what was to come.

"My Dear Husband, no doubt you are back at Leavenworth by now. I really had my misgivings yesterday tho' it being Friday the 13th. I was sure the train would wreck or you'd get hurt. You know my superstitious nature.[62]

"I have a much worse cold today. Have just sent after some Vicks Vapor rub [sic] and I really feel sick, but will be all right soon I hope. I will be awfully glad when I leave here. Anything for a change, however, two of the jailers here have been awfully kind and nice to me, the others hate me, I suppose.

"It is much more lonely for me, Dear, since you left. Just the thought of you here in the building was worth a lot. I do hope I can be with mother to cheer her up. I am going to try my best to be a model prisoner if with her and perhaps she can make parole, if I can't later. As for me personally, I'd just as soon be inside as out, without you, and you know that. So, don't worry about me, Honey. My life is so wrapped up with you I wouldn't enjoy my pleasure outside without you anyway, Dear.[63]

"I do hope you will try to be a good prisoner, Sweetheart. The cards are stacked against you, so, be man enough to realize it and don't give them a chance to murder you. That's what they want. I know how good and sweet you are, Dear, and I will always adore you and that's all that really matters. You have been and will always be the one great love of my life and if it is God's will to separate us forever that cannot destroy our love. And I don't believe that is his will for he alone realizes that you and I never harmed anyone and that we've helped hundreds of the needy. And I think we will be together in the future.

"None of the accused have been given justice here. You know, and a very bad picture has been painted of us and poor old sweet mother, but Honey, the public doesn't know, so don't feel hard about it. Nobody likes a squealer and altho' they deserved it, let the smart guys figure it out, if they can. They could have cleared me but rather than talk, I'd rather be here.[64]

"Think of me, Sweetheart, and I shall be thinking of you constantly. Try to be satisfied and don't worry. Just remember the happy hours we've enjoyed together. Nobody can take those away and we have been happier in the past three years than most people have thro' a lifetime, Darling.

"With a heart full of love and a big Kiss. Until death us do part. Your very own. Kathryn."[65]

If Judge Vaught had his way, Kelly wouldn't have been allowed to live to receive love letters from the woman who claimed in court to have been afraid of him. The judge would have sentenced Kelly to the gallows if he'd had the option. He made his thoughts known to Homer Stille Cummings, attorney general of the United States, a month after the Kellys were tried. He urged the appointed official to amend the Federal Kidnapping Law to provide for the death penalty. The judge argued that it was cruel to the survivors of such horror to continue struggling to get beyond the trauma of such an ordeal while the guilty moved forward, refusing to recognize the severity of their actions.[66]

CHAPTER 12

THE VERDICT

THE MISSOURI-KANSAS-TEXAS passenger train clattered mournfully on well-worn tracks as it headed toward the Union Station in Kansas City, Missouri. George "Machine Gun" Kelly sat shackled and handcuffed, staring out the steel-meshed, covered window of the specially built prisoner car. It was mid-October 1933, and the green flags of the trees had become sepia toned, waving in the southerly wind. Within the multitude of soft chocolatey browns, a mixture of golds and reds were shining through. Had he not been bound for the Leavenworth Penitentiary, Kelly might have taken more notice of the majestic colors that came with the late-changing season. Instead, he sat in silence, impassive, emotionless.[1]

Beyond the trees was a panorama of rolling hills and the muddy Missouri River. Traveling through the area three months prior to collect the ransom money for kidnap victim Charles Urschel, Kelly was filled with promise for the future for himself and his wife, Kathryn. Going forward all was bleak and hopeless, but the convicted felon had no intention of letting the armed Bureau of Investigation agents around him know that's what he was feeling. He wouldn't give them the satisfaction.

The officers were on heightened alert when the M-K-T train slowed to a stop at Union Station. Fearful some of Kelly's fellow criminals would try to help him escape, the authorities were ready to battle anyone who posed a threat. They'd not been prepared in June 1933, when the Kansas City Massacre occurred. Law enforcement agents escorting Kelly to the prison hadn't any intention of seeing history repeat itself.[2]

The October 14, 1933, edition of the *Commercial Appeal* reported that an army of federal, state, county, and city officers were present at the railyard when the train carrying Kelly pulled into the popular station. They took positions on either side of the vehicle, brandishing weapons of every type. Reporters were allowed up to the car but not inside. One of the Bureau agents shared with the press that Kelly had boasted on the trip from Oklahoma City that "the prison walls weren't been built strong" and that he would "be out of stir inside of eight days."[3]

Kelly had no way of knowing that even as he issued the threat, Alcatraz in San Francisco Bay, a military prison since 1859, had been transferred from the War Department to the Department of Justice and was in the process of being prepared to receive the nation's six hundred most vicious captives. Kelly would be one of them. His stay at Leavenworth would be temporary. Among his future penitentiary roommates at Alcatraz would be his old friend Harvey Bailey, Irish mobster Terry Druggan, and Al Capone.[4]

After allowing US Marshal W. C. "Rube" Geers and seven of his deputies, all of whom would serve as added security to assure Kelly's arrival at Leavenworth, to board in Kansas City, the train crept forward. It would not stop again until it reached the Kansas penitentiary. Kelly gave a wave to the G-men lining the track. He then stared quietly out the window and watched the cityscape fade from sight.

Throughout the duration of J. Edgar Hoover's time as director of the Bureau of Investigation, he perpetuated the myth that Kelly was the first to refer to his agents as G-men. The Bureau's part in capturing Machine Gun Kelly and other notorious gangsters like John Dillinger proved to the American public that the organization could wage war against crime and win. The mistakes the Bureau had made overseeing the Lindbergh baby kidnapping, which threatened to end the organization, had been corrected. The agency went on to develop a national fingerprinting system, and successfully pushed to have forced abductions recognized as a federal crime in order that the Bureau could pursue criminals across state lines.[5]

Director Hoover, a master at public relations, frequently announced the accomplishments of his agency, which included stories about how lawbreakers were fearful of the Bureau. The tenacity of Hoover's G-men and the many arrests they made prompted the government to expand the agency's powers. In 1935, the Bureau of Investigation officially became the Federal Bureau of Investigation. According to Hoover, "In the lawless era of the 1930s, this institution was the answer of progressive police agencies to the momentous crisis which confronted law enforcement and law-abiding citizens. ... The dangerous tenor of the times demanded immediate remedial action."[6]

Hoover served as the head of the FBI for more than three decades. When asked about his achievements in criminology, he readily admitted that "The most effective weapon against crime is cooperation. ... It's the efforts of all law enforcement agencies with the support and understanding of the American people." Hoover recognized the support and significant role Charles Urschel played in helping the Bureau apprehend his kidnappers. "Perhaps I should have at an earlier date advised you of my gratification because of your wholehearted cooperation with this Division in its conduct of the investigation of the kidnapping of which you are the victim," Hoover wrote to Charles Urschel in November 1933. "I thank you sincerely for your cooperation and extend to you my congratulations upon the successful presentation of this case, to which you contributed in no little degree."[7]

The editors of the *Oklahoma News* also acknowledged the oil tycoon's assistance. "Urschel's resourcefulness and nerve were the most important factors in the solution of the crime," an article in the October 31, 1933, edition of the publication read.[8]

The courage and commendable conduct of Charles Urschel and the combined efforts of numerous investigators led to the arrest and conviction of more than fifteen people in the Urschel kidnapping case, including those who helped launder the ransom money and harbored the fugitives who perpetrated the crime. All had been sentenced and were sent to various institutions throughout the country, including Kathryn Kelly.

On Monday, October 16, 1933, Kathryn and her mother, Ora Shannon, were ushered under heavy guard from the Oklahoma County jail to the train station, where they were placed aboard the Rock Island train. US Marshal Geers, who had just returned to Oklahoma from accompanying Kelly to Leavenworth, was placed in charge of shepherding Kathryn and her mother to their next stop. The two women were allowed a brief visit with Boss Shannon before they left the area. The three broke into tears as they said their goodbyes.[9]

Ora Shannon was to be delivered to the penal farm in Shelby County, Tennessee. Kathryn would go on to the Cincinnati work-house. Unbeknownst to Bureau agents, until mother and daughter were en route to the two prisons, the desperate Mrs. Kelly had offered E. E. Herron, the night jailer at the Oklahoma County jail, several thousand dollars to help her escape. She told the man that if he would allow her to "call a certain telephone number in Oklahoma City" that a male friend, who had been in the vicinity the entire time, would come to a specific block of the jail to help her. Kathryn told Herron that if he took her to that block she would give him fifteen thousand dollars. She told the jailer that she had another twelve thousand (presumably ransom money) she claimed to have buried. She informed him that she "would let it rot there before giving it up" and promised to discuss the additional funds with the guard when he came to take her to the block of the jail, where she could make her getaway.[10]

Kathryn and Ora spoke occasionally to each other during the trip. At one point, Kathryn was overheard telling her mother, "I can really be a good woman when I want to. They think I'm a bad woman." Ora was heard saying, "Kathryn, I've always been a good woman. I wouldn't know how to be otherwise."[11]

The women were nearly inconsolable when they parted company at the train station in Memphis. They hugged each other and sobbed loudly. As they led Ora off the train, Kathryn promised her mother she would be a "model" prisoner.

"They've crucified me," Ora called out to her daughter. "They are pinning me to the cross for something I don't know anything about. The only thing we were guilty of is having too much confidence in other people." She waved and blew a kiss to her daughter as authorities led her toward a vehicle to transport her to the institution.[12]

"Mother won't live long in prison," Kathryn told US Marshal Geers as she watched the grieving woman being loaded into a paddy wagon. "Someday I'm going to write a book about this and get some money to take care of Pauline," she said aloud to no one in particular. "I can write. I used to write short stories. I should be able to sell the kind of book I'm thinking about. A lot of thieves probably would read it, anyway."[13]

Like her mother, Kathryn was made to work in the sewing room when she arrived at the Ohio institution. Prisoners made all the clothes worn there. She ran a sewing machine, knitted, and darned. The only writing she did, though, was in the letters penned to her mother, daughter, Kelly, and J. Edgar Hoover. In November 1933, Kathryn wrote to Hoover, trying to negotiate her release. If she was allowed to leave the prison, she promised to lead the authorities to known wanted criminals and the individual who knew the whereabouts of several thousands of dollars of the Urschel money yet to be accounted for.[14]

"This will be a very difficult proposition, as the wanted people are not only dangerous but clever, but after a careful study from every angle, I am sure my plan cannot fail. If you desire to assist me, I know these people, I know their ways, and I know just how cautious they are. I will not do anything for the government in the hopes of obtaining leniency for myself, for I am doing fine. My life doesn't matter much anyway, but I do pray that my mother and father are given some consideration. They are not criminals but honest, good citizens, loving our government.[15]

"Kelly is responsible for their imprisonment. You people know that and you don't realize how good and honest mother and father are and to give them a sentence like Kelly and Bates is unjust. They would be an asset to society if released instead of a nuisance and my little daughter needs my mother so badly now.

"I know you are doing all you can to rid the country of the criminal element but if some of the bigshots were convicted it would cause so much fear among the smaller fry they might turn to a legitimate method of earning a livelihood. I am awfully square, Mr. Hoover, everyone that knows me can vouch for that. I don't double-cross anybody and a promise is sacred with me. This terrible notoriety from the press paints me quite a different person, but most of that source of publicity was lies.[16]

"I have no desire to escape prison only honorably. My people mean more to me than all the world I would gladly sit in the electric chair to free them anytime.

"There are now among you my close acquaintances Miller, Phillips, LaRue, Bentz, and probably a dozen more in the Twin Cities, and Chicago, and I will devote my entire life toward aiding you if you can be sure of talking to the right parties from your office. And my plan isn't parole, for they would be suspicious of that instantly and my worries wouldn't be over. I do desire to cooperate with you in every way possible, hoping I may aid my parents. And if you are interested, you may talk with me or send someone you have confidence in.

"Yours Truly, Kathryn Kelly."[17]

Director Hoover did not respond to Kathryn's letter or take her up on the offer to help the Bureau do their job. Until early 1934, additional correspondence from her to the FBI was also ignored. The deal Kathryn proposed in March of that year sparked an interest with Bureau officials, however. She promised to provide investigators with valuable information about the key players involved in the Kansas City Massacre in exchange for radio privileges and permission to exchange letters with her daughter. The information Kathryn offered proved to be important and her requests were granted.[18]

Less than a year after Kelly arrived at Leavenworth, he was moved to San Francisco. On September 4, 1934, he was transported by train to the Bay Area, where he was placed on a boat and taken to Alcatraz. Conditions at the newly opened facility were less than idyllic. The first glimpse filled him with grim foreboding. There was little vegetation on the rock island. It was always foggy and damp, and even in the summer it could be cold. The prison warden insisted on strict routines and obedient guards kept inmates in line.[19]

For the first six years, Kelly was limited to the number of letters he could write Kathryn or receive from her. Also, their correspondence was scrutinized by the guards at Alcatraz, which irritated Kelly. He hated having his letters to his wife censored. His frustration with the situation crept over in the notes he sent Kathryn. He threatened to stop writing because he was so annoyed at how the guards redacted sections that described his love and desire for her. Her response at times was biting. She was experiencing her own issues with being confined. Prison had changed her, and personal reflection had led her to see things differently than she had when they were first married.[20]

"My Dearest Bear, I have thought in vain of how to word a reply to you that would express exactly how I feel about us," Kathryn wrote Kelly in September 1940, "and I find that it is most difficult to do. Your letter touched my heart. In fact, I cried when I read it as I expected quite a different wording. I shrink from hurting you. That is the farthest desire of my heart. Naturally I did not think that you would be very hurt as long as you had cancelled your correspondence to me. I suppose the best thing I can do is to simply speak plainly and exactly how I feel.[21]

"First, please understand that I'm not 'cracking up', neither is prison getting me down, and in dismissing the love angle, which I admit is hard to do, I feel like this: that to help you in any manner I would gladly give my life, but I can't feel that I have added to you in any manner by consistently trying to encourage you by writing you the long cheerful letters that I have these years. I tried my level best to help you in doing your time, but it seems I failed miserably. Don't think that I even considered you less strong than myself. I haven't but I always feel that if either of us needed encouragement, I should attempt to give it to you because my surroundings have no doubt been more pleasing than yours.[22]

"I longed for you to avoid trouble, to stand on your own feet for what you know is right and minutely be the man you really are. Well, it seems you fell down on the job. I know you have acted up in some manner, so I feel that if maintaining your position as a prison politician, big shot, or something comes first in your thoughts. Then why should I hang onto a dream that could never come true? Unless you have changed a lot, darling. Even if we two were free tomorrow we should be forced to say goodbye. Why? Well, because I'm happy to say that I know I shall never place myself nor permit myself to be placed in a position to ever re-enter prison. I shall be just a little fish so speaking if I am fortunate enough to get that one chance and like it. No more 'big dough' for me in any place. In other words, I find that I am completely cured of any craving for un-legitimate luxuries and my sincere hopes and plans for the future are of a sane, balanced mode in living. I'll never change on that viewpoint. I have gone through hell and still am plainly speaking, seeing mother as a daily reminder of my own mistake. The mistake was in my love and marriage to you.[23]

"Not that I censure you, I don't. I blame myself. However, I've woke up. I hoped you would but I'm not sure of what goes on in your mind. As you know, I like to finish things immediately and I feel if our goodbye is to come, why not now? The hurt will at least be dimmed in the years of incarceration yet ahead of both of us. I've never told you that I did not love you and I never shall. I said that 'I would be happier even in prison' and I would. For I do worry about you and wonder. Love isn't everything in life. A content, peaceful existence, free from worry is most essential and I can dismiss love from my heart when my brain informs me it's best.[24]

"The reason you gave for cancelling your correspondence was a small rebellious boy's reason. Rules are rules in an institution and necessary. And I know that no mail censor would select your letters to heavily censor. You are just another number, the same as I, and the quicker you grasp that fact the better off you'll be.

". . . I know you thoroughly, honey, so don't think I'm harsh. What you need to do is to forget 'Machine Gun' Kelly and what he stood for and interest yourself in being plain, kind George, who is just another con like myself.[25]

". . . You should have found your true, honest self by now. You were never bad. We both simply thought wrong. . . . I will write you on the 1st, so keep smiling and try to see our problem as I see it and don't feel bad. I am devotedly yours, Kathryn."[26]

Like his wife, Kelly penned letters to government officials asking to be released. In a note sent to U S Attorney General Homer Cummings dated February 3, 1936, Kelly proposed he spend his time in a way that would be more beneficial to the country.

"Dear Sir, I am writing you regarding a plan I have had in mind for several months. I realize it is unusual and that no precedent has ever been set for such issue but I understand that as Attorney General it is within your power to designate the place a federal prisoner must serve his sentence. As you know, I am serving a life sentence for kidnapping, without any possible chance of ever being paroled.[27]

"The United States government has uninhabited islands in the Pacific, smaller than Wake or Midway. There is Admiral Byrd's abandoned camp at the South Pole, also extremely isolated outposts in Alaska. I feel certain there is at least one of these or some other place, where the government would like the atmospheric conditions studied over a long period of time. I know with the proper instruments and books I could make a meteorology survey of such a place that would be of benefit to science and the government.

"My idea is that such a place that has never been thoroughly studied, would be too lonesome and desolate for any free man to care to stay there longer than a few months, even if he had company.

"I could be taken from here secretly, placed on a boat in the Bay, and transported with what supplies I would need. This could be managed in such a way that the crew need never know who I was or even that I was a prisoner from Alcatraz. Some kind of arrangement could be made for a boat to stop say every year or two, leave supplies and take back what data I had accumulated.[28]

"By this method, I would be doing some useful work, serving my sentence and I believe by the time I was eligible for parole I would be shown some consideration.

"With the rapid strides that aviation is making, wind conditions and air currents will have to be studied all over the world. Two years ago, the islands the China Clipper was using on its flights to Manila were practically useless, but today they are the steppingstones to the Orient, and meteorology conditions must be known at such places, and lots of time and money would be saved by knowing their conditions in advance.

"This may seem like a hairbrained proposition to you, but I think it altogether feasible.[29]

"Hoping something can be done along those lines. I remain, Yours Truly, Geo. R. Kelly."[30]

Kelly wrote more than one letter asking to be transferred to another institution. He complained that the lack of sunshine and the cold, high winds at Alcatraz were affecting his health. He also wanted to be at a prison where he could work to earn some money to send Kathryn and her mother. He felt guilty that his wife "rarely has any money for the few trifles that she needs such as a newspaper, rouge, lipstick, and cigarettes."[31]

In early April 1940, Kelly was given permission to write a letter to Charles Urschel. He wanted to make sure the oil tycoon knew how much he had suffered since being locked away. He stopped short of apologizing for what he'd done to him but did admit he was ashamed of his actions toward him in court. "These five words seem written in fire on the walls of my cell," Kelly shared with Urschel, "Nothing can be worth this!"[32]

Kelly's requests to be relocated were granted in June 1951, when he was sent back to Leavenworth. He died of a heart attack the day before his fifty-fourth birthday on July 17, 1954. His father-in-law, Boss Shannon, who had been released in 1944, after President Franklin Roosevelt reduced his sentence, had Kelly buried at the Cottondale Community Cemetery, five miles from the Shannon farm in Paradise.[33]

Albert Bates, Kelly's accomplice in the kidnapping, had died six years earlier of a heart attack on July 4, 1948, while continuing to serve his time at Alcatraz. He was fifty-seven years old.[34]

In 1942, Kathryn was transferred to the Alderson Reformatory for Women in Alderson, West Virginia, where her mother had been transferred. In the fall of 1948, both women applied for parole after serving fifteen years each. The parole board denied their petitions.

In 1951, David Dressler, director of the New York State Division of Parole, speculated that Kathryn and Ora's parole was denied because their records showed that women gangsters in the 1930s proved to be deadlier than males.

"In 1933, some 22,948 females were arrested for major crimes," Dressler told a reporter with the *San Angelo Evening Standard*. "Women are natural gun-toters. Mobsters' molls have become common. Women like Kathryn Kelly, they comfort their men, carry the rods so that a cop's frisk won't reveal anything incriminating on the male suspect. Kathryn not only used a gun but blueprinted her husband's jobs and instilled in the cowardly George enough courage to carry out the plan."[35]

In late 1957, Kathryn and Ora sought help from a criminal lawyer named James Laughlin. The attorney had represented high-profile clients such as serial killer Charles Starkweather and American broadcaster-turned-Nazi propagandist Mildred Gillars. On March 20, 1958, Laughlin filed a motion for the release of the mother and daughter from prison. The motions contended that in the 1933 trials in federal court, "the constitutional rights of the women were violated because they did not have proper representation, false testimony was used against them, and their trials were conducted amidst publicity which prevented fair and impartial hearings."[36]

According to an article in the March 20, 1958, edition of the *Daily Oklahoman*, in the affidavit, Kathryn Kelly alleges, "She was not given ample time to prepare a defense." She noted that the lawyers didn't want to attempt to confer with their clients because the Bureau of Investigation insisted they listen in on all conversations between them. Kathryn claimed that "the day she was brought to trial she walked alongside her husband" and that both were handcuffed and chained and surrounded by thirty Bureau agents and Texas Rangers, and at least ten of those individuals had drawn shotguns. "As she was led into the building," the affidavit continued, "she was subjected to hissing, booing, and shouting. . . . Many people tried to strike her." It also alleged that her attorneys were intimidated because all defense attorneys were suspected of receiving ransom money.[37]

Ora Shannon's affidavit complained her attorneys were subjected to "merciless interrogation" by the Bureau of Investigation and "there always loomed large the danger of criminal prosecution." She also charged that E. E. Kirkpatrick, brother-in-law of Charles Urschel, was permitted to sit at the trial table and that this was prejudicial to her defense. It also was alleged that her defense was further prejudiced by the trial being held while newspapers were full of the story of the search for her notorious son-in-law, who was still at large.[38]

A hearing was granted for Kathryn and her mother and set for June 9, 1958. When Kathryn took the stand, she testified that Bureau of Investigation agents who arrested her in 1933 refused to allow her to get a lawyer until she had been questioned and threatened by at least eighty officers. "They told me they were going to sentence me to life or death in the electric chair and I didn't need counsel," she told the court.[39]

Herbert Hyde, former prosecuting attorney, testified on behalf of the government and defended the initial court cases against both women. He denied Kathryn's claim that eighty officers had questioned her about the case. Hyde noted that only seven or eight agents were assigned to the case.[40]

Kathryn said her attorney, James Mathers, and presiding judge, Edgar Vaught, urged her to plead guilty. Ora Shannon said one statement she allegedly signed was "mostly false and another was not even made by her."[41]

James Mathers was called to address Kathryn's statements about the threatening letters written to kidnap victim Charles Urschel. "Mrs. Kelly told me she wrote those notes, and that her husband made her do it and she was afraid she'd be killed if she didn't," Mathers testified.[42]

After more than a week reexamining the particulars of both trials, Judge William Wallace set aside the life sentences for the women and granted them new trials. The US Justice Department fought the judge's decision but lost. A new trial was never rescheduled; it is believed because J. Edgar Hoover did not want the FBI subjected to scrutiny. The director was against handing over twenty-five-year-old documents pertaining to the case. Judge Wallace's nullification of Kathryn and Ora's sentence stood.[43]

When Kathryn Kelly and Ora Shannon were released from prison in mid-June 1958, they were fifty-four and seventy years old. Both were now widows. Boss Shannon had passed away at his farm on Christmas Day in 1956.[44]

Mother and daughter settled in Oklahoma, where Kathryn got a job as a bookkeeper at a nursing home. She supported herself and Ora on a two hundred dollar a month salary. Kathryn visited Kelly's grave only once, in 1959. She and her mother returned to Paradise for a family reunion and she drove to the cemetery to pay her respects. The original grave marker her stepfather had purchased for Kelly's grave had been stolen and replaced with a headstone.[45]

Although Kathryn and her mother tried to live a quiet life out of the media spotlight, newspaper reporters came calling whenever a special anniversary associated with the famous Urschel kidnapping occurred. In 1962, the *Saturday Evening Post* printed a story about the crime and published facts about the case that hadn't been brought to life until then—facts such as Kathryn's attempt to bribe a prison official to help her escape prison. "Why can't they leave us alone?!" Kathryn tearfully replied when a reporter from the *Daily Oklahoman* visited her to ask about the *Post* article. "All we ask is to be allowed to live like everybody else," she said. "My mother is seventy-two years old* and these constant reminders are hard on her. . . . I'm afraid I'm going to lose my job if this constant barrage of publicity keeps up."[46]

Kathryn decided to begin life again in Oklahoma because that was where her daughter, Pauline, had been living while she was in prison. Pauline did well in school and was able to attend East Central University in Ada, Oklahoma, through the benevolence of Charles Urschel. For years, Pauline believed Judge Edgar Vaught was providing the funds, but he had merely been acting on the instructions of the Urschel family. In the summer of 1938, Pauline married a

---

* Ora was older than seventy-two. Perhaps Kathryn forgot her actual age or was too flustered to remember correctly.

schoolteacher named Olin Glen Horn. The pair had two children together.[47]

Oil tycoon and philanthropist Charles Urschel passed away on September 26, 1970. He and his wife had relocated to San Antonio after the Kellys' trial. His wife, Berenice, had died in 1969. Both were in their eighties. Although his accomplishments across the globe were many, newspapers recalled the famous kidnapping case in every article about him at the time of his demise.[48]

Kathryn Kelly died on May 28, 1985, at the age of eighty-one. She was buried beside her mother at the Tecumseh Cemetery in Tecumseh, Oklahoma. Ora had passed away on May 21, 1980. Kathryn's daughter, Pauline, passed away on December 31, 2005. She was eighty-six.[49]

Geralene Arnold made her last appearance before a live audience to tell of her experiences with Kathryn and Machine Gun Kelly in late June 1934, after a drawn-out legal battle to acquire the fifteen-thousand-dollar reward offered for the outlaws "dead or alive." C. F. Colcord, Charles Urschel's wealthy friend who underwrote the substantial reward, argued that Geralene, who provided information to the authorities that led them to Kathryn and Kelly, was not entitled to any of the money. He claimed Bureau agents already had the information she furnished and therefore was owed nothing.[50]

Luther Arnold retained an attorney for his daughter to fight for the funds, and on June 18, 1934, the court agreed that the young girl should be given four thousand dollars of the reward. After legal fees were paid, Geralene was left with two thousand dollars. Her parents purchased clothes for the family, a new car, and had plans to buy a chicken ranch in Tucson, Arizona.[51]

Flossie and Luther did not let Geralene's entertainment manager, K. Lee Williams, know they were pulling their daughter out of the vaudeville circuit he had arranged for her to take part in. When she failed to appear at a theater in Oklahoma City, Williams traveled from his office in Dallas to look for her. He learned then that the trio had departed for the Southwest.[52]

By September 1934, the Arnolds were living in Albuquerque, New Mexico, and doing everything they could to avoid the public spotlight. Geralene was schooled at home by a private tutor until she graduated high school.[53] On April 26, 1937, Geralene married a welder named Clifford Courtney. The couple had a daughter in December 1941, and were divorced in the summer of 1948.[54]

When Geralene left the limelight in June 1934, nine-year-old Charles Demsey Floyd, son of Pretty Boy Floyd, took her place on stage. Audiences complained that "little Charles's life as a son of a gangster was nowhere near as exciting as Geralene Arnold's time on the run from the law with the Kellys."[55]

ACKNOWLEDGMENTS

J. EDGAR HOOVER ONCE SAID, "There's something addictive about secrets." I want to thank Gary Goldstein for the opportunity to explore the secrets of Kathryn Thorne and her unfortunate husband, George "Machine Gun" Kelly. It truly was addictive.

Among those I owe a debt of gratitude for helping me uncover the Kellys' secrets are John Slate at the Dallas Municipal Archives, Jon May, photograph archives specialist at the Oklahoma Historical Society, and author Laurie Cockerell for accompanying me to Paradise, Texas, where the research for the story began. I'm grateful to the National Archives staff in Washington, DC, who aided in tracking down the Federal Bureau of Investigation documents relating to the Kellys and the other gangsters with whom they were associated.

BIBLIOGRAPHY

BOOKS

Barnes, Bruce, *Machine Gun Kelly: To Right a Wrong* (Perris, CA: Tipper Publications, 1991).

Burrough, Bryan, *Public Enemies: America's Greatest Crime Wave and the Birth of the FBI, 1933–34* (New York: Penguin, 2004).

Casey, Barbara, *Kathryn Kelly: The Moll Behind "Machine Gun" Kelly* (Rock Hill, SC: Strategic Media Books, Inc., 2016).

Casey, Orben J. *And Justice for All: The Legal Profession in Oklahoma, 1821–1989* (Oklahoma City, OK: Oklahoma Heritage Association, 1989).

Cook, William A. *The Lindbergh Baby Kidnapping* (Mechanicsburg, PA, Sunbury Press, 2014).

Cox, Carolyn, *The Snatch Racket: The Kidnapping Epidemic That Terrorized 1930s America* (Lincoln, NE, Potomac Books, 2021).

Flynn, Elizabeth Gurley, *The Alderson Story: My Life as a Political Prisoner* (New York: International Publishers, 1963).

Halye, J. Evetts, *Robbing Banks Was My Business: The Story of J. Harvey Bailey, America's Most Successful Bank Robber* (Canyon, TX: Palo Duro Press, 1973).

Hamilton, Stanley. *Machine Gun Kelly's Last Stand* (Lawrence, KS: University of Kansas, 2003).

Houts, Marshall, *From Gun to G.avel: The Courtroom Recollections of James Mathers of Oklahoma as Told to Marshall Houts* (New York: William Morrow & Company, 1954).

Kirkpatrick, E. E. *Crimes' Paradise: The Authentic Inside Story of the Urschel Kidnapping* (San Antonio, TX, The Naylor Company, 1934).

———, *Voices from Alcatraz: The Authentic Inside Story of the Urschel Kidnapping* (San Antonio, TX: The Naylor Company, 1947).

Newton, Michael, *The Encyclopedia of Robberies, Heists, and Capers* (New York: Checkmark Books, 2002).

River, Charles, *Machine Gun Kelly: The Notorious Life and Crimes of the Depression Era Gangster* (Ann Arbor, MI: Charles River Editors, 2019).

Sinclair, Andrew, *Era of Excess: A Social History of the Prohibition Movement* (New York: Harper, 1964).

Smith, Robert B. & Yadon, Lawrence J., *Oklahoma Scoundrels: History's Most Notorious Outlaws, Bandits & Gangsters* (Charleston, SC: The History Press, 2016).

Theoharis, Athan, *From the Secret Files of J. Edgar Hoover* (Chicago: Ivan R. Dee, 1993).

Urschel, Joe, *The Year of Fear: Machine Gun Kelly and the Manhunt That Changed the Nation* (New York: Minotaur Books, 2015).

Weiner, Tim, *Enemies: A History of the FBI* (New York: Random House, 2013).

Encyclopedias/Historical Archives/Journals

Division of Investigation, US Department of Justice, Washington, DC, George R. Kelly Arrest Record, USP-AC Form 175-11-26-35-400

Frontier Times Magazine, Vol. 21, No. 1, Gus T. Jones Retires from FBI, August 29, 1934

Funk & Wagnalls *New Encyclopedia,* Vol. 15, Federal Bureau of Investigation, pg. 293–8

Funk & Wagnalls *New Encyclopedia,* Vol. 19, Pfitzner to Punic Wars, pg. 383–4

George Kelly letter to Attorney General Homer Cummings dated February 3, 1936

George Kelly letter to Warden Jas. A. Johnstow dated September 26, 1941

George Kelly letter to Warden Jas. A. Johnstow dated April 7, 1945

J. Edgar Hoover letter to Law Enforcement Officials dated July 1, 1955

Kathryn Kelly letter to George R. Kelly dated September 11, 1940

Kathryn Kelly letter to J. Edgar Hoover dated November 1933

Minnesota Historical Society, St. Paul Gangster History Collection, Keating, Francis L. "Jimmy" (robber); Federal Bureau of Prisons File, 1928–1946, 2 Folders; Keating-Holden-Nash (National Archives record group 129, file 4-4-11-10 regarding escaped federal prisoners), 2 Folders

Special Agent in Charge Colvin letter to Bureau Director J. Edgar Hoover, dated October 24, 1933, Regarding Kathryn Kelly's Attempt to Bribe Jailer

Special Agent in Charge Melvin Purvis letter to Bureau Director J. Edgar Hoover dated December 18, 1933

Special Agent in Charge Whitley letter to Bureau Director J. Edgar Hoover, dated November 8, 1933, Regarding Louise Donavon Background/Aliases

Tennessee Quarterly, Vol. 24, No. 4, Memphis, Tennessee, 1965

US Bureau of Investigation, Department of Justice, Washington, DC, #56111, July 25, 1933

US Bureau of Investigation Report, Vol. 2, No. 6, Fugitives Wanted by Police by J. Edgar Hoover, June 1933

US Bureau of Investigation, Transcript of Interview between BI Agent Gus Jones and Charles Urschel dated August 8, 1933

US Department of Justice, Federal Bureau of Investigation, Albert Bates File

US Department of Justice, Federal Bureau of Investigation, Bremer Kidnapping Part D09

US Department of Justice, Federal Bureau of Investigation, Letter from Agent F. J. Blake RE: Louise Donavon to Mary B. Harris, Federal Industrial Institution for Women, Dated July 24, 1933

US Department of Justice, Federal Bureau of Investigation, George (Machine Gun) Kelly File

US Department of Justice, Federal Bureau of Investigation, George (Machine Gun) Kelly & Kathryn Kelly, Geralene Arnold Statement & Testimony

US Department of Justice, Federal Bureau of Investigation, George (Machine Gun) Kelly & Kathryn Kelly Court/Trial Transcripts

US Department of Justice, Federal Bureau of Investigation, Kathryn Thorne Kelly File

Newspapers

Ada Morning Times, Ada, OK June 29, 1938

Albuquerque Journal, Albuquerque, NM March 5, 1927

Altus Times Democrat, Altus, OK October 9, 1933

Alva Review, Alva, OK October 6, 1933

Anadarko Daily News, Anadarko, OK October 11, 1933

Argus Press, Owosso, MI June 23, 1932

Austin American, Austin, TX July 24, 1933

Austin American, Austin, TX October 1, 1933

Austin American Statesman, Austin, TX August 23, 1930

Austin American Statesman, Austin, TX April 21, 1931

Austin American Statesman, Austin, TX May 5, 1933

Baltimore Sun, Baltimore, MD September 25, 1933

Bartlesville Daily Enterprise, Bartlesville, OK September 25, 1933

Bartlesville Daily Enterprise, Bartlesville, OK October 3, 1933

Bartlesville Daily Enterprise, Bartlesville, OK October 7, 1933

Bartlesville Daily Enterprise, Bartlesville, OK October 9, 1933

Bartlesville Daily Enterprise, Bartlesville, OK October 14, 1933

Blackwell Morning Tribune, Blackwell, OK August 1, 1933

Blackwell Morning Tribune, Blackwell, OK August 2, 1933

Bristow Daily Record, Bristow, OK October 11, 1933

Bristol Herold Courier, Bristol, TN September 27, 1933

Bristol News Bulletin, Bristol, TN September 26, 1933

Bristol News Bulletin, Bristol, TN September 27, 1933

Bryan County Democrat, Durant, OK October 12, 1933

Carnegie Herald, Carnegie, OK October 18, 1933

Chattanooga Daily Times, Chattanooga, TN October 2, 1933

Chattanooga Daily Times, Chattanooga, TN October 13, 1933

Chelsea Reporter, Chelsea, OK April 26, 1934

Chicago American, Chicago, IL September 26, 1933

Chicago Tribune, Chicago, IL September 18, 1933

Chicago Tribune, Chicago, IL September 27, 1933

Chicago Tribune, Chicago, IL September 29, 1933

Clarion Ledger, Jackson, MS August 25, 1933

Clinton Daily News, Clinton, OK October 9, 1933

Coleman Democrat, Coleman, TX February 2, 1928

Commercial Appeal, Memphis, TN November 10, 1917

Commercial Appeal, Memphis, TN October 8, 1919

Commercial Appeal, Memphis, TN October 23, 1920

Commercial Appeal, Memphis, TN November 16, 1920

Commercial Appeal, Memphis, TN January 31, 1922

Commercial Appeal, Memphis, TN February 5, 1922

Commercial Appeal, Memphis, TN March 8, 1922

Commercial Appeal, Memphis, TN April 30, 1922

Commercial Appeal, Memphis, TN August 8, 1922

Commercial Appeal, Memphis, TN October 29, 1926

Commercial Appeal, Memphis, TN October 30, 1926

Commercial Appeal, Memphis, TN January 19, 1927

Commercial Appeal, Memphis, TN September 22, 1933

Commercial Appeal, Memphis, TN September 26, 1933

Commercial Appeal, Memphis, TN September 27, 1933

Commercial Appeal, Memphis, TN September 28, 1933

Commercial Appeal, Memphis, TN September 29, 1933

Commercial Appeal, Memphis, TN October 1, 1933

Commercial Appeal, Memphis, TN October 2, 1933

Commercial Appeal, Memphis, TN October 12, 1933

Commercial Appeal, Memphis, TN October 13, 1933

Commercial Appeal, Memphis, TN October 14, 1933

Commercial Appeal, Memphis, TN October 18, 1933

Commercial Appeal, Memphis, TN October 22, 1933

Commercial Appeal, Memphis, TN October 29, 1933

Commercial Appeal, Memphis, TN June 19, 1934

Corsicana Daily Sun, Corsicana, TX April 30, 1928

Corsicana Daily Sun, Corsicana, TX April 7, 1931

Courier Gazette, McKinney, TX September 28, 1970

Cushing Daily Citizen, Cushing, OK October 2, 1933

Cushing Daily Citizen, Cushing, OK October 9, 1933

Cushing Daily Citizen, Cushing, OK October 11, 1933

Cushing Daily Citizen, Cushing, OK October 18, 1933

Coweta Times Sun, Coweta, OK May 17, 1934

Daily Ardmoreite, Ardmore, OK July 26, 1933

Daily Ardmoreite, Ardmore, OK October 10, 1933

Daily Herald, Biloxi, MS August 30, 1933

Daily Herald, Biloxi, MS November 30, 1932

Daily Journal Capital, Pawhuska, OK October 1, 1933

Daily News Journal, Murfreesboro, TN September 25, 1933

Daily Oklahoman, Oklahoma City, OK January 20, 1930

Daily Oklahoman, Oklahoma City, OK November 27, 1932

Daily Oklahoman, Oklahoma City, OK December 8, 1932

Daily Oklahoman, Oklahoma City, OK December 15, 1932

Daily Oklahoman, Oklahoma City, OK April 6, 1933

Daily Oklahoman, Oklahoma City, OK April 16, 1933

Daily Oklahoman, Oklahoma City, OK July 25, 1933

Daily Oklahoman, Oklahoma City, OK July 27, 1933

Daily Oklahoman, Oklahoma City, OK August 1, 1933

Daily Oklahoman, Oklahoma City, OK August 2, 1933

Daily Oklahoman, Oklahoma City, OK September 20, 1933

Daily Oklahoman, Oklahoma City, OK September 22, 1933

Daily Oklahoman, Oklahoma City, OK September 25, 1933

Daily Oklahoman, Oklahoma City, OK September 28, 1933

Daily Oklahoman, Oklahoma City, OK October 2, 1933

Daily Oklahoman, Oklahoma City, OK October 3, 1933

Daily Oklahoman, Oklahoma City, OK October 8, 1933

Daily Oklahoman, Oklahoma City, OK October 10, 1933

Daily Oklahoman, Oklahoma City, OK October 11, 1933

Daily Oklahoman, Oklahoma City, OK October 12, 1933

Daily Oklahoman, Oklahoma City, OK September 16, 1934

Daily Oklahoman, Oklahoma City, OK March 20, 1958

Daily Oklahoman, Oklahoma City, OK October 10, 1958

Daily Oklahoman, Oklahoma City, OK June 17, 1962

Democrat Voice, Coleman, TX May 2, 1928

Denton Record Chronicle, Denton, TX February 6, 1932

Denton Record Chronicle, Denton, TX July 25, 1933

Denton Record Chronicle, Denton, TX August 14, 1933

Des Moines Register, Des Moines, IA August 15, 1933

Des Moines Tribune, Des Moines, IA August 15, 1933

Dixon Evening Telegraph, Dixon, IL January 29, 1932

Drumright Weekly, Derrick Drumright, OK October 8, 1933

Duncan Banner, Duncan, OK October 3, 1933

El Paso Herald Post, El Paso, TX June 20, 1934

El Paso Herald Post, El Paso, TX September 14, 1934

El Paso Times, El Paso, TX March 5, 1927

El Paso Times, El Paso, TX July 24, 1933

El Paso Times, El Paso, TX June 20, 1934

El Reno Daily Tribune, El Reno, OK October 4, 1933

Elk City Daily News, Elk City, OK October 9, 1933

Enid Daily Eagle, Enid, OK October 3, 1933

Enid Daily Eagle, Enid, OK October 11, 1933

Enid Daily Eagle, Enid, OK October 12, 1933

Enid Morning News, Enid, OK October 3, 1933

Enid Morning News, Enid, OK October 11, 1933

Evansville Press, Evansville, IN October 3, 1933

Evening Derrick, Derrick, OK November 2, 1927

Evening Sun, Baltimore, MD May 7, 1931

Fletcher Herald, Fletcher, OK August 23, 1933

Fort Collins Express, Fort Collins, CO August 16, 1933

Fort Worth Record Telegram, Fort Worth, TX May 14, 1928

Fort Worth Record Telegram, Fort Worth, TX June 23, 1928

Fort Worth Record Telegram, Fort Worth, TX September 3, 1928

Fort Worth Record Telegram, Fort Worth, TX July 2, 1929

Fort Worth Star-Telegram, Fort Worth, TX September 11, 1927

Fort Worth Star-Telegram, Fort Worth, TX September 3, 1928

Fort Worth Star-Telegram, Fort Worth, TX November 19, 1929

Fort Worth Star-Telegram, Fort Worth, TX January 17, 1930

Fort Worth Star-Telegram, Fort Worth, TX January 25, 1930

Fort Worth Star-Telegram, Fort Worth, TX February 23, 1930

Fort Worth Star-Telegram, Fort Worth, TX May 4, 1930

Fort Worth Star-Telegram, Fort Worth, TX January 8, 1932

Fort Worth Star-Telegram, Fort Worth, TX February 7, 1932

Fort Worth Star-Telegram, Fort Worth, TX October 18, 1932

Fort Worth Star-Telegram, Fort Worth, TX October 21, 1932

Fort Worth Star-Telegram, Fort Worth, TX November 2, 1932

Fort Worth Star-Telegram, Fort Worth, TX November 13, 1932

Fort Worth Star-Telegram, Fort Worth, TX July 23, 1933

Fort Worth Star-Telegram, Fort Worth, TX August 15, 1933

Fort Worth Star-Telegram, Fort Worth, TX August 18, 1933

Fort Worth Star-Telegram, Fort Worth, TX August 19, 1933

Fort Worth Star-Telegram, Fort Worth, TX September 25, 1933

Fort Worth Star-Telegram, Fort Worth, TX September 26, 1933

Fort Worth Star-Telegram, Fort Worth, TX October 1, 1933

Fort Worth Star-Telegram, Fort Worth, TX October 7, 1933

Fort Worth Star-Telegram, Fort Worth, TX June 21, 1934

Fort Worth Star-Telegram, Fort Worth, TX November 1, 1944

Fort Worth Star-Telegram, Fort Worth, TX July 16, 1948

Fort Worth Star-Telegram, Fort Worth, TX June 9, 1958

Fort Worth Star-Telegram, Fort Worth, TX May 31, 1959

Frederick Leader, Frederick, OK July 24, 1933

Frederick Leader, Frederick, OK October 12, 1933

Gazette, Cedar Rapids, IA September 9, 1930

Greeley Daily Tribune, Greeley, CO August 16, 1933

Guthrie Daily Leader, Guthrie, OK September 17, 1933

Guthrie Daily Leader, Guthrie, OK October 12, 1933

Hobart Democrat Chief, Hobart, OK October 9, 1933

Holdenville Daily News, Holdenville, OK October 9, 1933

Hugo Daily News, Hugo, OK August 4, 1933

Hugo Daily News, Hugo, OK October 9, 1933

Hugo Daily News, Hugo, OK October 12, 1933

Hugo Daily News, Hugo, OK October 17, 1933

Indianapolis News, Indianapolis, IN February 26, 1932

Indianapolis News, Indianapolis, IN June 25, 1932

Indianapolis Star, Indianapolis, IN January 30, 1932

Iowa City Press Citizen, Iowa City, IA March 5, 1932

Kiowa County Review, Hobart, OK February 24, 1928

Knoxville News Sentinel, Knoxville, TN September 25, 1933

Kokomo Tribune, Kokomo, IN January 27, 1932

Lampasas Leader, Lampasas, TX September 29, 1933

Lawton Constitution, Lawton, OK October 9, 1933

Lawton News Review, Lawton, OK August 31, 1933

Lubbock Evening Journal, Lubbock, TX November 9, 1948

M'Alester News Capital, McAlester, OK October 17, 1933

M'Alester News Capital, McAlester, OK May 31, 1934

Mangum Daily Star, Mangum, OK October 5, 1933

Manhattan Mercury, Manhattan, KS March 1, 1930

Maud Daily Enterprise, Maud, OK October 10, 1933

Memphis Press Scimitar, Memphis, TN September 27, 1933

Memphis Press Scimitar, Memphis, TN September 28, 1933

Memphis Press Scimitar, Memphis, TN October 12, 1933

Memphis Press Scimitar, Memphis, TN October 13, 1933

Miami Daily News, Miami, OK July 27, 1933

Miami Daily News, Miami, OK September 20, 1933

Miami Daily News, Miami, OK October 9, 1933

Miami Daily News, Miami, OK October 9, 1933

Miami Daily News, Miami, OK October 17, 1933

Miami Daily News, Miami, OK April 29, 1934

Miami Daily News, Miami, OK March 20, 1958

Minneapolis Star, Minneapolis, MN August 8, 1933

Minneapolis Star, Minneapolis, MN August 9, 1933

Morning Examiner, Bartlesville, OK September 28, 1933

Morning Examiner, Bartlesville, OK October 13, 1933

Morning Tulsa Daily World, Tulsa, OK August 12, 1927

Muldrow Sun, Sallisaw, OK July 4, 1930

Muskogee Daily Phoenix, Muskogee, OK September 21, 1933

Muskogee Daily Phoenix, Muskogee, OK September 23, 1933

Muskogee Daily Phoenix, Muskogee, OK October 5, 1933

Muskogee Daily Phoenix, Muskogee, OK October 9, 1933

Muskogee Daily Phoenix, Muskogee, OK October 11, 1933

Muskogee Times Democrat, Muskogee, OK October 11, 1933

Nashua Reporter, Charles City, IA September 24, 1930

News Journal, Wilmington, DE March 2, 1932

New York Times, New York, NY March 3, 1932

New York Times, New York, NY October 1, 1963

Oklahoma County News, Jones, OK June 29, 1934

Oklahoma Daily, Norman, OK October 11, 1933

Oklahoma News, Oklahoma City, OK November 5, 1927

Oklahoma News, Oklahoma City, OK November 27, 1932

Oklahoma News, Oklahoma City, OK December 15, 1932

Oklahoma News, Oklahoma City, OK February 9, 1933

Oklahoma News, Oklahoma City, OK February 15, 1933

Oklahoma News, Oklahoma City, OK April 12, 1933

Oklahoma News, Oklahoma City, OK July 10, 1933

Oklahoma News, Oklahoma City, OK July 23, 1933

Oklahoma News, Oklahoma City, OK July 24, 1933

Oklahoma News, Oklahoma City, OK July 25, 1933

Oklahoma News, Oklahoma City, OK July 27, 1933

Oklahoma News, Oklahoma City, OK August 1, 1933

Oklahoma News, Oklahoma City, OK August 3, 1933

Oklahoma News, Oklahoma City, OK August 4, 1933

Oklahoma News, Oklahoma City, OK September 17, 1933

Oklahoma News, Oklahoma City, OK September 19, 1933

Oklahoma News, Oklahoma City, OK September 21, 1933

Oklahoma News, Oklahoma City, OK September 26, 1933

Oklahoma News, Oklahoma City, OK October 2, 1933

Oklahoma News, Oklahoma City, OK October 8, 1933

Oklahoma News, Oklahoma City, OK October 9, 1933

Oklahoma News, Oklahoma City, OK October 10, 1933

Oklahoma News, Oklahoma City, OK October 11, 1933

Oklahoma News, Oklahoma City, OK October 12, 1933

Oklahoma News, Oklahoma City, OK October 13, 1933

Oklahoma News, Oklahoma City, OK October 16, 1933

Oklahoma News, Oklahoma City, OK October 31, 1933

Oklahoma News, Oklahoma City, OK April 6, 1934

Oklahoma News, Oklahoma City, OK July 8, 1934

Oklahoma News Sun, Oklahoma City, OK September 19, 1933

Okmulgee Daily Times, Okmulgee, OK July 25, 1933

Okmulgee Daily Times, Okmulgee, OK August 2, 1933

Okmulgee Daily Times, Okmulgee, OK October 13, 1933

Okmulgee Daily Times, Okmulgee, OK October 18, 1933

Owosso Argus Press, Owosso, MI June 23, 1932

Pampa Daily News, Pampa, TX July 24, 1933

Parsons Sun, Parsons, KS June 17, 1958

Pensacola News Journal, Pensacola, FL October 13, 1933

Pineville Herald, Pineville, MO May 22, 1931

Pittsburg Press, Pittsburg, PA October 13, 1933

Reading Times, Reading, PA October 13, 1933

Reporter Times, Martinsville, IN January 27, 1932

Rushville Republican, Rushville, IN January 27, 1932

San Angelo Evening Standard, San Angelo, TX April 30, 1928

San Angelo Evening Standard, San Angelo, TX May 25, 1951

San Angelo Evening Standard, San Angelo, TX June 10, 1958

San Angelo Examiner, San Angelo, TX June 10, 1958

San Angelo Examiner, San Angelo, TX June 11, 1958

San Angelo Standard Times, San Angelo, TX July 18, 1954

San Antonio Express, San Antonio, TX August 29, 1933

San Francisco Examiner, San Francisco, CA July 6, 1948

Sapulpa Herald, Sapulpa, OK October 6, 1933

Sapulpa Herald, Sapulpa, OK October 9, 1933

Sapulpa Herald, Sapulpa, OK June 9, 1958

Sauk Centre Herald, Sauk Centre, MN July 24, 1930

Sayre Headlight, Sayre, OK October 3, 1933

Sayre Headlight, Sayre, OK October 5, 1933

Seminole Morning News, Seminole, OK March 13, 1930

Seminole Producer, Seminole, OK October 6, 1933

Shawnee Morning News, Shawnee, OK December 30, 1919

Shawnee Morning News, Shawnee, OK August 27, 1920

Shawnee Morning News, Shawnee, OK November 26, 1920

Shawnee Morning News, Shawnee, OK March 26, 1921

Shawnee Morning News, Shawnee, OK June 18, 1921

Shawnee Morning News, Shawnee, OK June 25, 1921

Shawnee Morning News, Shawnee, OK August 24, 1921

Shawnee Morning News, Shawnee, OK December 5, 1922

Shawnee Morning News, Shawnee, OK March 8, 1927

Shawnee Morning News, Shawnee, OK July 26, 1933

Shawnee Morning News, Shawnee, OK October 8, 1933

Shawnee Evening Star, Shawnee, OK October 10, 1933

Shawnee News Star, Shawnee, OK October 3, 1933

Shawnee News Star, Shawnee, OK October 4, 1933

Shawnee News Star, Shawnee, OK October 17, 1933

Southeastern Oklahoma Citizen, Durant, OK October 12, 1933

Spokesman Review, Spokane, WA September 23, 1932

St. Cloud Times, St. Cloud, MN July 16, 1930

St. Cloud Times, St. Cloud, MN August 15, 1930

St. Paul Daily News, St. Paul, MN March 8, 1933

Star Tribune, Minneapolis, MN July 16, 1930

Star Tribune, Minneapolis, MN July 17, 1930

Star Tribune, Minneapolis, MN September 26, 1930

Star Tribune, Minneapolis, MN August 9, 1933

Stillwater Democrat, Stillwater, OK July 28, 1927

Stillwater Democrat, Stillwater, OK February 9, 1928

Stillwater Democrat, Stillwater, OK September 27, 1928

Stillwater Gazette, Stillwater, OK July 29, 1927

Stillwater Gazette, Stillwater, OK December 14, 1928

Stillwater Gazette, Stillwater, OK October 6, 1933

Sun Sentinel, Charleston, MS December 1, 1932

Tacoma Daily Ledger, Tacoma, WA September 22, 1932

Tacoma Daily Ledger, Tacoma, WA September 28, 1932

Times Record News, Wichita Falls, KS September 28, 1948

Times Record News, Wichita Falls, KS December 26, 1956

Times Union, Albany, NY March 2, 1932

Tipton Daily Tribune, Tipton, IN March 31, 1932

Tulare Advance Register, Visalia, CA July 7, 1948

Tulsa Daily World, Tulsa, OK July 26, 1933

Tulsa Tribune, Tulsa, OK July 25, 1927

Tulsa Tribune, Tulsa, OK January 9, 1928

Tulsa Tribune, Tulsa, OK January 13, 1928

Tulsa Tribune, Tulsa, OK October 14, 1932

Tulsa Tribune, Tulsa, OK September 24, 1933

Tulsa Tribune, Tulsa, OK October 3, 1933

Tulsa Tribune, Tulsa, OK October 11, 1933

Tulsa Tribune, Tulsa, OK June 12, 1962

Tulsa World, Tulsa, OK February 19, 1933

Tyler Daily Courier Times, Tyler, TX February 16, 1930

Tyler Daily Courier Times, Tyler, TX July 23, 1933

Tyler Morning Telegraph, Tyler, TX November 9, 1932

Tyler Morning Telegraph, Tyler, TX September 4, 1934

Vinita Daily Journal, Vinita, OK October 9, 1933

Vinita Daily Journal, Vinita, OK October 11, 1933

Waco News Tribune, Waco, TX October 11, 1933

West Central Tribune, Willmar, MN March 18, 2010

Wichita Falls Record. Wichita, KS June 20, 1934

Winona Daily News, Winona, MN May 6, 1984

Winston County Journal, Louisville, MS December 2, 1932

Wise County Messenger, Decatur, TX July 22, 1954

World News, Roanoke, VA September 4, 1934

WEBSITES

ancestry.com, Charles Thorne Certificate of Death

ancestry.com, Deed Record Charlie and Kathryn Thorne

ancestry.com, Geralene Arnold

ancestry.com, Lera Cleo "Kathryn" "Kay" Brooks

ancestry.com, Lera Cleo and Lennie Brewer Marriage Record

ancestry.com, Mrs. Elizabeth K. Barnes Death Certificate

ancestry.com, R. G. Shannon

babyfacenelsonjournal.com, The Outlaw Journals

fbi.gov/history/brief-history, The FBI and the American Gangster,
1924-1938

fbi.gov/history/famous-cases/lindbergh-kidnapping, Lindbergh
Kidnapping

fbi.gov/history/brief-history, The Mann Act

fbi.gov/history/brief-history, The Nation Calls

findagrave.com/memorial/35409674/lera-cleo-kelly, Kathryn Kelly

genealogy.com/ftm/r/o/r/John-Davis-Rorer/FILE/0002page.html,
Machine Gun Kelly

historylink.org/File/9315, Three Gangsters Rob First Savings & Trust
Bank in Colfax

okhistory.org/publications/enc/entry.php?entry=UR009, A Heroic
Example for Every American

paradisehistoricalsociety.org/2011-earlier/, Robert "Boss" Shannon

tennesseeencyclopedia.net/entries/temperance/, Temperance

thislandpress.com/2011/10/15/
tigress-the-life-and-times-of-kathryn-kelly/

sdpb.sd.gov/VerneMiller/timeline.asp, Verne Miller Timeline

ENDNOTES

Chapter 1: In the Company of the Kellys

1. *Coweta Times Sun*, May 17, 1934; *The M'Alester News Capital*, May 31, 1934

2. *The Oklahoma News*, April 6, 1934

3. US Department of Justice, Federal Bureau of Investigation, George (Machine Gun) Kelly & Kathryn Kelly, Geralene Arnold Statement & Testimony

4. Ibid.

5. Ibid.

6. Ibid.

7. Ibid.

8. Ibid.; *Miami Daily News*, April 29, 1934

9. *Coweta Times Sun*, May 17, 1934; US Department of Justice, Federal Bureau of Investigation, George (Machine Gun) Kelly & Kathryn Kelly, Geralene Arnold Statement & Testimony

10. *Coweta Times Sun*, May 17, 1934; *The Chelsea Reporter*, April 26, 1934; *The Oklahoma News*, April 6, 1934

11. *Machine Gun Kelly: To Right a Wrong*, pg. 201–2; *The Pittsburgh Press*, October 13, 1933; *Funk & Wagnalls New Encyclopedia*, Volume 15, pg. 293–8; *Seminole Morning News*, March 13, 1930

12. *The Muldrow Sun*, July 4, 1930

13. Ibid.

14. Ibid.

15. *Kathryn Kelly: The Moll Behind "Machine Gun" Kelly*, pg. 8–11

16. *From the Secret Files of J. Edgar Hoover*, pg. 114–6

17. *Reading Times*, October 13, 1933

18. Ibid.; *Kathryn Kelly: The Moll Behind "Machine Gun" Kelly*, pg. 8–9; ancestry.com, Lera Cleo "Kathryn" "Kay" Brooks

19. *Shawnee Morning News*, June 18, 1921; *Shawnee Morning News*, December 30, 1919

20. *Shawnee Morning News*, June 25, 1921; ancestry.com, Lera Cleo and Lennie Brewer Marriage Record

21. *Shawnee Morning News*, August 24, 1921

22. *Coleman Democrat*, February 2, 1928; *Fort Worth Star-Telegram*, September 11, 1927

23. *Kathryn Kelly: The Moll Behind "Machine Gun" Kelly*, pg. 10–1; *Reading Times*, October 13, 1933

24. *San Angelo Evening Standard*, April 30, 1928; *Kathryn Kelly: The Moll Behind "Machine Gun" Kelly*, pg. 10–1

25. *San Angelo Evening Standard*, April 30, 1928; *Kathryn Kelly: The Moll Behind "Machine Gun" Kelly*, pg. 10–1; *The Democrat Voice*, May 2, 1928

26. *Corsicana Daily Sun*, April 30, 1928; ancestry.com, Charles Thorne Certificate of Death

27. ancestry.com, Charles Thorne Certificate of Death; *The Democrat Voice*, May 2, 1928; *Kathryn Kelly: The Moll Behind "Machine Gun" Kelly*, pg. 11

28. *Fort Worth Star-Telegram*, September 3, 1928; *Fort Worth Record Telegram*, May 14, 1928; *Fort Worth Record Telegram*, June 23, 1928

29. ancestry.com, Deed Record Charlie and Kathryn Thorne; *From Gun to Gavel: The Courtroom Recollections of James Mathers of Oklahoma as Told to Marshall Houts*, pg. 226–227.

30. *From Gun to Gavel*, pg. 226–7

31. *Fort Worth Star-Telegram*, February 23, 1930

32. *Fort Worth Star-Telegram*, November 19, 1929

33. *Fort Worth Star-Telegram*, May 4, 1930; *Kathryn Kelly: The Moll Behind "Machine Gun" Kelly*, pg. 1–3

34. *Fort Worth Star-Telegram*, May 4, 1930; *Kathryn Kelly: The Moll Behind "Machine Gun" Kelly*, pg. 12–3

35. *The Pittsburgh Press*, October 13, 1933; *From Gun to Gavel*, pg. 226–7

36. *Fort Worth Star-Telegram*, January 25, 1930; *Tyler Daily Courier*, February 16, 1930; *Austin American Statesman*, August 23, 1930

37. *Wise County Messenger*, July 22, 1954; *Kathryn Kelly: The Moll Behind "Machine Gun" Kelly*, pg. 12–3

38. *The Daily Oklahoman*, January 1, 1930

39. *Funk & Wagnalls New Encyclopedia*, Volume 19, pg. 383–384

40. *The Evening Derrick*, November 2, 1927; Division of Investigation, US Department of Justice, Washington, DC, George R. Kelly Arrest Record

CHAPTER 2: Bootleggers to Bank Robbers

1. *Tennessee Quarterly*, Vol. 24, No. 4, 1965

2. http://tennesseeencyclopedia.net/temperance; *Tennessee Quarterly*, Vol. 24, No. 4, 1965

3. *Machine Gun Kelly: To Right a Wrong*, pg. 52–54

4. Ibid.

5. *Machine Gun Kelly: To Right a Wrong*, pg. 60–61

6. Ibid.; *Commercial Appeal*, November 10, 1917; ancestry.com, Mrs. Elizabeth K. Barnes Death Certificate

7. *Machine Gun Kelly: To Right a Wrong*, pg. 65–70

8. Ibid.

9. Ibid.

10. Ibid.

11. *Machine Gun Kelly: To Right a Wrong*, pg. 71, 79–85

12. *Machine Gun Kelly: To Right a Wrong*, pg. 91–93; *Commercial Appeal*, October 8, 1919

13. *Commercial Appeal*, October 8, 1919

14. *Machine Gun Kelly: To Right a Wrong*, pg. 132–137; *Commercial Appeal*, October 23, 1920

15. *Commercial Appeal*, November 16, 1920

16. *Machine Gun Kelly: To Right a Wrong*, pg. 155–158

17. Ibid.

18. Ibid.; *Commercial Appeal*, January 31, 1922

19. *Commercial Appeal*, January 31, 1922

20. Ibid.

21. Ibid.

22. *Machine Gun Kelly: To Right a Wrong*, pg. 167–168

23. Ibid.; *Commercial Appeal*, March 8, 1922

24. *Machine Gun Kelly: To Right a Wrong*, pg. 168–169; *Commercial Appeal*, October 28, 1926; *Commercial Appeal*, October 29, 1926; *Commercial Appeal*, October 30, 1926; *Commercial Appeal*, January 19, 1927

25. *Machine Gun Kelly: To Right a Wrong*, pg. 179–184

26. *Machine Gun Kelly: To Right a Wrong*, pg. 189–192

27. Ibid.; US Department of Justice, Washington, DC, George R. Kelly Arrest Record; *Albuquerque Journal*, March 5, 1927

28. US Department of Justice, Washington, DC, George R. Kelly Arrest Record; *Machine Gun Kelly: To Right a Wrong*, pg. 190–192

29. *Machine Gun Kelly: To Right a Wrong*, pg. 192–193; *Tulsa Tribune*, July 25, 1927

30. *Stillwater Democrat*, July 28, 1927; *Stillwater Democrat*, July 29, 1927; *Stillwater Democrat*, August 12, 1927

31. *Tulsa Tribune*, January 9, 1928; *Tulsa Tribune*, January 13, 1928

32. *Tulsa Tribune*, January 13, 1928

33. *Stillwater Democrat*, February 9, 1928; *Kiowa County Review*, February 24, 1928

34. *Manhattan Mercury*, March 1, 1930

35. Ibid.

36. Ibid.

37. Ibid.

38. Ibid.

39. US Department of Justice, Washington, DC, George R. Kelly Arrest Record

40. *Machine Gun Kelly: To Right a Wrong*, pg. 194–197

41. Minnesota Historical Society, St. Paul Gangster History Collection

42. *St. Cloud Times*, July 16, 1930

43. Ibid.; *Star Tribune*, July 16, 1930; *Sauk Centre Herald*, July 24, 1930

44. *West Central Tribune*, March 18, 2010

45. *Star Tribune*, July 16, 1930

46. *St. Cloud Times*, August 15, 1930

47. *Gazette*, September 9, 1930

48. Ibid.

49. Ibid.

50. Ibid.; *Nashua Reporter*, September 24, 1930; sdpb.sd.gov/VerneMiller/timeline.asp, Verne Miller Timeline

51. *Machine Gun Kelly: To Right a Wrong*, pg. 198-200

52. *Pittsburg Press*, October 13, 1933; *Star Tribune*, September 26, 1930

CHAPTER 3: Adventures in Kidnapping

1. *Machine Gun Kelly: To Right a Wrong*, pg. 201–203

2. Ibid.

3. ancestry.com, R. G. Shannon; *Oklahoma News*, September 17, 1933

4. ancestry.com, R. G. Shannon; *Oklahoma News*, September 17, 1933

5. *Machine Gun Kelly: To Right a Wrong*, pg. 203–206

6. Ibid.

7. *Machine Gun Kelly: To Right a Wrong*, pg. 207–209

8. Ibid.; *Star Tribune*, July 16, 1930; *Star Tribune*, July 17, 1930

9. *Robbing Banks Was My Business*, pg. 76–81

10. *Corsicana Daily Sun*, April 7, 1931

11. Ibid.

12. Ibid.

13. Ibid.

14. Ibid.

15. *Machine Gun Kelly: To Right a Wrong*, pg. 210–211

16. Ibid.

17. *Robbing Banks Was My Business*, pg. 89–90

18. US Department of Justice, Federal Bureau of Investigation, Albert Bates File

19. Ibid.; *Machine Gun Kelly: To Right a Wrong*, pg. 212–220

20. US Department of Justice, Federal Bureau of Investigation, Albert Bates File

21. *Evening Sun*, May 7, 1931; *Pineville Herald*, May 22, 1931

22. *Machine Gun Kelly: To Right a Wrong*, pg. 221–222; *Kathryn Kelly: The Moll Behind "Machine Gun" Kelly*, pg. 83–85

23. *Dixon Evening Telegram*, January 29, 1932; US Department of Justice, Federal Bureau of Investigation, Bremer Kidnapping Part D09

24. *Reporter Times*, January 27, 1932; *Kokomo Tribune*, January 27, 1932

25. *Rushville Republican*, January 27, 1932

26. Ibid.

27. Ibid.

28. *Indianapolis Star*, January 30, 1932; US Department of Justice, Federal Bureau of Investigation, Bremer Kidnapping Part D09; *Tipton Daily Tribune*, March 3, 1932

29. *Machine Gun Kelly: The Notorious Life and Crimes of the Depression Era Gangster*, pg. 22–24, US Department of Justice, Federal Bureau of Investigation, Albert Bates File; *Denton Record Chronicle*, February 6, 1932; *Fort Worth Star-Telegram*, February 7, 1932

30. US Department of Justice, Federal Bureau of Investigation, George (Machine Gun) Kelly File; *Kathryn Kelly: The Moll Behind "Machine Gun" Kelly*, pg. 32–33; *Fort Worth Star-Telegram*, January 8, 1932; babyfacenelsonjournal.com

31. *Public Enemies: America's Greatest Crime Wave and the Birth of the FBI, 1933-34*, pg. 74–75; *The Snatch Racket: The Kidnapping Epidemic That Terrorized 1930s America*, pg. 140–142

32. *Public Enemies: America's Greatest Crime Wave and the Birth of the FBI, 1933-34*, pg. 74–75; *The Snatch Racket: The Kidnapping Epidemic That Terrorized 1930s America*, pg. 140–142

33. *Times Union*, March 2, 1932; *News Journal*, March 2, 1932

34. *Iowa City Press Citizen*, March 5, 1932

35. *Indianapolis News*, February 26, 1932

36. *Machine Gun Kelly: To Right a Wrong*, pg. 221–222

37. *Spokesman Review*, September 23, 1932; *Tacoma Daily Ledger*, September 22, 1932; *Tacoma Daily Ledger*, September 28, 1932

38. *Tacoma Daily Ledger*, September 22, 1932; *Tacoma Daily Ledger*, September 28, 1932

39. *Tyler Morning Telegraph*, November 9, 1932; *Fort Worth Star-Telegram*, November 13, 1932; historylink.org/File/9315

40. *Machine Gun Kelly: The Notorious Life and Crimes of the Depression Era Gangster*, pg. 13–14; *Machine Gun Kelly: To Right a Wrong*, pg. 206–207; *Kathryn Kelly: The Moll Behind "Machine Gun" Kelly*, pg. 28–30

41. *Sun Sentinel*, December 1, 1932; *Daily Herald*, November 30, 1932

42. *Winston County Journal*, December 2, 1932

43. Ibid.

44. *Indianapolis News*, June 25, 1932

45. Ibid.

46. US Department of Justice, Federal Bureau of Investigation, Kathryn Thorne Kelly File

CHAPTER 4: The Abduction of Charles Urschel

1. *New York Times*, March 3, 1932

2. US Bureau of Investigation, Report, Vol. 2, No. 6; fbi.gov/history/brief-history, *The Mann Act*; *Enemies: A History of the FBI*, pg. 22–24; *Public Enemies: America's Greatest Crime Wave and the Birth of the FBI, 1933–34*, pg. 11–12

3. fbi.gov/history/brief-history, *The FBI and the American Gangster, 1924–1938*

4. *The Lindbergh Baby Kidnapping*, pg. 25–26

5. Ibid.; fbi.gov/history/famous-cases/lindbergh-kidnapping, *Lindbergh Kidnapping*

6. *Kathryn Kelly: The Moll Behind "Machine Gun" Kelly*, pg. 32–33; *Machine Gun Kelly: To Right a Wrong*, pg. 221–222; *Fort Worth Star-Telegram*, October 21, 1932; *Fort Worth Star-Telegram*, October 18, 1932

7. *Daily Oklahoman*, November 27, 1932; *Oklahoma News*, November 27, 1932; *Daily Oklahoman*, December 8, 1932; *Oklahoma News*, December 15, 1932

8. *Oklahoma News,* December 15, 1932

9. *Machine Gun Kelly: To Right a Wrong,* pg. 221–222; *Oklahoma News,* February 15, 1933; *Oklahoma News,* April 12, 1933; *Daily Oklahoman,* April 16, 1933; *Daily Oklahoman,* April 6, 1933

10. *Oklahoma News,* April 12, 1933; *Daily Oklahoman,* April 16, 1933; *Machine Gun Kelly: To Right a Wrong,* pg. 221–222; *Kathryn Kelly: The Moll Behind "Machine Gun" Kelly,* 38–39; US Department of Justice, Federal Bureau of Investigation, George (Machine Gun) Kelly File

11. *Machine Gun Kelly: To Right a Wrong,* pg. 221–222

12. US Department of Justice, Federal Bureau of Investigation, George (Machine Gun) Kelly File; US Department of Justice, Federal Bureau of Investigation, Albert Bates File; *Machine Gun Kelly: To Right a Wrong,* pg. 223–224

13. *Tulsa World,* February 19, 1933

14. *Oklahoma News,* February 9, 1933; *Oklahoma News,* July 10, 1933; US Department of Justice, Federal Bureau of Investigation, George (Machine Gun) Kelly File; US Department of Justice, Federal Bureau of Investigation, Albert Bates File

15. US Department of Justice, Federal Bureau of Investigation, George (Machine Gun) Kelly File; US Department of Justice, Federal Bureau of Investigation, Albert Bates File

16. US Department of Justice, Federal Bureau of Investigation, George (Machine Gun) Kelly File; US Department of Justice, Federal Bureau of Investigation, Albert Bates File; US Department of Justice, Federal Bureau of Investigation, George (Machine Gun) Kelly & Kathryn Kelly Court/Trial Transcripts

17. US Department of Justice, Federal Bureau of Investigation, George (Machine Gun) Kelly File; US Department of Justice, Federal Bureau of Investigation, Albert Bates File; US Department of Justice, Federal Bureau of Investigation, George (Machine Gun) Kelly & Kathryn Kelly Court/Trial Transcripts

18. US Department of Justice, Federal Bureau of Investigation, George (Machine Gun) Kelly File, US Department of Justice, Federal Bureau of Investigation, Albert Bates File; US Department of Justice, Federal Bureau of Investigation, George (Machine Gun) Kelly & Kathryn Kelly Court/Trial Transcripts: US Bureau of Investigation, Department of Justice, Washington, DC, #56111, July 25, 1933

19. US Department of Justice, Federal Bureau of Investigation, George (Machine Gun) Kelly File; US Department of Justice, Federal Bureau of Investigation, Albert Bates File; US Department of Justice, Federal Bureau of Investigation, George (Machine Gun) Kelly & Kathryn Kelly Court/Trial Transcripts; *Machine Gun Kelly: To Right a Wrong*, pg. 231–234; US Bureau of Investigation, Department of Justice, Washington, DC #56111, July 25, 1933

20. US Department of Justice, Federal Bureau of Investigation, George (Machine Gun) Kelly File; US Department of Justice, Federal Bureau of Investigation, Albert Bates File; US Department of Justice, Federal Bureau of Investigation, George (Machine Gun) Kelly & Kathryn Kelly Court/Trial Transcripts; US Bureau of Investigation, Department of Justice, Washington, DC #56111, July 25, 1933

21. US Department of Justice, Federal Bureau of Investigation, George (Machine Gun) Kelly File; US Department of Justice, Federal Bureau of Investigation, Albert Bates File: US Department of Justice, Federal Bureau of Investigation, George (Machine Gun) Kelly & Kathryn Kelly Court/Trial Transcripts: US Bureau of Investigation, Department of Justice, Washington, DC #56111, July 25, 1933; *Machine Gun Kelly: To Right a Wrong*, pg. 232–233

22. US Department of Justice, Federal Bureau of Investigation, George (Machine Gun) Kelly File; US Department of Justice, Federal Bureau of Investigation, Albert Bates File; US Department of Justice, Federal Bureau of Investigation, George (Machine Gun) Kelly & Kathryn Kelly Court/Trial Transcripts; US Bureau of Investigation, Department of Justice, Washington, DC #56111

23. US Department of Justice, Federal Bureau of Investigation, George (Machine Gun) Kelly File; US Department of Justice, Federal Bureau of Investigation, Albert Bates File; US Department of Justice, Federal Bureau of Investigation, George (Machine Gun) Kelly & Kathryn Kelly Court/Trial Transcripts; US Bureau of Investigation, Department of Justice, Washington, DC #56111

24. US Department of Justice, Federal Bureau of Investigation, George (Machine Gun) Kelly File: US Department of Justice, Federal Bureau of Investigation, Albert Bates File; US Department of Justice, Federal Bureau of Investigation, George (Machine Gun) Kelly & Kathryn Kelly Court/Trial Transcripts; US Bureau of Investigation, Department of Justice, Washington, DC #56111; *Crimes' Paradise: The Authentic Inside Story of the Urschel Kidnapping*, 9–10

25. *Oklahoma News*, July 23, 1933

26. Ibid.

27. Ibid.

28. *Crimes' Paradise: The Authentic Inside Story of the Urschel Kidnapping*, pg. 88–89; US Department of Justice, Federal Bureau of Investigation, George (Machine Gun) Kelly & Kathryn Kelly Court/Trial Transcripts; US Bureau of Investigation, Transcript of Interview between BI Agent Gus Jones and Charles Urschel dated August 8, 1933

29. US Department of Justice, Federal Bureau of Investigation, George (Machine Gun) Kelly & Kathryn Kelly Court/Trial Transcripts; US Bureau of Investigation, Transcript of Interview between BI Agent Gus Jones and Charles Urschel dated August 8, 1933

30. Federal Bureau of Investigation, George (Machine Gun) Kelly & Kathryn Kelly Court/Trial Transcripts; US Bureau of Investigation

31. Ibid.

32. Ibid.

33. Ibid.

34. Ibid.

35. *Oklahoma News*, July 24, 1933

36. Ibid.

37. Ibid.

38. George (Machine Gun) Kelly & Kathryn Kelly Court/Trial Transcripts; US Bureau of Investigation, Transcript of Interview between BI Agent Gus Jones and Charles Urschel dated August 8, 1933

39. George (Machine Gun) Kelly & Kathryn Kelly Court/Trial Transcripts; US Bureau of Investigation, Transcript of Interview between BI Agent Gus Jones and Charles Urschel dated August 8, 1933

40. *Kathryn Kelly: The Moll Behind "Machine Gun" Kelly*, pg. 43–44; George (Machine Gun) Kelly & Kathryn Kelly Court/Trial Transcripts; US Bureau of Investigation, Transcript of Interview between BI Agent Gus Jones and Charles Urschel dated August 8, 1933

41. *El Paso Times*, July 24, 1933; *Tyler Daily Courier*, July 23, 1933

42. *El Paso Times*, July 24, 1933; *Tyler Daily Courier*, July 23, 1933

43. *El Paso Times*, July 24, 1933, *Tyler Daily Courier*, July 23, 1933

44. George (Machine Gun) Kelly & Kathryn Kelly Court/Trial Transcripts; US Bureau of Investigation, Transcript of Interview between BI Agent Gus Jones and Charles Urschel dated August 8, 1933; *Kathryn Kelly: The Moll Behind "Machine Gun" Kelly*, pg. 43–44; *Machine Gun Kelly: To Right a Wrong*, pg. 235–237

45. George (Machine Gun) Kelly & Kathryn Kelly Court/Trial Transcripts; US Bureau of Investigation, Transcript of Interview between BI Agent Gus Jones and Charles Urschel dated August 8, 1933; *Kathryn Kelly: The Moll Behind "Machine Gun" Kelly*, pg. 43–44; *Machine Gun Kelly: To Right a Wrong*, pg. 235–237

46. George (Machine Gun) Kelly & Kathryn Kelly Court/Trial Transcripts; US Bureau of Investigation, Transcript of Interview between BI Agent Gus Jones and Charles Urschel dated August 8, 1933; *Kathryn Kelly: The Moll Behind "Machine Gun" Kelly*, pg. 43–44; *Machine Gun Kelly: To Right a Wrong*, pg. 235–237

47. *Fort Worth Telegram*, July 23, 1933; George (Machine Gun) Kelly & Kathryn Kelly Court/Trial Transcripts; US Bureau of Investigation, Transcript of Interview between BI Agent Gus Jones and Charles Urschel dated August 8, 1933; *Kathryn Kelly: The Moll Behind "Machine Gun" Kelly*, pg. 43–44; *Machine Gun Kelly: To Right a Wrong*, pg. 235–237

48. George (Machine Gun) Kelly & Kathryn Kelly Court/Trial Transcripts; US Bureau of Investigation, Transcript of Interview between BI Agent Gus Jones and Charles Urschel dated August 8, 1933; *Kathryn Kelly: The Moll Behind "Machine Gun" Kelly*, pg. 43–44; *Machine Gun Kelly: To Right a Wrong*, pg. 235–237; US Department of Justice, Federal Bureau of Investigation, Albert Bates File

49. George (Machine Gun) Kelly & Kathryn Kelly Court/Trial Transcripts; US Bureau of Investigation, Transcript of Interview between BI Agent Gus Jones and Charles Urschel dated August 8, 1933; *Kathryn Kelly: The Moll Behind "Machine Gun" Kelly*, pg. 43–44; *Machine Gun Kelly: To Right a Wrong*, pg. 235–237; US Department of Justice, Federal Bureau of Investigation, Albert Bates File

50. *Pampa Daily News*, July 24, 1933

51. *Denton Record Chronicle*, July 25, 1933

52. *Austin American*, July 24, 1933

CHAPTER 5: The Ransom

1. George (Machine Gun) Kelly & Kathryn Kelly Court/Trial Transcripts; US Bureau of Investigation, Transcript of Interview between BI Agent Gus Jones and Charles Urschel dated August 8, 1933

2. George (Machine Gun) Kelly & Kathryn Kelly Court/Trial Transcripts; US Bureau of Investigation, Transcript of Interview between BI Agent Gus Jones and Charles Urschel dated August 8, 1933

3. George (Machine Gun) Kelly & Kathryn Kelly Court/Trial Transcripts; US Bureau of Investigation, Transcript of Interview between BI Agent Gus Jones and Charles Urschel dated August 8, 1933; *Machine Gun Kelly: To Right a Wrong*, pg. 236–237

4. George (Machine Gun) Kelly & Kathryn Kelly Court/Trial Transcripts; US Bureau of Investigation, Transcript of Interview between BI Agent Gus Jones and Charles Urschel dated August 8, 1933; *Machine Gun Kelly: To Right a Wrong*, pg. 236–237

5. *Crimes' Paradise: The Authentic Inside Story of the Urschel Kidnapping*, pg. 90–92; *Frederick Leader*, July 24, 1933; George (Machine Gun) Kelly & Kathryn Kelly Court/Trial Transcripts; US Bureau of Investigation

6. George (Machine Gun) Kelly & Kathryn Kelly Court/Trial Transcripts; US Bureau of Investigation, Transcript of Interview between BI Agent Gus Jones and Charles Urschel dated August 8, 1933

7. *Daily Ardmoreite*, July 26, 1933; *Miami Daily News Record*, July 27, 1933

8. *Daily Ardmoreite*, July 26, 1933; *Miami Daily News Record*, July 27, 1933

9. *Okmulgee Daily Times*, July 25, 1933; *Oklahoma News*, July 25, 1933; *Daily Oklahoman*, July 25, 1933

10. *Okmulgee Daily Times*, July 25, 1933; *Oklahoma News*, July 25, 1933; *Daily Oklahoman*, July 25, 1933

11. *Machine Gun Kelly's Last Stand*, pg. 30–32

12. George (Machine Gun) Kelly & Kathryn Kelly Court/Trial Transcripts; US Bureau of Investigation, Transcript of Interview between BI Agent Gus Jones and Charles Urschel dated August 8, 1933; *Machine Gun Kelly: To Right a Wrong*, pg. 236–237

13. George (Machine Gun) Kelly & Kathryn Kelly Court/Trial Transcripts; US Bureau of Investigation, Transcript of Interview between BI Agent Gus Jones and Charles Urschel dated August 8, 1933; *Machine Gun Kelly: To Right a Wrong*, pg. 236–237

14. *Machine Gun Kelly's Last Stand*, pg. 61–63

15. *Machine Gun Kelly: To Right a Wrong*, pg. 237–238, *Kathryn Kelly: The Moll Behind "Machine Gun" Kelly*, pg. 46–48; *Machine Gun Kelly's Last Stand*, pg. 30–32

16. *Machine Gun Kelly's Last Stand*, pg. 30–32; US Department of Justice, Federal Bureau of Investigation, George (Machine Gun) Kelly File

17. *Machine Gun Kelly's Last Stand*, pg. 30–32; US Department of Justice, Federal Bureau of Investigation, George (Machine Gun) Kelly File

18. *Machine Gun Kelly's Last Stand*, pg. 30–32; US Department of Justice, Federal Bureau of Investigation, George (Machine Gun) Kelly File

19. *Machine Gun Kelly's Last Stand*, pg. 30–32; US Department of Justice, Federal Bureau of Investigation, George (Machine Gun) Kelly File

20. US Department of Justice, Federal Bureau of Investigation, George (Machine Gun) Kelly & Kathryn Kelly Court/Trial Transcripts

21. US Department of Justice: Federal Bureau of Investigation, George (Machine Gun) Kelly & Kathryn Kelly Court/Trial Transcripts

22. George (Machine Gun) Kelly & Kathryn Kelly Court/Trial Transcripts, US Bureau of Investigation, Transcript of Interview between BI Agent Gus Jones and Charles Urschel dated August 8, 1933; *Machine Gun Kelly: To Right a Wrong*, pg. 238–239

23. *Public Enemies: America's Greatest Crime Wave and the Birth of the FBI, 1933–34*, pg. 75–78

24. *Tulsa Daily World*, July 26, 1933; *Shawnee Evening Star*, July 26, 1933

25. *Daily Oklahoman*, July 27, 1933; *Voices from Alcatraz*, pg. 18–23

26. *Voices from Alcatraz*, pg. 18–23

27. Ibid.

28. Ibid.

29. George (Machine Gun) Kelly & Kathryn Kelly Court/Trial Transcripts; US Bureau of Investigation

30. Ibid.; *Public Enemies: America's Greatest Crime Wave and the Birth of the FBI, 1933–34*, pg. 81–82

31. *The Year of Fear: Machine Gun Kelly and the Manhunt That Changed the Nation*, pg. 104–105; *Crimes' Paradise*, pg. 40–44

32. *Oklahoma News*, July 27, 1933

33. Ibid.

34. *Crimes' Paradise*, pg. 60–65; George (Machine Gun) Kelly & Kathryn Kelly Court/Trial Transcripts; US Bureau of Investigation

35. George (Machine Gun) Kelly & Kathryn Kelly Court/Trial Transcripts; U. S. Bureau of Investigation

36. Ibid.

37. Ibid.

38. Ibid.; *Voices from Alcatraz*, pg. 26–34

39. George (Machine Gun) Kelly & Kathryn Kelly Court/Trial Transcripts; US Bureau of Investigation

40. Ibid.; Transcript of Interview between BI Agent Gus Jones and Charles Urschel dated August 8, 1933

41. *Voices from Alcatraz*, pg. 26–34; *Machine Gun Kelly: To Right a Wrong*, pg. 241–242

42. *Crimes' Paradise*, pg. 56–58; US Department of Justice, Federal Bureau of Investigation, George (Machine Gun) Kelly File

43. George (Machine Gun) Kelly & Kathryn Kelly Court/Trial Transcripts; US Bureau of Investigation

44. *Voices from Alcatraz*, pg. 31–34; George (Machine Gun) Kelly & Kathryn Kelly Court/Trial Transcripts; US Bureau of Investigation

45. *Voices from Alcatraz*, pg. 31–34; George (Machine Gun) Kelly & Kathryn Kelly Court/Trial Transcripts; US Bureau of Investigation

46. *Voices from Alcatraz*, pg. 31–34; George (Machine Gun) Kelly & Kathryn Kelly Court/Trial Transcripts; US Bureau of Investigation

47. *Voices from Alcatraz*, pg. 31–34; George (Machine Gun) Kelly & Kathryn Kelly Court/Trial Transcripts; US Bureau of Investigation

48. *Machine Gun Kelly: To Right a Wrong*, pg. 244–245

49. *Kathryn Kelly: The Moll Behind "Machine Gun" Kelly*, pg. 51–53

50. Ibid.

51. US Department of Justice, Federal Bureau of Investigation, Albert Bates File; Transcript of Interview between BI Agent Gus Jones and Charles Urschel dated August 8, 1933

52. US Department of Justice, Federal Bureau of Investigation, Albert Bates File; Transcript of Interview between BI Agent Gus Jones and Charles Urschel dated August 8, 1933

53. US Department of Justice, Federal Bureau of Investigation, Albert Bates File; Transcript of Interview between BI Agent Gus Jones and Charles Urschel dated August 8, 1933

54. US Department of Justice,, Federal Bureau of Investigation, Albert Bates File; Transcript of Interview between BI Agent Gus Jones and Charles Urschel dated August 8, 1933; *Oklahoma News*, August 1, 1933

55. US Department of Justice, Federal Bureau of Investigation, Albert Bates File; Transcript of Interview between BI Agent Gus Jones and Charles Urschel dated August 8, 1933; *Kathryn Kelly: The Moll Behind "Machine Gun" Kelly*, pg. 52–53

56. US Department of Justice, Federal Bureau of Investigation, Albert Bates File; Transcript of Interview between BI Agent Gus Jones and Charles Urschel dated August 8, 1933; *Kathryn Kelly: The Moll Behind "Machine Gun" Kelly*, pg. 52–53

57. *Voices from Alcatraz*, pg. 32–34

58. Ibid.; George (Machine Gun) Kelly & Kathryn Kelly Court/Trial Transcripts; US Bureau of Investigation

59. George (Machine Gun) Kelly & Kathryn Kelly Court/Trial Transcripts; US Bureau of Investigation; *Voices from Alcatraz*, pg. 35–37

60. *Crimes' Paradise*, pg. 65–68

CHAPTER 6: Outlaws in Paradise

1. US Department of Justice, Federal Bureau of Investigation, George (Machine Gun) Kelly & Kathryn Kelly, Geralene Arnold Statement & Testimony

2. US Department of Justice, Federal Bureau of Investigation, George (Machine Gun) Kelly & Kathryn Kelly, Geralene Arnold Statement & Testimony; US Department of Justice, Federal Bureau of Investigation, Albert Bates File

3. US Department of Justice, Federal Bureau of Investigation, George (Machine Gun) Kelly & Kathryn Kelly, Geralene Arnold Statement & Testimony; US Department of Justice, Federal Bureau of Investigation, George (Machine Gun) Kelly File

4. US Department of Justice, Federal Bureau of Investigation, George (Machine Gun) Kelly File; US Department of Justice, Federal Bureau of Investigation, George (Machine Gun) Kelly & Kathryn Kelly

5. *Minneapolis Star*, August 8, 1933; *Minneapolis Star*, August 9, 1933; *Star Tribune*, August 9, 1933; *Voices from Alcatraz*, pg. 85–86

6. *Minneapolis Star*, August 8, 1933

7. US Department of Justice,, Federal Bureau of Investigation, George (Machine Gun) Kelly & Kathryn Kelly, Geralene Arnold Statement & Testimony; US Department of Justice, Federal Bureau of Investigation, George (Machine Gun) Kelly File

8. *Oklahoma News*, September 26, 1933

9. *Daily Oklahoman*, August 1, 1933

10. *Oklahoma News*, August 1, 1933

11. Ibid.

12. Ibid.

13. *Crimes' Paradise*, pg. 66–68; *Oklahoma News*, August 3, 1933

14. *Crimes' Paradise*, pg. 66–68; *Oklahoma News*, August 3, 1933

15. *Crimes' Paradise*, pg. 66–68; *Oklahoma News*, August 3, 1933

16. *Crimes' Paradise*, pg. 66–68; *Oklahoma News*, August 3, 1933

17. *Crimes' Paradise*, pg. 66–68; *Oklahoma News*, August 3, 1933

18. *Crimes' Paradise*, pg. 72–74; *Oklahoma News*, August 4, 1933; *Hugo Daily News*, August 4, 1933

19. *Oklahoma News*, August 4, 1933

20. Ibid.

21. *Crimes' Paradise*, pg. 72–74

22. US Department of Justice, Federal Bureau of Investigation, George (Machine Gun) Kelly & Kathryn Kelly Court/Trial Transcripts; *Daily Oklahoman*, August 2, 1933; *Okmulgee Daily Times*, August 2, 1933; *Crimes' Paradise*, pg. 86–88

23. US Bureau of Investigation, Transcript of Interview between BI Agent Gus Jones and Charles Urschel dated August 8, 1933

24. Ibid.; *Crimes' Paradise*, pg. 100–101

25. US Department of Justice, Federal Bureau of Investigation, George (Machine Gun) Kelly & Kathryn Kelly Court/Trial Transcripts; *Voices from Alcatraz*, pg. 51–53

26. US Department of Justice, Federal Bureau of Investigation, George (Machine Gun) Kelly & Kathryn Kelly Court/Trial Transcripts; *Crimes' Paradise*, pg. 110–113

27. US Department of Justice, Federal Bureau of Investigation, George (Machine Gun) Kelly & Kathryn Kelly Court/Trial Transcripts; *Crimes' Paradise*, pg. 110–113

28. US Department of Justice, Federal Bureau of Investigation, George (Machine Gun) Kelly & Kathryn Kelly Court/Trial Transcripts; *Crimes' Paradise*, pg. 112–114

29. US Department of Justice, Federal Bureau of Investigation, George (Machine Gun) Kelly & Kathryn Kelly Court/Trial Transcripts; *Crimes' Paradise*, pg. 112–114; Federal Bureau of Investigation, Albert Bates File

30. Federal Bureau of Investigation, Albert Bates File; *Crimes' Paradise*, pg. 120–121

31. Federal Bureau of Investigation, Albert Bates File; *Crimes' Paradise*, pg. 122–123

32. Federal Bureau of Investigation, Albert Bates File; *Crimes' Paradise*, pg. 120–121

33. *Fort Worth Star-Telegram*, August 15, 1933; *Fletcher Herald*, August 23, 1933

34. *Denton Record Chronicle*, August 14, 1933

35. *Public Enemies: America's Greatest Crime Wave and the Birth of the FBI, 1933–34*, pg. 92–93

36. *The Year of Fear: Machine Gun Kelly and the Manhunt That Changed the Nation*, pg. 130–131

37. *Greely Daily Tribune*, August 16, 1933

38. *Fort Worth Star-Telegram*, August 15, 1933

39. *Fort Collins Express Courier*, August 16. 1933

40. *Lawton News Review*, August 31, 1933

41. Ibid.

42. *Voices from Alcatraz*, pg. 59–60

43. US Department of Justice, Federal Bureau of Investigation, George (Machine Gun) Kelly File; *Public Enemies: America's Greatest Crime Wave and the Birth of the FBI, 1933–34*, pg. 92–93; US Department of Justice, Federal Bureau of Investigation, Letter from Agent F. J. Blake RE: Louise Donavon to Mary B. Harris, Federal Industrial Institution for Women dated July 24, 1933

44. *Des Moines Register*, August 15, 1933; *Des Moines Tribune*, August 15, 1933

45. *Des Moines Tribune*, August 15, 1933

46. *The Year of Fear: Machine Gun Kelly and the Manhunt That Changed the Nation*, pg. 139–140

47. US Department of Justice, Federal Bureau of Investigation, George (Machine Gun) Kelly & Kathryn Kelly Court/Trial Transcripts

48. US Department of Justice, Federal Bureau of Investigation, George (Machine Gun) Kelly & Kathryn Kelly Court/Trial Transcripts; US Department of Justice, Federal Bureau of Investigation, Kathryn Thorne Kelly File; US Department of Justice, Federal Bureau of Investigation, George (Machine Gun) Kelly File

49. US Department of Justice, Federal Bureau of Investigation, George (Machine Gun) Kelly & Kathryn Kelly Court/Trial Transcripts

50. Ibid.

51. Ibid.

52. Ibid.

CHAPTER 7: Letters from Gangsters

1. US Department of Justice, Federal Bureau of Investigation, George (Machine Gun) Kelly & Kathryn Kelly Court/Trial Transcripts

2. *Fort Worth Star-Telegram*, August 19, 1933; *Public Enemies: America's Greatest Crime Wave and the Birth of the FBI, 1933–34*, pg. 116–117

3. *Clarion Ledger*, August 25, 1933; *Daily Herald*, August 27, 1933; US Department of Justice, Federal Bureau of Investigation, George (Machine Gun) Kelly File; US Department of Justice, Federal Bureau of Investigation, Albert Bates File

4. US Department of Justice, Federal Bureau of Investigation, George (Machine Gun) Kelly File; US Department of Justice, Federal Bureau of Investigation, George (Machine Gun) Kelly & Kathryn Kelly Court/Trial Transcripts

5. US Department of Justice, Federal Bureau of Investigation, George (Machine Gun) Kelly File; US Department of Justice, Federal Bureau of Investigation, George (Machine Gun) Kelly & Kathryn Kelly Court/Trial Transcripts

6. US Department of Justice, Federal Bureau of Investigation, George (Machine Gun) Kelly File; US Department of Justice, Federal Bureau of Investigation, George (Machine Gun) Kelly & Kathryn Kelly Court/Trial Transcripts

7. US Department of Justice, Federal Bureau of Investigation, George (Machine Gun) Kelly File; US Department of Justice, Federal Bureau of Investigation, George (Machine Gun) Kelly & Kathryn Kelly Court/Trial Transcripts; *Austin American*, May 5, 1933

8. US Department of Justice, Federal Bureau of Investigation, George (Machine Gun) Kelly File; US Department of Justice, Federal Bureau of Investigation, George (Machine Gun) Kelly & Kathryn Kelly Court/Trial Transcripts; *Fort Worth Star-Telegram*, August 18, 1933; *Fort Worth Star-Telegram*, August 19, 1933

9. US Department of Justice, Federal Bureau of Investigation, Kathryn Thorne Kelly File; US Department of Justice, Federal Bureau of Investigation, George (Machine Gun) Kelly & Kathryn Kelly Court/Trial Transcripts; *Crimes' Paradise*, pg. 156–157

10. US Department of Justice, Federal Bureau of Investigation, Kathryn Thorne Kelly File; US Department of Justice, Federal Bureau of Investigation, George (Machine Gun) Kelly & Kathryn Kelly Court/Trial Transcripts

11. US Department of Justice, Federal Bureau of Investigation, Kathryn Thorne Kelly File; US Department of Justice, Federal Bureau of Investigation, George (Machine Gun) Kelly & Kathryn Kelly Court/Trial Transcripts; *Public Enemies: America's Greatest Crime Wave and the Birth of the FBI, 1933–34*, pg. 117–118

12. US Department of Justice, Federal Bureau of Investigation, Kathryn Thorne Kelly File; US Department of Justice, Federal Bureau of Investigation, George (Machine Gun) Kelly & Kathryn Kelly Court/Trial Transcripts: *Public Enemies: America's Greatest Crime Wave and the Birth of the FBI, 1933–34*, pg. 117–118

13. US Department of Justice, Federal Bureau of Investigation, Kathryn Thorne Kelly File; US Department of Justice, Federal Bureau of Investigation, George (Machine Gun) Kelly & Kathryn Kelly Court/Trial Transcripts

14. US Department of Justice, Federal Bureau of Investigation, George (Machine Gun) Kelly File; US Department of Justice: Federal Bureau of Investigation, George (Machine Gun) Kelly & Kathryn Kelly Court/Trial Transcripts: US Department of Justice, Federal Bureau of Investigation, Kathryn Thorne Kelly File

15. US Department of Justice, Federal Bureau of Investigation, George (Machine Gun) Kelly File: US Department of Justice, Federal Bureau of Investigation, George (Machine Gun) Kelly & Kathryn Kelly Court/Trial Transcripts; US Department of Justice, Federal Bureau of Investigation, Kathryn Thorne Kelly File

16. US Department of Justice, Federal Bureau of Investigation, George (Machine Gun) Kelly File: US Department of Justice, Federal Bureau of Investigation, George (Machine Gun) Kelly & Kathryn Kelly Court/Trial Transcripts; US Department of Justice, Federal Bureau of Investigation, Kathryn Thorne Kelly File

17. US Department of Justice, Federal Bureau of Investigation, George (Machine Gun) Kelly File: US Department of Justice, Federal Bureau of Investigation, George (Machine Gun) Kelly & Kathryn Kelly Court/Trial Transcripts; US Department of Justice, Federal Bureau of Investigation, Kathryn Thorne Kelly File

18. US Department of Justice, Federal Bureau of Investigation, George (Machine Gun) Kelly File: US Department of Justice, Federal Bureau of Investigation, George (Machine Gun) Kelly & Kathryn Kelly Court/Trial Transcripts; US Department of Justice: Federal Bureau of Investigation, Kathryn Thorne Kelly File

19. US Department of Justice: Federal Bureau of Investigation, George (Machine Gun) Kelly File: US Department of Justice, Federal Bureau of Investigation, George (Machine Gun) Kelly & Kathryn Kelly Court/Trial Transcripts; US Department of Justice, Federal Bureau of Investigation, Kathryn Thorne Kelly File

20. US Department of Justice, Federal Bureau of Investigation, George (Machine Gun) Kelly File; US Department of Justice, Federal Bureau of Investigation, George (Machine Gun) Kelly & Kathryn Kelly Court/Trial Transcripts; US Department of Justice, Federal Bureau of Investigation, Kathryn Thorne Kelly File

21. US Department of Justice, Federal Bureau of Investigation, George (Machine Gun) Kelly File; US Department of Justice, Federal Bureau of Investigation, George (Machine Gun) Kelly & Kathryn Kelly Court/Trial Transcripts; US Department of Justice, Federal Bureau of Investigation, Kathryn Thorne Kelly File

22. US Department of Justice, Federal Bureau of Investigation, George (Machine Gun) Kelly File; US Department of Justice, Federal Bureau of Investigation, George (Machine Gun) Kelly & Kathryn Kelly Court/Trial Transcripts; US Department of Justice, Federal Bureau of Investigation, Kathryn Thorne Kelly File

23. US Department of Justice, Federal Bureau of Investigation, George (Machine Gun) Kelly File; US Department of Justice, Federal Bureau of Investigation, George (Machine Gun) Kelly & Kathryn Kelly Court/Trial Transcripts; US Department of Justice, Federal Bureau of Investigation, Kathryn Thorne Kelly File; *Machine Gun Kelly: To Right a Wrong*, pg. 261–262

24. US Department of Justice, Federal Bureau of Investigation, George (Machine Gun) Kelly File; US Department of Justice, Federal Bureau of Investigation, George (Machine Gun) Kelly & Kathryn Kelly Court/Trial Transcripts, US Department of Justice, Federal Bureau of Investigation, Kathryn Thorne Kelly File; *St. Paul Daily News*, March 8, 1933

25. US Department of Justice, Federal Bureau of Investigation, George (Machine Gun) Kelly File; US Department of Justice, Federal Bureau of Investigation, George (Machine Gun) Kelly & Kathryn Kelly Court/Trial Transcripts; US Department of Justice, Federal Bureau of Investigation, Kathryn Thorne Kelly File

26. US Department of Justice, Federal Bureau of Investigation, George (Machine Gun) Kelly File; US Department of Justice, Federal Bureau of Investigation, George (Machine Gun) Kelly & Kathryn Kelly Court/Trial Transcripts; US Department of Justice, Federal Bureau of Investigation, Kathryn Thorne Kelly File

27. *New York Times*, October 1, 1933; *San Antonio Express*, August 29, 1933; US Department of Justice, Federal Bureau of Investigation, George (Machine Gun) Kelly File; US Department of Justice, Federal Bureau of Investigation, George (Machine Gun) Kelly & Kathryn Kelly Court/Trial Transcripts; US Department of Justice, Federal Bureau of Investigation, Kathryn Thorne Kelly File

28. US Department of Justice, Federal Bureau of Investigation, George (Machine Gun) Kelly File; US Department of Justice, Federal Bureau of Investigation, George (Machine Gun) Kelly & Kathryn Kelly Court/Trial Transcripts; US Department of Justice, Federal Bureau of Investigation, Kathryn Thorne Kelly File

29. US Department of Justice, Federal Bureau of Investigation, George (Machine Gun) Kelly File; US Department of Justice, Federal Bureau of Investigation, George (Machine Gun) Kelly & Kathryn Kelly Court/Trial Transcripts; US Department of Justice, Federal Bureau of Investigation, Kathryn Thorne Kelly File

30. US Department of Justice, Federal Bureau of Investigation, George (Machine Gun) Kelly File; US Department of Justice, Federal Bureau of Investigation, George (Machine Gun) Kelly & Kathryn Kelly Court/Trial Transcripts; US Department of Justice, Federal Bureau of Investigation, Kathryn Thorne Kelly File; *Enid Daily Eagle*, October 3, 1933; *Shawnee New Star*, October 3, 1933; *Guthrie Daily Leader*, September 17, 1933; *Oklahoma News*, September 17, 1933

31. US Department of Justice, Federal Bureau of Investigation, George (Machine Gun) Kelly File; US Department of Justice, Federal Bureau of Investigation, George (Machine Gun) Kelly & Kathryn Kelly Court/Trial Transcripts; US Department of Justice, Federal Bureau of Investigation, Kathryn Thorne Kelly File

32. US Department of Justice, Federal Bureau of Investigation, George (Machine Gun) Kelly File; US Department of Justice, Federal Bureau of Investigation, George (Machine Gun) Kelly & Kathryn Kelly Court/Trial Transcripts; US Department of Justice, Federal Bureau of Investigation, Kathryn Thorne Kelly File; US Department of Justice, Federal Bureau of Investigation, George (Machine Gun) Kelly & Kathryn Kelly, Geralene Arnold Statement & Testimony

33. US Department of Justice, Federal Bureau of Investigation, George (Machine Gun) Kelly File; US Department of Justice, Federal Bureau of Investigation, George (Machine Gun) Kelly & Kathryn Kelly Court/Trial Transcripts; US Department of Justice, Federal Bureau of Investigation, Kathryn Thorne Kelly File; US Department of Justice, Federal Bureau of Investigation, George (Machine Gun) Kelly & Kathryn Kelly, Geralene Arnold Statement & Testimony

34. US Department of Justice, Federal Bureau of Investigation, George (Machine Gun) Kelly File; US Department of Justice, Federal Bureau of Investigation, George (Machine Gun) Kelly & Kathryn Kelly Court/Trial Transcripts; US Department of Justice, Federal Bureau of Investigation, Kathryn Thorne Kelly File; US Department of Justice, Federal Bureau of Investigation, George (Machine Gun) Kelly & Kathryn Kelly, Geralene Arnold Statement & Testimony

35. US Department of Justice, Federal Bureau of Investigation, George (Machine Gun) Kelly File; US Department of Justice, Federal Bureau of Investigation, George (Machine Gun) Kelly & Kathryn Kelly Court/Trial Transcripts; US Department of Justice, Federal Bureau of Investigation, Kathryn Thorne Kelly File; US Department of Justice, Federal Bureau of Investigation, George (Machine Gun) Kelly & Kathryn Kelly, Geralene Arnold Statement & Testimony; *Crimes' Paradise*, pg. 183–184

36. US Department of Justice, Federal Bureau of Investigation, George (Machine Gun) Kelly File; US Department of Justice, Federal Bureau of Investigation, George (Machine Gun) Kelly & Kathryn Kelly Court/Trial Transcripts; US Department of Justice, Federal Bureau of Investigation, Kathryn Thorne Kelly File; US Department of Justice, Federal Bureau of Investigation, George (Machine Gun) Kelly & Kathryn Kelly, Geralene Arnold Statement & Testimony; *Crimes' Paradise*, pg. 183–184; *Public Enemies: America's Greatest Crime Wave and the Birth of the FBI, 1933–34*, pg. 123–124

37. *The Oklahoma News Sun*, September 18, 1933; *Chicago Tribune*, September 18, 1933; *Public Enemies: America's Greatest Crime Wave and the Birth of the FBI, 1933–34*, pg. 123–124

38. *Voices from Alcatraz*, pg. 81–82; US Department of Justice, Federal Bureau of Investigation, George (Machine Gun) Kelly File; US Department of Justice, Federal Bureau of Investigation, George (Machine Gun) Kelly & Kathryn Kelly Court/Trial Transcripts; US Department of Justice, Federal Bureau of Investigation, Kathryn Thorne Kelly File; US Department of Justice, Federal Bureau of Investigation, George (Machine Gun) Kelly & Kathryn Kelly, Geralene Arnold Statement & Testimony

39. *Voices from Alcatraz*, pg. 81–82; US Department of Justice, Federal Bureau of Investigation, George (Machine Gun) Kelly File; US Department of Justice, Federal Bureau of Investigation, George (Machine Gun) Kelly & Kathryn Kelly Court/Trial Transcripts; US Department of Justice, Federal Bureau of Investigation, Kathryn Thorne Kelly File; US Department of Justice, Federal Bureau of Investigation, George (Machine Gun) Kelly & Kathryn Kelly, Geralene Arnold Statement & Testimony

40. *Voices from Alcatraz*, pg. 81–82, 89–90; US Department of Justice, Federal Bureau of Investigation, George (Machine Gun) Kelly File; US Department of Justice, Federal Bureau of Investigation, George (Machine Gun) Kelly & Kathryn Kelly Court/Trial Transcripts; US Department of Justice, Federal Bureau of Investigation, Kathryn Thorne Kelly File; US Department of Justice, Federal Bureau of Investigation, George (Machine Gun) Kelly & Kathryn Kelly, Geralene Arnold Statement & Testimony

41. *Voices from Alcatraz*, pg. 81–82; US Department of Justice, Federal Bureau of Investigation, George (Machine Gun) Kelly File; US Department of Justice, Federal Bureau of Investigation, George (Machine Gun) Kelly & Kathryn Kelly Court/Trial Transcripts; US Department of Justice, Federal Bureau of Investigation, Kathryn Thorne Kelly File; US Department of Justice, Federal Bureau of Investigation, George (Machine Gun) Kelly & Kathryn Kelly, Geralene Arnold Statement & Testimony

42. *Voices from Alcatraz*, pg. 81–82; US Department of Justice, Federal Bureau of Investigation, George (Machine Gun) Kelly File; US Department of Justice, Federal Bureau of Investigation, George (Machine Gun) Kelly & Kathryn Kelly Court/Trial Transcripts; US Department of Justice, Federal Bureau of Investigation, Kathryn Thorne Kelly File; US Department of Justice, Federal Bureau of Investigation, George (Machine Gun) Kelly & Kathryn Kelly, Geralene Arnold Statement & Testimony

43. *Voices from Alcatraz*, pg. 81–82; US Department of Justice, Federal Bureau of Investigation, George (Machine Gun) Kelly File; US Department of Justice, Federal Bureau of Investigation, George (Machine Gun) Kelly & Kathryn Kelly Court/Trial Transcripts; US Department of Justice, Federal Bureau of Investigation, Kathryn Thorne Kelly File; US Department of Justice, Federal Bureau of Investigation, George (Machine Gun) Kelly & Kathryn Kelly, Geralene Arnold Statement & Testimony

44. *Voices from Alcatraz*, pg. 81–82, 89–90; US Department of Justice, Federal Bureau of Investigation, George (Machine Gun) Kelly File; US Department of Justice, Federal Bureau of Investigation, George (Machine Gun) Kelly & Kathryn Kelly Court/Trial Transcripts; US Department of Justice, Federal Bureau of Investigation, Kathryn Thorne Kelly File; US Department of Justice, Federal Bureau of Investigation, George (Machine Gun) Kelly & Kathryn Kelly, Geralene Arnold Statement & Testimony; *Public Enemies: America's Greatest Crime Wave and the Birth of the FBI, 1933–34*, pg. 123–124

45. *Voices from Alcatraz*, pg. 81–82, 89–90; US Department of Justice, Federal Bureau of Investigation, George (Machine Gun) Kelly File; US Department of Justice, Federal Bureau of Investigation, George (Machine Gun) Kelly & Kathryn Kelly Court/Trial Transcripts; US Department of Justice, Federal Bureau of Investigation, Kathryn Thorne Kelly File; US Department of Justice, Federal Bureau of Investigation, George (Machine Gun) Kelly & Kathryn Kelly, Geralene Arnold Statement & Testimony; *Public Enemies: America's Greatest Crime Wave and the Birth of the FBI, 1933–34*, pg. 123–124

46. *Voices from Alcatraz*, pg. 81-82, 89–90; US Department of Justice, Federal Bureau of Investigation, George (Machine Gun) Kelly File; US Department of Justice, Federal Bureau of Investigation, George (Machine Gun) Kelly & Kathryn Kelly Court/Trial Transcripts; US Department of Justice, Federal Bureau of Investigation, Kathryn Thorne Kelly File; US Department of Justice, Federal Bureau of Investigation, George (Machine Gun) Kelly & Kathryn Kelly, Geralene Arnold Statement & Testimony; *Public Enemies: America's Greatest Crime Wave and the Birth of the FBI, 1933–34*, pg. 123–124

47. US Department of Justice, Federal Bureau of Investigation, George (Machine Gun) Kelly File; US Department of Justice, Federal Bureau of Investigation, George (Machine Gun) Kelly & Kathryn Kelly Court/Trial Transcripts; US Department of Justice, Federal Bureau of Investigation, Kathryn Thorne Kelly File; US Department of Justice, Federal Bureau of Investigation, George (Machine Gun) Kelly & Kathryn Kelly, Geralene Arnold Statement & Testimony; *Machine Gun Kelly's Last Stand*, pg. 95–96

48. US Department of Justice, Federal Bureau of Investigation, George (Machine Gun) Kelly File; US Department of Justice, Federal Bureau of Investigation, George (Machine Gun) Kelly & Kathryn Kelly Court/Trial Transcripts; US Department of Justice, Federal Bureau of Investigation, Kathryn Thorne Kelly File; US Department of Justice, Federal Bureau of Investigation, George (Machine Gun) Kelly & Kathryn Kelly, Geralene Arnold Statement & Testimony

49. *Daily Oklahoman*, October 10, 1933

50. Ibid.

51. Ibid.

52. Ibid.

53. Ibid.

54. US Department of Justice: Federal Bureau of Investigation, George (Machine Gun) Kelly File: US Department of Justice, Federal Bureau of Investigation, George (Machine Gun) Kelly & Kathryn Kelly Court/Trial Transcripts; US Department of Justice, Federal Bureau of Investigation, Kathryn Thorne Kelly File; US Department of Justice, Federal Bureau of Investigation, George (Machine Gun) Kelly & Kathryn Kelly, Geralene Arnold Statement & Testimony

55. Agent Melvin Purvis letter to Bureau Director J. Edgar Hoover dated December 18, 1933

CHAPTER 8: Capturing the Kellys

1. *Daily Oklahoman*, September 20, 1933, *Miami Daily Record*, September 20, 1933

2. *Muskogee Daily Phoenix*, September 23, 1933

3. US Department of Justice, Federal Bureau of Investigation, George (Machine Gun) Kelly & Kathryn Kelly, Geralene Arnold Statement & Testimony

4. *Oklahoma News*, September 19, 1933

5. *Daily Oklahoman*, September 22, 1933; US Department of Justice, Federal Bureau of Investigation, Albert Bates File

6. *Muskogee Daily Phoenix*, September 21, 1933; *Muskogee Times Democrat*, October 11, 1933; US Department of Justice, Federal Bureau of Investigation, George (Machine Gun) Kelly & Kathryn Kelly, Geralene Arnold Statement & Testimony

7. US Department of Justice, Federal Bureau of Investigation, George (Machine Gun) Kelly File; US Department of Justice, Federal Bureau of Investigation, George (Machine Gun) Kelly & Kathryn Kelly Court/Trial Transcripts; US Department of Justice, Federal Bureau of Investigation, Kathryn Thorne Kelly File

8. US Department of Justice, Federal Bureau of Investigation, George (Machine Gun) Kelly File; US Department of Justice, Federal Bureau of Investigation, George (Machine Gun) Kelly & Kathryn Kelly Court/Trial Transcripts; US Department of Justice, Federal Bureau of Investigation, Kathryn Thorne Kelly File

9. US Department of Justice, Federal Bureau of Investigation, George (Machine Gun) Kelly File; US Department of Justice, Federal Bureau of Investigation, George (Machine Gun) Kelly & Kathryn Kelly Court/Trial Transcripts; US States Department of Justice, Federal Bureau of Investigation, Kathryn Thorne Kelly File

10. *Kathryn Kelly: The Moll Behind "Machine Gun" Kelly*, pg. 102–104; US Department of Justice, Federal Bureau of Investigation, George (Machine Gun) Kelly File; US Department of Justice, Federal Bureau of Investigation, George (Machine Gun) Kelly & Kathryn Kelly Court/Trial Transcripts; US Department of Justice, Federal Bureau of Investigation, Kathryn Thorne Kelly File; US Department of Justice, Federal Bureau of Investigation, George (Machine Gun) Kelly & Kathryn Kelly, Geralene Arnold Statement & Testimony

11. US Department of Justice, Federal Bureau of Investigation, George (Machine Gun) Kelly File; US Department of Justice, Federal Bureau of Investigation, George (Machine Gun) Kelly & Kathryn Kelly Court/Trial Transcripts; US Department of Justice, Federal Bureau of Investigation, Kathryn Thorne Kelly File; US Department of Justice, Federal Bureau of Investigation, George (Machine Gun) Kelly & Kathryn Kelly, Geralene Arnold Statement & Testimony; *Tulsa Tribune*, September 24, 1933

12. US Department of Justice, Federal Bureau of Investigation, George (Machine Gun) Kelly File; US Department of Justice, Federal Bureau of Investigation, George (Machine Gun) Kelly & Kathryn Kelly Court/Trial Transcripts; US Department of Justice, Federal Bureau of Investigation, Kathryn Thorne Kelly File; US Department of Justice, Federal Bureau of Investigation, George (Machine Gun) Kelly & Kathryn Kelly, Geralene Arnold Statement & Testimony; *Baltimore Sun*, September 25, 1933; *Bartlesville Daily Enterprise*, September 25, 1933

13. US Department of Justice, Federal Bureau of Investigation, George (Machine Gun) Kelly File; US Department of Justice, Federal Bureau of Investigation, George (Machine Gun) Kelly & Kathryn Kelly Court/Trial Transcripts; US Department of Justice, Federal Bureau of Investigation, Kathryn Thorne Kelly File; US Department of Justice, Federal Bureau of Investigation, George (Machine Gun) Kelly & Kathryn Kelly, Geralene Arnold Statement & Testimony *Fort Worth Star-Telegram*, September 25, 1933

14. US Department of Justice, Federal Bureau of Investigation, George (Machine Gun) Kelly File; US Department of Justice, Federal Bureau of Investigation, George (Machine Gun) Kelly & Kathryn Kelly Court/Trial Transcripts; US Department of Justice, Federal Bureau of Investigation, Kathryn Thorne Kelly File; US Department of Justice, Federal Bureau of Investigation, George (Machine Gun) Kelly & Kathryn Kelly, Geralene Arnold Statement & Testimony

15. US Department of Justice, Federal Bureau of Investigation, George (Machine Gun) Kelly File; US Department of Justice, Federal Bureau of Investigation, George (Machine Gun) Kelly & Kathryn Kelly Court/Trial Transcripts; US Department of Justice, Federal Bureau of Investigation, Kathryn Thorne Kelly File; US Department of Justice, Federal Bureau of Investigation, George (Machine Gun) Kelly & Kathryn Kelly, Geralene Arnold Statement & Testimony; *Kathryn Kelly: The Moll Behind "Machine Gun" Kelly*, pg. 103–104; *Voices from Alcatraz*, pg. 105–106

16. US Department of Justice, Federal Bureau of Investigation, George (Machine Gun) Kelly File; US Department of Justice, Federal Bureau of Investigation, George (Machine Gun) Kelly & Kathryn Kelly Court/Trial Transcripts; US Department of Justice: Federal Bureau of Investigation, Kathryn Thorne Kelly File: US Department of Justice, Federal Bureau of Investigation, George (Machine Gun) Kelly & Kathryn Kelly, Geralene Arnold Statement & Testimony

17. US Department of Justice, Federal Bureau of Investigation, George (Machine Gun) Kelly File; US Department of Justice, Federal Bureau of Investigation, George (Machine Gun) Kelly & Kathryn Kelly Court/Trial Transcripts; US Department of Justice, Federal Bureau of Investigation, Kathryn Thorne Kelly File; US Department of Justice, Federal Bureau of Investigation, George (Machine Gun) Kelly & Kathryn Kelly, Geralene Arnold Statement & Testimony

18. US Department of Justice, Federal Bureau of Investigation, George (Machine Gun) Kelly File; US Department of Justice, Federal Bureau of Investigation, George (Machine Gun) Kelly & Kathryn Kelly Court/Trial Transcripts; US Department of Justice, Federal Bureau of Investigation, Kathryn Thorne Kelly File; US Department of Justice, Federal Bureau of Investigation, George (Machine Gun) Kelly & Kathryn Kelly, Geralene Arnold Statement & Testimony

19. US Department of Justice, Federal Bureau of Investigation, George (Machine Gun) Kelly File; US Department of Justice, Federal Bureau of Investigation, George (Machine Gun) Kelly & Kathryn Kelly Court/Trial Transcripts; US Department of Justice, Federal Bureau of Investigation, Kathryn Thorne Kelly File; US Department of Justice, Federal Bureau of Investigation, George (Machine Gun) Kelly & Kathryn Kelly, Geralene Arnold Statement & Testimony

20. *Commercial Appeal*, September 22, 1933; *Commercial Appeal*, September 27, 1933; *Memphis Press Scimitar*, September 28, 1933

21. *Knoxville News Sentinel*, September 25, 1933

22. *Daily News Journal*, September 25, 1933; *Daily Oklahoman*, September 25, 1933; *Voices of Alcatraz*, pg. 107–108

23. *Fort Worth Star-Telegram*, September 26, 1933; *Bristol Herald*, September 27, 1933; *Voices from Alcatraz*, pg. 106–108

24. *Commercial Appeal*, September 27, 1933

25. US Department of Justice, Federal Bureau of Investigation, George (Machine Gun) Kelly File; US Department of Justice, Federal Bureau of Investigation, George (Machine Gun) Kelly & Kathryn Kelly Court/Trial Transcripts; US Department of Justice, Federal Bureau of Investigation, Kathryn Thorne Kelly File

26. US Department of Justice, Federal Bureau of Investigation, George (Machine Gun) Kelly File; US Department of Justice, Federal Bureau of Investigation, George (Machine Gun) Kelly & Kathryn Kelly Court/Trial Transcripts; US Department of Justice, Federal Bureau of Investigation, Kathryn Thorne Kelly File

27. US Department of Justice, Federal Bureau of Investigation, George (Machine Gun) Kelly File; US Department of Justice, Federal Bureau of Investigation, George (Machine Gun) Kelly & Kathryn Kelly Court/Trial Transcripts; US Department of Justice, Federal Bureau of Investigation, Kathryn Thorne Kelly File

28. US Department of Justice, Federal Bureau of Investigation, George (Machine Gun) Kelly File; US Department of Justice, Federal Bureau of Investigation, George (Machine Gun) Kelly & Kathryn Kelly Court/Trial Transcripts; US Department of Justice, Federal Bureau of Investigation, Kathryn Thorne Kelly File

29. US Department of Justice, Federal Bureau of Investigation, George (Machine Gun) Kelly File; US Department of Justice, Federal Bureau of Investigation, George (Machine Gun) Kelly & Kathryn Kelly Court/Trial Transcripts; US Department of Justice: Federal Bureau of Investigation, Kathryn Thorne Kelly File

30. *Bristol Herald Courier*, September 27, 1933; US Department of Justice, Federal Bureau of Investigation, George (Machine Gun) Kelly File; US Department of Justice, Federal Bureau of Investigation, George (Machine Gun) Kelly & Kathryn Kelly Court/Trial Transcripts; US Department of Justice, Federal Bureau of Investigation, Kathryn Thorne Kelly File

31. US Department of Justice, Federal Bureau of Investigation, George (Machine Gun) Kelly File; US Department of Justice, Federal Bureau of Investigation, George (Machine Gun) Kelly & Kathryn Kelly Court/Trial Transcripts; US Department of Justice, Federal Bureau of Investigation, Kathryn Thorne Kelly File; *Fort Worth Star-Telegram*, September 26, 1933

32. US Department of Justice, Federal Bureau of Investigation, George (Machine Gun) Kelly File; US Department of Justice, Federal Bureau of Investigation, George (Machine Gun) Kelly & Kathryn Kelly Court/Trial Transcripts: US Department of Justice, Federal Bureau of Investigation, Kathryn Thorne Kelly File; *Fort Worth Star-Telegram*, September 26, 1933

33. *Bristol Herald Courier*, September 27, 1933; *Bristol News Bulletin*, September 26, 1933; *Lampasas Leader*, September 29, 1933; *Machine Gun Kelly: To Right a Wrong*, pg. 262–265

34. *Bristol Herald Courier*, September 27, 1933; *Bristol News Bulletin*, September 26, 1933; *Lampasas Leader*, September 29, 1933; *Machine Gun Kelly: To Right a Wrong*, pg. 262–265

35. *Memphis Press Scimitar*, September 27, 1933

36. US Department of Justice, Federal Bureau of Investigation, George (Machine Gun) Kelly File; US Department of Justice, Federal Bureau of Investigation, George (Machine Gun) Kelly & Kathryn Kelly Court/Trial Transcripts; US Department of Justice, Federal Bureau of Investigation, Kathryn Thorne Kelly File; *Memphis Press Scimitar*, September 27, 1933; *Commercial Appeal*, September 28, 1933

37. US Department of Justice, Federal Bureau of Investigation, George (Machine Gun) Kelly File; US Department of Justice, Federal Bureau of Investigation, George (Machine Gun) Kelly & Kathryn Kelly Court/Trial Transcripts; US Department of Justice, Federal Bureau of Investigation, Kathryn Thorne Kelly File; *Memphis Press Scimitar*, September 27, 1933; *Commercial Appeal*, September 28, 1933

38. US Department of Justice, Federal Bureau of Investigation, George (Machine Gun) Kelly File; US Department of Justice, Federal Bureau of Investigation, George (Machine Gun) Kelly & Kathryn Kelly Court/Trial Transcripts; US Department of Justice, Federal Bureau of Investigation, Kathryn Thorne Kelly File; *Memphis Press Scimitar*, September 27, 1933; *Commercial Appeal*, September 28, 1933

39. US Department of Justice, Federal Bureau of Investigation, George (Machine Gun) Kelly File; US Department of Justice, Federal Bureau of Investigation, George (Machine Gun) Kelly & Kathryn Kelly Court/Trial Transcripts; US Department of Justice, Federal Bureau of Investigation, Kathryn Thorne Kelly File; *Memphis Press Scimitar*, September 27, 1933; *Commercial Appeal*, September 28, 1933

40. US Department of Justice, Federal Bureau of Investigation, George (Machine Gun) Kelly File; US Department of Justice, Federal Bureau of Investigation, George (Machine Gun) Kelly & Kathryn Kelly Court/Trial Transcripts; US Department of Justice, Federal Bureau of Investigation, Kathryn Thorne Kelly File; *Memphis Press Scimitar*, September 27, 1933; *Commercial Appeal*, September 28, 1933

41. US Department of Justice, Federal Bureau of Investigation, George (Machine Gun) Kelly File; US Department of Justice, Federal Bureau of Investigation, George (Machine Gun) Kelly & Kathryn Kelly Court/Trial Transcripts; US Department of Justice, Federal Bureau of Investigation, Kathryn Thorne Kelly File; *Memphis Press Scimitar*, September 27, 1933; *Commercial Appeal*, September 28, 1933

42. US Department of Justice, Federal Bureau of Investigation, George (Machine Gun) Kelly File; US Department of Justice, Federal Bureau of Investigation, George (Machine Gun) Kelly & Kathryn Kelly Court/Trial Transcripts; US Department of Justice, Federal Bureau of Investigation, Kathryn Thorne Kelly File; US Department of Justice, Federal Bureau of Investigation, George (Machine Gun) Kelly & Kathryn Kelly, Geralene Arnold Statement & Testimony; *Commercial Appeal*, September 28, 1933; *Crimes' Paradise*, pg. 216–219

43. US Department of Justice, Federal Bureau of Investigation, George (Machine Gun) Kelly File; US Department of Justice, Federal Bureau of Investigation, George (Machine Gun) Kelly & Kathryn Kelly Court/Trial Transcripts; US Department of Justice, Federal Bureau of Investigation, Kathryn Thorne Kelly File; US Department of Justice, Federal Bureau of Investigation, George (Machine Gun) Kelly & Kathryn Kelly, Geralene Arnold Statement & Testimony

44. US Department of Justice, Federal Bureau of Investigation, George (Machine Gun) Kelly File; US Department of Justice, Federal Bureau of Investigation, George (Machine Gun) Kelly & Kathryn Kelly Court/Trial Transcripts; US Department of Justice, Federal Bureau of Investigation, Kathryn Thorne Kelly File; US Department of Justice, Federal Bureau of Investigation, George (Machine Gun) Kelly & Kathryn Kelly, Geralene Arnold Statement & Testimony

45. US Department of Justice, Federal Bureau of Investigation, George (Machine Gun) Kelly File; US Department of Justice, Federal Bureau of Investigation, George (Machine Gun) Kelly & Kathryn Kelly Court/Trial Transcripts; US Department of Justice, Federal Bureau of Investigation, Kathryn Thorne Kelly File; US Department of Justice, Federal Bureau of Investigation, George (Machine Gun) Kelly & Kathryn Kelly, Geralene Arnold Statement & Testimony; *Commercial Appeal*, September 27, 1933; *Memphis Press Scimitar*, September 27, 1933

46. *Commercial Appeal*, September 27, 1933; *Memphis Press Scimitar*, September 27, 1933

47. *Commercial Appeal*, September 27, 1933; *Memphis Press Scimitar*, September 27, 1933

48. *Commercial Appeal*, September 27, 1933; *Memphis Press Scimitar*, September 27, 1933

49. US Department of Justice, Federal Bureau of Investigation, George (Machine Gun) Kelly File; US Department of Justice, Federal Bureau of Investigation, George (Machine Gun) Kelly & Kathryn Kelly Court/Trial Transcripts; US Department of Justice, Federal Bureau of Investigation, Kathryn Thorne Kelly File; US Department of Justice, Federal Bureau of Investigation, George (Machine Gun) Kelly & Kathryn Kelly, Geralene Arnold Statement & Testimony; *Commercial Appeal*, September 27, 1933; *Memphis Press Scimitar*, September 27, 1933

50. US Department of Justice, Federal Bureau of Investigation, George (Machine Gun) Kelly File; US Department of Justice, Federal Bureau of Investigation, George (Machine Gun) Kelly & Kathryn Kelly Court/Trial Transcripts; US Department of Justice, Federal Bureau of Investigation, Kathryn Thorne Kelly File; *Commercial Appeal*, September 27, 1933; *Memphis Press Scimitar*, September 27, 1933

51. US Department of Justice, Federal Bureau of Investigation, George (Machine Gun) Kelly File; US Department of Justice, Federal Bureau of Investigation, George (Machine Gun) Kelly & Kathryn Kelly Court/Trial Transcripts; US Department of Justice, Federal Bureau of Investigation, Kathryn Thorne Kelly File; *Bristol News Bulletin*, September 27, 1933

52. *Commercial Appeal*, September 28, 1933; *Commercial Appeal*, September 29, 1933

53. *Commercial Appeal*, October 12, 1933; *Voices from Alcatraz*, pg. 221–225; *Crimes' Paradise*, pg. 220–221

CHAPTER 9: Leaving Memphis

1. *Fort Worth Star-Telegram*, October 1, 1933; *Commercial Appeal*, October 2, 1933

2. *Fort Worth Star-Telegram*, October 1, 1933; *Commercial Appeal*, October 2, 1933

3. *Fort Worth Star-Telegram*, October 1, 1933; *Commercial Appeal*, October 2, 1933

4. *Fort Worth Star-Telegram*, October 1, 1933; *Commercial Appeal*, October 2, 1933

5. *Fort Worth Star-Telegram*, October 1, 1933; *Commercial Appeal*, October 2, 1933

6. *Fort Worth Star-Telegram*, October 1, 1933; *Commercial Appeal*, October 2, 1933

7. *Commercial Appeal*, September 28, 1933; *Memphis Press Scimitar*, September 28, 1933; *Memphis Press Scimitar*, September 29, 1933; *Daily Oklahoman*, September 28, 1933

8. *Chattanooga Daily Times*, October 2, 1933; *Austin American*, October 1, 1933

9. *Oklahoma News*, October 2, 1933

10. Ibid.

11. *Daily Journal Capital*, October 1, 1933

12. *Owosso Argus Press*, June 23, 1932

13. *Daily Journal Capital*, October 1, 1933

14. *Oklahoma News*, October 2, 1933; US Department of Justice, Federal Bureau of Investigation, George (Machine Gun) Kelly & Kathryn Kelly Court/Trial Transcripts

15. US Department of Justice, Federal Bureau of Investigation, George (Machine Gun) Kelly & Kathryn Kelly Court/Trial Transcripts; *Blackwell Morning Tribune*, October 2, 1933

16. US Department of Justice, Federal Bureau of Investigation, George (Machine Gun) Kelly & Kathryn Kelly Court/Trial Transcripts; *Commercial Appeal*, October 1, 1933

17. US Department of Justice, Federal Bureau of Investigation, George (Machine Gun) Kelly & Kathryn Kelly Court/Trial Transcripts; *Cushing Daily Citizen*, October 2, 1933

18. US Department of Justice, Federal Bureau of Investigation, George (Machine Gun) Kelly & Kathryn Kelly Court/Trial Transcripts

19. *Oklahoma News*, September 21, 1933

20. Ibid.

21. *Tulsa Tribune*, October 3, 1933; US Department of Justice, Federal Bureau of Investigation, George (Machine Gun) Kelly & Kathryn Kelly Court/Trial Transcripts

22. *Sayre Headlight*, October 5, 1933; *Daily Oklahoman*, October 3, 1933; US Department of Justice, Federal Bureau of Investigation, George (Machine Gun) Kelly & Kathryn Kelly Court/Trial Transcripts

23. *Bartlesville Daily Enterprise*, October 3, 1933; US Department of Justice, Federal Bureau of Investigation, George (Machine Gun) Kelly & Kathryn Kelly Court/Trial Transcripts; *Sayre Daily Headlight Journal*, October 3, 1933

24. *El Reno Daily Tribune*, October 4, 1933

25. *Shawnee Morning News*, October 4, 1933

26. US Department of Justice, Federal Bureau of Investigation, George (Machine Gun) Kelly & Kathryn Kelly Court/Trial Transcripts; *Pittsburgh Press*, October 13, 1933; *Enid Morning News*, October 3, 1933; *Duncan Banner*, October 3, 1933, *From Gun to Gavel: The Courtroom Recollections of James Mathers of Oklahoma as Told to Marshall Houts*, pg. 231–233

27. US Department of Justice, Federal Bureau of Investigation, George (Machine Gun) Kelly & Kathryn Kelly Court/Trial Transcripts; *Evansville Press*, October 3, 1933; *Reading Times*, October 13, 1933

28. US Department of Justice, Federal Bureau of Investigation, George (Machine Gun) Kelly & Kathryn Kelly Court/Trial Transcripts; *Muskogee Daily Phoenix*, October 5, 1933; *From Gun to Gavel: The Courtroom Recollections of James Mathers of Oklahoma as Told to Marshall Houts*, pg. 232–233

29. US Department of Justice, Federal Bureau of Investigation, George (Machine Gun) Kelly & Kathryn Kelly Court/Trial Transcripts; *Muskogee Daily Phoenix*, October 5, 1933

30. US Department of Justice, Federal Bureau of Investigation, George (Machine Gun) Kelly & Kathryn Kelly Court/Trial Transcripts

31. US Department of Justice, Federal Bureau of Investigation, George (Machine Gun) Kelly & Kathryn Kelly Court/Trial Transcripts; *Sapulpa Herald*, October 6, 1933; *Alva Review Courier*, October 6, 1933; *Daily Oklahoman*, October 3, 1933

32. US Department of Justice, Federal Bureau of Investigation, George (Machine Gun) Kelly & Kathryn Kelly Court/Trial Transcripts; *Daily Oklahoman*, October 8, 1933

33. US Department of Justice, Federal Bureau of Investigation, George (Machine Gun) Kelly & Kathryn Kelly Court/Trial Transcripts

34. US Department of Justice, Federal Bureau of Investigation, George (Machine Gun) Kelly & Kathryn Kelly Court/Trial Transcripts; *Mangum Daily Star*, October 5, 1933

35. US Department of Justice, Federal Bureau of Investigation, George (Machine Gun) Kelly & Kathryn Kelly Court/Trial Transcripts; *From Gun to Gavel: The Courtroom Recollections of James Mathers of Oklahoma as Told to Marshall Houts*, pg. 231–233

36. US Department of Justice, Federal Bureau of Investigation, George (Machine Gun) Kelly & Kathryn Kelly Court/Trial Transcripts; *From Gun to Gavel: The Courtroom Recollections of James Mathers of Oklahoma as Told to Marshall Houts*, pg. 231–233

37. US Department of Justice, Federal Bureau of Investigation, George (Machine Gun) Kelly & Kathryn Kelly Court/Trial Transcripts

38. *Oklahoma News*, October, 8, 1933; US Department of Justice, Federal Bureau of Investigation, George (Machine Gun) Kelly & Kathryn Kelly Court/Trial Transcripts

39. *Oklahoma News*, October, 8, 1933; US Department of Justice, Federal Bureau of Investigation, George (Machine Gun) Kelly & Kathryn Kelly Court/Trial Transcripts

40. *Oklahoma News*, October, 8, 1933; US Department of Justice, Federal Bureau of Investigation, George (Machine Gun) Kelly & Kathryn Kelly Court/Trial Transcripts

41. *Oklahoma News*, October, 8, 1933; US Department of Justice, Federal Bureau of Investigation, George (Machine Gun) Kelly & Kathryn Kelly Court/Trial Transcripts

42. *Oklahoma News*, October, 8, 1933; US Department of Justice, Federal Bureau of Investigation, George (Machine Gun) Kelly & Kathryn Kelly Court/Trial Transcripts; *Shawnee Morning News*, October 8, 1933

43. *Oklahoma News*, October, 8, 1933; US Department of Justice, Federal Bureau of Investigation, George (Machine Gun) Kelly & Kathryn Kelly Court/Trial Transcripts; *Shawnee Morning News*, October 8, 1933; *Drumright Weekly Derrick*, October 8, 1933

44. *Oklahoma News*, October, 8, 1933; US Department of Justice, Federal Bureau of Investigation, George (Machine Gun) Kelly & Kathryn Kelly Court/Trial Transcripts; *Fort Worth Star-Telegram*, October 7, 1933; *Oklahoma News*, October 8, 1933; *Daily Oklahoman*, October 10, 1933

45. *Oklahoma News*, October, 8, 1933; US Department of Justice, Federal Bureau of Investigation, George (Machine Gun) Kelly & Kathryn Kelly Court/Trial Transcripts; *Fort Worth Star-Telegram*, October 7, 1933; *Oklahoma News*, October 8, 1933; *Daily Oklahoman*, October 10, 1933

46. *Fort Worth Star-Telegram*, October 7, 1933

47. Ibid.; *Crimes' Paradise*, pg. 228–229

48. *Pittsburgh Press*, October 13, 1933

49. Ibid.

50. *Seminole Producer*, October 6, 1933

51. US Department of Justice, Federal Bureau of Investigation, George (Machine Gun) Kelly & Kathryn Kelly Court/Trial Transcripts; *Miami Daily News*, October 9, 1933

52. *Hugo Daily News*, October 9, 1933

53. Ibid.

54. *Miami Daily News*, October 9, 1933

55. US Department of Justice, Federal Bureau of Investigation, George (Machine Gun) Kelly & Kathryn Kelly Court/Trial Transcripts; *Oklahoma News*, October 9, 1933

56. US Department of Justice, Federal Bureau of Investigation, George (Machine Gun) Kelly & Kathryn Kelly Court/Trial Transcripts; *Muskogee Daily Phoenix*, October 9, 1933

57. *Bartlesville Daily Enterprise*, October 9, 1933

58. Ibid.

CHAPTER 10: The Kellys on Trial

1. *Voices from Alcatraz*, pg. 112–115; *Daily Oklahoman*, October 10, 1933

2. *Voices from Alcatraz*, pg. 112–115; *Daily Oklahoman*, October 10, 1933

3. *Voices from Alcatraz*, pg. 112–115; *Daily Oklahoman*, October 10, 1933

4. *Voices from Alcatraz*, pg. 112–115; *Daily Oklahoman*, October 10, 1933

5. *Voices from Alcatraz*, pg. 112–115; *Daily Oklahoman*, October 10, 1933

6. *Voices from Alcatraz*, pg. 112–115; *Daily Oklahoman*, October 10, 1933; *Altus Times Democrat*, October 9, 1933

7. *Daily Oklahoman*, October 10, 1933; *Altus Times Democrat*, October 9, 1933

8. *Cushing Daily Citizen*, October 9, 1933; *Elk City Daily News*, October 9, 1933

9. *Altus Times Democrat*, October 9, 1933; US Department of Justice, Federal Bureau of Investigation, George (Machine Gun) Kelly & Kathryn Kelly Court/Trial Transcripts

10. US Department of Justice, Federal Bureau of Investigation, George (Machine Gun) Kelly & Kathryn Kelly Court/Trial Transcripts; *Oklahoma News*, October 9, 1933; *Lawton Constitution*, October 9, 1933

11. US Department of Justice, Federal Bureau of Investigation, George (Machine Gun) Kelly & Kathryn Kelly Court/Trial Transcripts; *Oklahoma News*, October 9, 1933

12. US Department of Justice, Federal Bureau of Investigation, George (Machine Gun) Kelly & Kathryn Kelly Court/Trial Transcripts; *Oklahoma News*, October 9, 1933; *Altus Times Democrat*, October 9, 1933

13. US Department of Justice, Federal Bureau of Investigation, George (Machine Gun) Kelly & Kathryn Kelly Court/Trial Transcripts; *Oklahoma News*, October 9, 1933; *Altus Times Democrat*, October 9, 1933

14. US Department of Justice, Federal Bureau of Investigation, George (Machine Gun) Kelly & Kathryn Kelly Court/Trial Transcripts; *Oklahoma News*, October 9, 1933; *Altus Times Democrat*, October 9, 1933; *Hobart Democrat Chief*, October 9, 1933; *Holdenville Daily News*, October 9, 1933; *Clinton Daily News*, October 9, 1933

15. US Department of Justice, Federal Bureau of Investigation, George (Machine Gun) Kelly & Kathryn Kelly Court/Trial Transcripts

16. Ibid.

17. Ibid.

18. Ibid.

19. Ibid.

20. US Department of Justice, Federal Bureau of Investigation, George (Machine Gun) Kelly & Kathryn Kelly Court/Trial Transcripts; *Daily Oklahoman*, October 10, 1933

21. US Department of Justice, Federal Bureau of Investigation, George (Machine Gun) Kelly & Kathryn Kelly Court/Trial Transcripts; *Sapulpa Herald*, October 9, 1933; *Shawnee Evening Star*, October 10, 1933; *Vinita Daily Journal*, October 9, 1933

22. *Holdenville Daily News*, October 9, 1933; *Clinton Daily News*, October 9, 1933; *Vinita Daily Journal*, October 9, 1933

23. US Department of Justice, Federal Bureau of Investigation, George (Machine Gun) Kelly & Kathryn Kelly Court/Trial Transcripts; *Oklahoma News*, October 10, 1933

24. US Department of Justice, Federal Bureau of Investigation, George (Machine Gun) Kelly & Kathryn Kelly Court/Trial Transcripts

25. Ibid.

26. Ibid.

27. Ibid.; *The Year of Fear: Machine Gun Kelly and the Manhunt That Changed the Nation*, pg. 204–205

28. US Department of Justice, Federal Bureau of Investigation, George (Machine Gun) Kelly & Kathryn Kelly Court/Trial Transcripts; *Daily Ardmoreite*, October 10, 1933; *Oklahoma News*, October 10, 1933

29. US Department of Justice, Federal Bureau of Investigation, George (Machine Gun) Kelly & Kathryn Kelly Court/Trial Transcripts

30. Ibid.

31. US Department of Justice, Federal Bureau of Investigation, George (Machine Gun) Kelly & Kathryn Kelly, Geralene Arnold Statement & Testimony; *Muskogee Daily Phoenix*, October 11, 1933

32. US Department of Justice, Federal Bureau of Investigation, George (Machine Gun) Kelly & Kathryn Kelly, Geralene Arnold Statement & Testimony; *Daily Oklahoman*, October 11, 1933

33. US Department of Justice, Federal Bureau of Investigation, George (Machine Gun) Kelly & Kathryn Kelly, Geralene Arnold Statement & Testimony

34. US Department of Justice, Federal Bureau of Investigation, George (Machine Gun) Kelly & Kathryn Kelly Court/Trial Transcripts; *Daily Oklahoman*, October 11, 1933

35. US Department of Justice, Federal Bureau of Investigation, George (Machine Gun) Kelly & Kathryn Kelly Court/Trial Transcripts; *Daily Oklahoman*, October 11, 1933

36. US Department of Justice, Federal Bureau of Investigation, George (Machine Gun) Kelly & Kathryn Kelly Court/Trial Transcripts; *Daily Oklahoman*, October 11, 1933

37. US Department of Justice, Federal Bureau of Investigation, George (Machine Gun) Kelly & Kathryn Kelly Court/Trial Transcripts; *Daily Oklahoman*, October 11, 1933

38. US Department of Justice, Federal Bureau of Investigation, George (Machine Gun) Kelly & Kathryn Kelly Court/Trial Transcripts; *Daily Oklahoman*, October 11, 1933

39. US Department of Justice, Federal Bureau of Investigation, George (Machine Gun) Kelly & Kathryn Kelly Court/Trial Transcripts; *Daily Oklahoman*, October 11, 1933

40. US Department of Justice, Federal Bureau of Investigation, George (Machine Gun) Kelly & Kathryn Kelly Court/Trial Transcripts; *Daily Oklahoman*, October 11, 1933

41. US Department of Justice, Federal Bureau of Investigation, George (Machine Gun) Kelly & Kathryn Kelly Court/Trial Transcripts; *Daily Oklahoman*, October 11, 1933

42. US Department of Justice, Federal Bureau of Investigation, George (Machine Gun) Kelly & Kathryn Kelly, Geralene Arnold Statement & Testimony

43. US Department of Justice, Federal Bureau of Investigation, George (Machine Gun) Kelly & Kathryn Kelly, Geralene Arnold Statement & Testimony; *Muskogee Daily Phoenix*, October 11, 1933

44. US Department of Justice, Federal Bureau of Investigation, George (Machine Gun) Kelly & Kathryn Kelly, Geralene Arnold Statement & Testimony; *Muskogee Daily Phoenix*, October 11, 1933

45. US Department of Justice, Federal Bureau of Investigation, George (Machine Gun) Kelly & Kathryn Kelly, Geralene Arnold Statement & Testimony; *Muskogee Daily Phoenix*, October 11, 1933

46. US Department of Justice, Federal Bureau of Investigation, George (Machine Gun) Kelly & Kathryn Kelly, Geralene Arnold Statement & Testimony; *Muskogee Daily Phoenix*, October 11, 1933

47. US Department of Justice, Federal Bureau of Investigation, George (Machine Gun) Kelly & Kathryn Kelly, Geralene Arnold Statement & Testimony; *Muskogee Daily Phoenix*, October 11, 1933

48. US Department of Justice, Federal Bureau of Investigation, George (Machine Gun) Kelly & Kathryn Kelly, Geralene Arnold Statement & Testimony; *Muskogee Daily Phoenix*, October 11, 1933; *Voices from Alcatraz*, pg. 113–116

49. US Department of Justice, Federal Bureau of Investigation, George (Machine Gun) Kelly & Kathryn Kelly Court/Trial Transcripts; *Muskogee Daily Phoenix*, October 11, 1933

50. US Department of Justice, Federal Bureau of Investigation, George (Machine Gun) Kelly & Kathryn Kelly Court/Trial Transcripts

51. Ibid.

52. Ibid.

53. Ibid.

54. Ibid.

55. *Oklahoma News*, October 13, 1933

56. Ibid.

57. Ibid.

58. US Department of Justice, Federal Bureau of Investigation, George (Machine Gun) Kelly & Kathryn Kelly Court/Trial Transcripts

59. *Vinita Daily Journal*, October 11, 1933

60. Ibid.

61. US States Department of Justice, Federal Bureau of Investigation, George (Machine Gun) Kelly & Kathryn Kelly Court/Trial Transcripts

62. Ibid.

63. Ibid.

64. Ibid.; *Oklahoma News*, October 12, 1933

65. *Waco News Tribune*, October 11, 1933

66. *Commercial Appeal*, October 22, 1933; *Memphis Press Scimitar*, October 12, 1933

67. US Department of Justice, Federal Bureau of Investigation, George (Machine Gun) Kelly & Kathryn Kelly Court/Trial Transcripts

68. Ibid.

69. *Oklahoma Daily*, October 11, 1933

70. Ibid.

71. US Department of Justice, Federal Bureau of Investigation, George (Machine Gun) Kelly & Kathryn Kelly Court/Trial Transcripts

72. Ibid.

CHAPTER 11: Defending Kathryn

1. *Voices from Alcatraz*, pg. 115–118; *Oklahoma News*, October 11, 1933

2. US Department of Justice, Federal Bureau of Investigation, George (Machine Gun) Kelly & Kathryn Kelly Court/Trial Transcripts; *Oklahoma News*, October 11, 1933

3. US Department of Justice, Federal Bureau of Investigation, George (Machine Gun) Kelly & Kathryn Kelly Court/Trial Transcripts

4. Ibid.

5. Ibid.

6. Ibid.

7. Ibid; *Cushing Daily Citizen*, October 11, 1933

8. US Department of Justice, Federal Bureau of Investigation, George (Machine Gun) Kelly & Kathryn Kelly Court/Trial Transcripts

9. Ibid; *Cushing Daily Citizen*, October 11, 1933

10. US Department of Justice, Federal Bureau of Investigation, George (Machine Gun) Kelly & Kathryn Kelly Court/Trial Transcripts

11. Ibid.

12. Ibid.

13. Ibid.

14. Ibid.

15. Ibid.

16. Ibid; *Cushing Daily Citizen*, October 11, 1933

17. US Department of Justice, Federal Bureau of Investigation, George (Machine Gun) Kelly & Kathryn Kelly Court/Trial Transcripts

18. US Department of Justice, Federal Bureau of Investigation, George (Machine Gun) Kelly & Kathryn Kelly Court/Trial Transcripts; *Oklahoma News*, October 12, 1933

19. US Department of Justice, Federal Bureau of Investigation, George (Machine Gun) Kelly & Kathryn Kelly Court/Trial Transcripts; *Voices from Alcatraz*, pg. 117–118

20. US Department of Justice, Federal Bureau of Investigation, George (Machine Gun) Kelly & Kathryn Kelly Court/Trial Transcripts; *Bryan County Democrat*, October 12, 1933; *Southeastern Oklahoma Citizen*, October 12, 1933

21. US Department of Justice, Federal Bureau of Investigation, George (Machine Gun) Kelly & Kathryn Kelly Court/Trial Transcripts; *Crimes' Paradise*, pg. 226–227; *Cushing Daily Citizen*, October 11, 1933

22. US Department of Justice, Federal Bureau of Investigation, George (Machine Gun) Kelly & Kathryn Kelly Court/Trial Transcripts; *Cushing Daily Citizen*, October 11, 1933

23. US Department of Justice, Federal Bureau of Investigation, George (Machine Gun) Kelly & Kathryn Kelly Court/Trial Transcripts

24. Ibid.

25. Ibid.

26. Ibid.; *Tulsa Tribune*, October 11, 1933; Special Agent in Charge Whitley to Bureau Director J. Edgar Hoover dated November 8, 1933 Regarding Louise Donavon Background/Aliases

27. US Department of Justice, Federal Bureau of Investigation, George (Machine Gun) Kelly & Kathryn Kelly Court/Trial Transcripts

28. Ibid.

29. US Department of Justice, Federal Bureau of Investigation, George (Machine Gun) Kelly & Kathryn Kelly Court/Trial Transcripts; *Oklahoma News*, October 11, 1933

30. US Department of Justice, Federal Bureau of Investigation, George (Machine Gun) Kelly & Kathryn Kelly Court/Trial Transcripts

31. Ibid.

32. Ibid.

33. Ibid.

34. Ibid.

35. Ibid.

36. Ibid.

37. Ibid.

38. Ibid.; *Muskogee Times Democrat*, October 11, 1933; *Bristow Daily Record*, October 11, 1933; *Anadarko News*, October 11, 1933

39. US Department of Justice, Federal Bureau of Investigation, George (Machine Gun) Kelly & Kathryn Kelly Court/Trial Transcripts; *Voices from Alcatraz*, pg. 117–119

40. US Department of Justice, Federal Bureau of Investigation, George (Machine Gun) Kelly & Kathryn Kelly Court/Trial Transcripts; *Daily Oklahoman*, October 12, 1933

41. US Department of Justice, Federal Bureau of Investigation, George (Machine Gun) Kelly & Kathryn Kelly Court/Trial Transcripts; *Hugo Daily News*, October 12, 1933

42. US Department of Justice, Federal Bureau of Investigation, George (Machine Gun) Kelly & Kathryn Kelly Court/Trial Transcripts; *Frederick Leader*, October 12, 1933

43. US Department of Justice, Federal Bureau of Investigation, George (Machine Gun) Kelly & Kathryn Kelly Court/Trial Transcripts; *Frederick Leader*, October 12, 1933; *Daily Oklahoman*, October 12, 1933; *Hugo Daily News*, October 12, 1933

44. US Department of Justice, Federal Bureau of Investigation, George (Machine Gun) Kelly & Kathryn Kelly Court/Trial Transcripts; *Frederick Leader*, October 12, 1933; *Daily Oklahoman*, October 12, 1933; *Hugo Daily News*, October 12, 1933

45. *Oklahoma News*, October 12, 1933

46. US Department of Justice, Federal Bureau of Investigation, George (Machine Gun) Kelly & Kathryn Kelly Court/Trial Transcripts

47. *Oklahoma News*, October 12, 1933

48. Ibid.

49. US Department of Justice, Federal Bureau of Investigation, George (Machine Gun) Kelly & Kathryn Kelly Court/Trial Transcripts; *Guthrie Daily Leader*, October 12, 1933; *Memphis Press Scimitar*, October 12, 1933

50. US Department of Justice, Federal Bureau of Investigation, George (Machine Gun) Kelly & Kathryn Kelly Court/Trial Transcripts

51. *Okmulgee Daily Times*, October 13, 1933

52. Ibid.

53. *Enid Daily Eagle*, October 12, 1933

54. Ibid.

55. Ibid.

56. *Pensacola News*, October 13, 1933

57. Ibid.

58. Ibid.

59. *Bartlesville Examiner Enterprise*, October 14, 1933

60. *Enid Daily Eagle*, October 12, 1933; *Morning Examiner*, October 13, 1933; *Chattanooga News*, October 13, 1933

61. *Enid Daily Eagle*, October 12, 1933; *Morning Examiner*, October 13, 1933; *Chattanooga News*, October 13, 1933

62. US Department of Justice, Federal Bureau of Investigation, Kathryn Thorne Kelly File

63. Ibid.

64. Ibid.

65. Ibid.

66. *Hugo Daily News*, October 12, 1933

CHAPTER 12: The Verdict

1. *Carnegie Herald*, October 18, 1933; *Cushing Daily Citizen*, October 18, 1933

2. *Commercial Appeal*, October 13, 1933; *Okmulgee Daily Times*, October 18, 1933; *Memphis Press Scimitar*, October 13, 1933

3. *Commercial Appeal*, October 14, 1933

4. *Commercial Appeal*, October 13, 1933, *Commercial Appeal*, October 14, 1933

5. *Winona Daily News*, May 6, 1984

6. *Funk & Wagnalls New Encyclopedia* , Volume 15; Federal Bureau of Investigation, J. Edgar Hoover letter to law enforcement officials dated July 1, 1955

7. okhistory.org/publications/enc/entry.php?entry=UR009 A Heroic Example for Every American

8. *Oklahoma News*, October 31, 1933

9. *Oklahoma News*, October 16, 1933; *Shawnee News Star*, October 17, 1933

10. Special Agent in Charge Colvin to Bureau Director J. Edgar Hoover, dated October 24, 1933, Regarding Kathryn Kelly's Attempt to Bribe Jailer; *Hugo Daily News*, October 17, 1933

11. *Miami News Record*, October 17, 1933

12. US Department of Justice, Federal Bureau of Investigation, Kathryn Thorne Kelly File

13. US Department of Justice, Federal Bureau of Investigation, Kathryn Thorne Kelly File; *M'Alester News Capital*, October 17, 1933

14. US Department of Justice, Federal Bureau of Investigation, Kathryn Thorne Kelly File; *Miami Daily News Record*, October 17, 1933; *Commercial Appeal*, October 18, 1933; Kathryn Kelly letter to J. Edgar Hoover dated November 1933

15. Kathryn Kelly letter to J. Edgar Hoover dated November 1933

16. Ibid.

17. Ibid.

18. US Department of Justice, Federal Bureau of Investigation, Kathryn Thorne Kelly File

19. US Department of Justice, Federal Bureau of Investigation, George (Machine Gun) Kelly File; *World News*, September 4, 1934; *Tyler Morning Telegraph*, September 4, 1934

20. US Department of Justice, Federal Bureau of Investigation, George (Machine Gun) Kelly File

21. US Department of Justice, Federal Bureau of Investigation, Kathryn Thorne Kelly File; US Department of Justice, Federal Bureau of Investigation, George (Machine Gun) Kelly File; Kathryn Kelly letter to George R. Kelly dated September 11, 1940

22. US Department of Justice, Federal Bureau of Investigation, Kathryn Thorne Kelly File; US Department of Justice, Federal Bureau of Investigation, George (Machine Gun) Kelly File; Kathryn Kelly letter to George R. Kelly dated September 11, 1940

23. US Department of Justice, Federal Bureau of Investigation, Kathryn Thorne Kelly File; US Department of Justice, Federal Bureau of Investigation, George (Machine Gun) Kelly File; Kathryn Kelly letter to George R. Kelly dated September 11, 1940

24. US Department of Justice, Federal Bureau of Investigation, Kathryn Thorne Kelly File; US Department of Justice, Federal Bureau of Investigation, George (Machine Gun) Kelly File; Kathryn Kelly letter to George R. Kelly dated September 11, 1940

25. US Department of Justice, Federal Bureau of Investigation, Kathryn Thorne Kelly File; US Department of Justice, Federal Bureau of Investigation, George (Machine Gun) Kelly File; Kathryn Kelly letter to George R. Kelly dated September 11, 1940

26. US Department of Justice, Federal Bureau of Investigation, Kathryn Thorne Kelly File; US Department of Justice, Federal Bureau of Investigation, George (Machine Gun) Kelly File; Kathryn Kelly letter to George R. Kelly dated September 11, 1940

27. George Kelly letter to Attorney General Homer Cummings dated February 3, 1936; US Department of Justice, Federal Bureau of Investigation, George (Machine Gun) Kelly File

28. George Kelly letter to Attorney General Homer Cummings dated February 3, 1936; US Department of Justice, Federal Bureau of Investigation, George (Machine Gun) Kelly File

29. George Kelly letter to Attorney General Homer Cummings dated February 3, 1936; US Department of Justice, Federal Bureau of Investigation, George (Machine Gun) Kelly File

30. George Kelly letter to Attorney General Homer Cummings dated February 3, 1936; US Department of Justice, Federal Bureau of Investigation, George (Machine Gun) Kelly File

31. US Department of Justice, Federal Bureau of Investigation, George (Machine Gun) Kelly File; George Kelly letter to Warden Jas. A. Johnstow dated September 26, 1941; George Kelly letter to Warden Jas. A. Johnstow dated April 7, 1945

32. *The Year of Fear: Machine Gun Kelly and the Manhunt That Changed the Nation*, pg. 256–257

33. US Department of Justice, Federal Bureau of Investigation, George (Machine Gun) Kelly File; *San Angelo Standard Times*, July 8, 1954; *Wise County Messenger*, July 22, 1954; *Fort Worth Star-Telegram*, November 1, 1954; *The Year of Fear: Machine Gun Kelly and the Manhunt That Changed the Nation*, pg. 259

34. *San Francisco Examiner*, July 6, 1948; *Tulare Advance Register*, July 7, 1948; US Department of Justice, Federal Bureau of Investigation, Albert Bates File

35. *San Angelo Evening Standard*, May 25, 1951; *Lubbock Evening Journal*, November 9, 1948; US Department of Justice, Federal Bureau of Investigation, Kathryn Thorne Kelly File; *Fort Worth Star-Telegram*, July 16, 1948; *Miami Daily News Record*, March 20, 1958

36. US Department of Justice, Federal Bureau of Investigation, Kathryn Thorne Kelly File; *Daily Oklahoman*, March 20, 1958; *Miami Daily News*, March 20, 1958; *Fort Worth Star-Telegram*, June 9, 1958

37. US Department of Justice, Federal Bureau of Investigation, Kathryn Thorne Kelly File; *Daily Oklahoman*, March 20, 1958

38. US Department of Justice, Federal Bureau of Investigation, Kathryn Thorne Kelly File; *Daily Oklahoman*, March 20, 1958

39. US Department of Justice, Federal Bureau of Investigation, Kathryn Thorne Kelly File; *Sapulpa Daily Herald*, June 9, 1958

40. US Department of Justice, Federal Bureau of Investigation, Kathryn Thorne Kelly File; *San Angelo Evening Standard*, June 10, 1958

41. US Department of Justice, Federal Bureau of Investigation, Kathryn Thorne Kelly File; *San Angelo Evening Standard*, June 10, 1958

42. US Department of Justice, Federal Bureau of Investigation, Kathryn Thorne Kelly File; *San Angelo Evening Standard*, June 10, 1958

43. US Department of Justice, Federal Bureau of Investigation, Kathryn Thorne Kelly File; *Parsons Sun*, June 17, 1958; *Daily Oklahoman*, October 10, 1958

44. *Fort Worth Star-Telegram*, May 31, 1959; *Times Record News*, December 26, 1956

45. *Tulsa Tribune*, June 12, 1962

46. *The Alderson Story: My Life as a Political Prisoner*, pg. 136–137; *Daily Oklahoman*, June 17, 1962

47. *Kathryn Kelly: The Moll Behind "Machine Gun" Kelly*, pg. 163–164; *Ada Morning Times*, June 29, 1938; *The Year of Fear: Machine Gun Kelly and the Manhunt That Changed the Nation*, pg. 266–267

48. *Tulsa World*, September 27, 1970; *Courier Gazette*, September 28, 1970

49. ancestry.com, Lera Cleo "Kathryn" "Kay" Brooks

50. *Commercial Appeal*, June 19, 1934; *Wichita Falls Record News*, June 20, 1934

51. *Commercial Appeal*, June 19, 1934; *Wichita Falls Record News*, June 20, 1934; *El Paso Herald Post*, June 20, 1934

52. *Fort Worth Star-Telegram*, June 21, 1934

53. *El Paso Herald Post*, September 14, 1934

54. ancestry.com, Geralene Arnold

55. *Oklahoma News*, July 8, 1934

INDEX

—